MW01057102

PROFILES IN RUSSIAN RESISTANCE

PROFILES IN RUSSIAN RESISTANCE

Irina Kirk

QUADRANGLE
The New York Times Book Company

The poem on page 111 was translated by Richard Pevear for this volume and is used by permission.

 For information, address: Quadrangle/The New York Times Book Co., 10 East 53 Street, New York, N.Y. 10022. Manufactured in the United States of America. Published simultaneously in Canada by Fitzhenry & Whiteside, Ltd., Toronto.

Library of Congress Cataloging in Publication Data

Kirk, Irina.
Profiles in Russian resistance.

1. Russia—Politics and government—1953–
2. Dissenters—Russia—Interviews. I. Title.
II. Title: Russian resistance.
DK274.K55 322.4'4'0947 74-77945
ISBN 0-8129-0484-2

Designed by Tere LoPrete

To

Mikhail Pankratov

AND

Yelena Semeka

CONTENTS

INTRODUCTION

This journey was more than a change of scenery, a bridging of distances and anticipation of gratified expectations. It was not a series of encounters with all the sentimental suggestiveness of chance meetings and the sharing of illusory affinities. The people I met were not natives who could initiate me into the mysteries of foreign lands. Like myself, they were strangers, caught between their dissolving mirages and the unknown. They had left their own country—the Soviet Union—often not realizing where they were going but only knowing why. At the time when I traveled to various parts of the world to meet them, their initial astonishment at having been severed from their homeland had not worn off. The fantasy with which they had invested the world outside Russia still persisted, as though to forestall the encroachment of the reality they were about to confront. They had come to that reality for some answers, and most of them did not yet know that it contained even more questions than the one they had left behind.

Their journey was not merely frontier crossing. It was not conceived suddenly. In fact, it was the final stage of a journey that had begun long before, while they were still in Russia: a journey to self-consciousness. Though for each of them it began differently, all shared a defiance of the existing order, an order that does not acknowledge an individual search for values but presupposes adherence to values already established as the highest good.

Such paths to consciousness are necessarily taken in isolation, but theirs, due to the peculiar circumstances of their life-style, had to have the support and unity of others.

My own interest in the Soviet dissidents began neither as a scholarly project nor a venture into foreign territory: that is, politics. It was rather the result of an impression received and absorbed, one of those fated moments committing one to act out the emotions and thoughts generated by an impression. In the fall of 1972 the first Russian dissidents began to arrive in America as émigrés. I had met the family of Dr. Yuri Glazov and went to spend a weekend with them in South Nyack, New York. It was a gesture of goodwill, welcoming a new arrival to my country, and a bit of curiosity. It was also a recollection of my own experience, the memory of how important it is in those first few months in a new country to receive reassurance that one will not remain here a stranger forever. But in our nightlong conversation the concern for their future never came up. Like the characters in Dostoevsky's novels, they discussed with passion and immediacy the questions of truth and justice. They were not troubled as to how they were going to live, whether their children would take to a new school, or even where they were going to find work. What they discussed endlessly was the fate of their friends in Russia: who could be arrested, who would or would not be allowed to leave, who needed urgent help and how to provide it.

Long ago, during the Japanese occupation in China, when food was scarce and one feared a knock in the middle of the night and the words, "Japanese Gendarmerie," we too had lived that way. The impermanence of positions, money, and even personal strength was our only certainty. We survived by depending on one another, by sharing, by communion.

In America I was taught the importance of self-reliance, the sacredness of privacy, the values of individualism. Translated into images, the principles of our Constitution and the Declaration of Independence evoked visions of successful personalities who triumphed over poverty and hardships by toil and perseverance and preferably without any help. And when the years of crisis in America had shaken our myths, it was the youth who banded together, who claimed monopoly in the search for consciousness, who proclaimed that anyone over 30 is not to be trusted. It was easy to be idealistic and to protest, said the older generation, when there is nothing to lose, when the parents had provided the material well-being.

The Glazovs, and the others whom I met later, were almost all over 30. Back in the Soviet Union they were established scholars or professionals, often with prestigious jobs and material security. Had they kept silent on certain matters they could have lived comfortably and provided their children with a rather carefree future. Instead, they adopted *glasnost'* as their motto, which resulted for some in the loss of jobs and for others in imprisonment. There is no single English word for glasnost'; it means to make public, to bring into the open. These people began to demand glasnost' for injustices and injuries that were done not to them but to others. They united to bring this about and began what is called the Democratic or the Dissident Movement.

"But have they achieved anything? Were there any concrete reforms?" asked my American colleagues and friends to whom I tried to convey the intensity and the passion that I encountered in these people. "And why did they leave if they believed in their cause? Why did the Soviet Government allow them to go?" I decided to find out.

But I did not plan to provide a window on the Soviet reality, nor to establish what the Intelligentsia thinks of its Government. Above all else I wanted to find out how a person defines his identity against the one that is imposed on him or her by the State. How, having found the premises of an ethical life, does a person act upon these convictions when such action may result not only in the loss of livelihood, but in the loss of liberty and even life? And how did these people manage to unite and trust one another in a country where decades of Stalinism had achieved disunity, suspicion, mistrust, and fear even among the closest friends and relatives? What I wanted to know could not be learned in libraries and archives, it had to be learned through personal encounters with various people, through seeing their faces and hearing their voices, and, if at all possible, through sharing their lives in some small measure.

In traveling through the United States, to Rome, London, Paris, and Israel, and in doing the interviews I often stayed in the homes of these most recent émigrés or at a nearby hotel so that I could observe their lives and not simply talk with them for a few hours. In learning about these individuals a certain pattern began to emerge, not in the ways in which they have searched for consciousness, but in regard to the events that impelled the search.

Most people I spoke with named the Twentieth Party Congress, at which Khrushchev had denounced Stalin, as the point of their awakening, or the beginning of the realization that questions had to be asked. The return of ZEKs (prisoners rehabilitated by Khrushchev) was another point in the ascendancy of awareness. "I never knew that my mother had a brother," said a young historian, "and suddenly he came back from the prison camp. We would gather every night to listen to his stories. But then there was hardly a home in Russia in which someone wasn't in prison or shot or had died in a labor camp."

But at the same time, it seems, a hope was born that the system would be liberalized. "For a time our attitude toward the government was, 'Let us help you make things better,' " a cyberneticist told me. Indeed, the publication of Solzhenitsyn's *One Day in the Life of Ivan Denisovich* supported that hope, and many of the Intelligentsia believed that freedom of expression would be granted. Such belief was first undermined by the trial of Joseph Brodsky, who was arrested in Leningrad in 1964 and tried for parasitism. Brodsky, the most talented poet to appear in the Soviet Union in decades, did not write anti-Soviet poems. His concerns were universal, but because he did not praise gods or sing heroes he had to be banished from the Republic. He was sentenced to five years; his time had been reduced to two after the transcript of his trial appeared in the West and resulted in unfavorable publicity for the Soviet Government. Within the Soviet Union the trial produced indignation, and a few telegrams had been sent in protest; still it did not result in any action among the Intelligentsia.

What finally brought an open reaction and the first public demonstration was the arrest in September, 1965, of the writers Andrei Sinyavsky and Yuli Daniel. Almost everyone I spoke with referred to that event as the final force that propelled them to the articulation of their frustrations: "I knew that to remain silent now would be to lose hope of ever being human." "I was indignant before about many things, but afraid to speak up. This trial made my anger stronger than the fear." "It was the moment of birth of the new Russian Intelligentsia. The moment when we understood that if we fail to act our destiny will remain the same as it was during Stalin."

On December 5, 1965, the day of the Soviet Constitution, a group of dissidents assembled in Pushkin Square. The passersby began to gather across the street wondering what it was all about. At 6 P.M. Alexander Yesenin-Volpin unrolled a poster which said, "Respect the Soviet Constitution." Yuri Titov [1] held another,

1. Yuri Titov, an underground artist who emigrated in 1972. At first he was told that he would not be allowed to take out his paintings (which were mainly

"Open trial for Sinyavsky and Daniel." The choice of Pushkin Square was not accidental; poets in Russia have always been the arbiters of consciousness. The demonstration was dispersed in minutes and the participants were taken to the police station. They were later released but the precedent had been set.

The severe sentence—Sinyavsky received seven years in a camp of strict regime and Daniel five [2]—marked the end of an illusion that the system would be liberalized and gave a new impetus to Samizdat. Aleksandr Ginzburg, a poet and a young sculling champion, with the help of Yuri Galanskov, also a poet (who died in a labor camp in 1973 at the age of 33 for failure to receive medical help) and two others, collected the transcript of the trial, the protest letters, and all available documents in connection with the trial and sent the typewritten *White Book* to the Supreme Soviet, to Kosygin, to the KGB, and abroad. All four were arrested.

The Trial of Four, as it came to be known, brought the explosion of an epistolary campaign; letters of protest were sent to various Soviet authorities, to the press, to the West. Pavel Litvinov and Larisa Bogoraz, Yuli Daniel's wife, made an appeal that was broadcast by BBC asking people everywhere to react against the injustice of the trial. On January 22, 1967, Vladimir Bukovsky and Viktor Khaustov organized a demonstration on Pushkin Square to protest the Trial of Four, and were in turn arrested. Bukovsky, who had already been arrested in 1963 for circulating Djilas's *New Class* and had spent two years in a punitive insane asylum, was given three years. In his final speech Bukovsky announced that as soon as he completed his sentence he would continue to act against repressions. "I absolutely refuse to repent for having organized the demonstration. And when I am free again I shall organize others like this one, in perfect conformity with the Soviet Law." Bukovsky kept his word. He was released in 1970 and in January, 1971, he wrote an "Appeal to the Psychiatrists" in which he documented the abuses of psychiatry for political repression in the Soviet Union. On March 10, 1971, the International Committee on Human Rights presented this document to the Western press in

---

religious), but later, when he refused to leave without them, he was given an exit visa. He brought all his paintings to the airport himself and saw that they were put in the baggage compartment of Aeroflot. On arriving at Rome and unpacking his works, he discovered that they had been destroyed by acid.

2. The labor camps are of four categories: general regime, reinforced regime, strict regime, and especially strict regime.

Paris and on March 29 Bukovsky was again arrested. He is now serving a 12-year sentence. This time he ended his last plea in court with the following words: "And no matter how long I will be imprisoned I will never renounce my convictions and will continue to express them, using the right which is provided by Article 125 of the Soviet Constitution. I will continue to fight for justice and for lawfulness. I only regret that during this short period of time in which I was free—one year, two months, and three days—I accomplished too little toward that end."

Vladimir Bukovsky's conduct was an important event in the dissident movement. Along with a few others he introduced a new model of behavior, an attempt to break the 50-year-old tradition of using fear to silence dissent. In a court where repentance is the norm, Sinyavsky and Daniel refused to plead guilty and Bukovsky announced his intention not to be "reeducated." It was a step in asserting human rights; it was also a step toward glasnost'.

For generations the mere letters "KGB" reduced everyone to a state of complete anxiety, and in many cases little else was needed by the Committee of State Security to obtain confessions or cooperation. It was taken for granted that a talk with the KGB was to be kept in the strictest confidence, and that no one would think of sharing the interrogation even with a friend. When in early 1967 Pavel Litvinov was called in for questioning by the KGB regarding Bukovsky, he was warned sternly that any attempt at making it public would result in "repressive measures" against him. Instead of heeding the warning, Litvinov wrote down the contents of the interrogation with the KGB agent, Gostev, and had it published in Samizdat and smuggled abroad. "You cannot imagine what a bomb it was for all of us," I was told in Moscow, "when we heard this broadcast over the foreign radio stations. We suddenly understood that one didn't have to follow the KGB orders." Said Yuri Glazov, "It was a beautiful evening when we sat and listened to the broadcast of Litvinov's talk with the KGB." And in the morning we woke up with a new perception of the world, that we are not in the world of Byzantium Orthodoxy where the responsibility for social order is solely Caesar's, but in a world in which Russia hadn't severed her ties with Europe." Later, when a group of scholars were called in by the KGB and asked to write a retraction of their letter to some Western newspaper, "because glasnost' is profitable for our enemies," they replied that glasnost' was precisely the point of their letter.

Whenever a visit to a labor camp was allowed it was also understood by the relatives of the inmate that nothing was to be related about the life of the prisoners. It was clear that it would do no good and it might even make the prisoner's life more difficult. In May, 1967, Larisa Bogoraz went to visit Yuli Daniel in his camp in Potma. She reported the inhuman conditions for the inmates in a document, *About One Journey*, which was circulated in Samizdat.

None of these people was breaking any of the Soviet laws in making all this public; they broke the unwritten laws by which everyone had lived for so long, the shackles of fear by which the secret police ran the country. Some of the dissidents decided that the most expedient way to bring about the liberalization was to force the authorities to uphold their own laws, and to educate the public in their civil rights. Alexander Yesenin-Volpin, having been through several prisons and insane asylums himself, studied the Soviet penal code and the constitution thoroughly and wrote out a "Memorandum" instructing citizens how to behave during interrogation or arrest and advising them on their rights under the Soviet law. Valery Chalidze, a physicist, and two well-known mathematicians, Yuli Telesin and Boris Tsukerman, became the unofficial counselors for all those who needed legal advice. People were instructed that they were morally obliged to report the contents of any talk or interrogation by the KGB so that others who might be called in the same case could be forewarned. The "Memorandum" was typed out by volunteers and circulated. As soon as the news of someone's interrogation would reach the dissidents, one of them would be dispatched to instruct this person in his or her rights and to warn of what psychological pressures might be applied during the subsequent interrogations. Soon the KGB, instead of obedience and diffidence, began to encounter resistance and refusals to answer certain questions on the basis of articles of the Soviet law. Courageous lawyers like Dina Kaminskaya began to take on cases of the dissidents in place of court-appointed attorneys anxious to serve the State. After she had taken on the defense of Bukovsky, Marchenko, Galanskov, and others, Kaminskaya was told to occupy herself with criminal cases from then on, but her speeches in court were another contribution to glasnost'. At the trial of Yuri Galanskov she had said of her client, "He is a remarkable, compassionate person. He wanted to fight all that seemed to him unjust. He could not remain passive. He sought neither riches nor career, nor glory for himself." Such words were not heard before in a Soviet court about someone who was accused of slandering the Soviet Union.

The glasnost' of these cases made people aware of those who were already in prisons and labor camps. Letter-writing campaigns were organized for the inmates to let them know that they were not forgotten.

"In Stalin's time," I was told by a man who had spent many years in prisons, "what made our life hopeless was the feeling of being forgotten. Once arrested one was left without any outside support. Often not even a mother knew where her son was being held. Today, many of us have survived only because we knew that some people on the outside and even in the West were concerned about our destiny." The prisoners in turn learned various methods by which to get their messages out so that glasnost' penetrated even the walls of such fortresses as Vladimir Prison.[3]

In their quest for ethical standards, some turned toward religion and were baptized as Christians. Because there were dissidents among the priests, there was no difficulty in performing the rituals in church. The Buddhists, on the other hand, had to meet in their own homes to observe their rites,[4] but even so a group of them were arrested in 1972.

In these and many other different ways the dissidents asserted their beliefs outside the established ones. They had no leaders, no manifestos, no political philosophy. In this sense there was no specific movement, if one understands a movement to be a definite structure with organizing principles and a political ideology. In many ways their fight was for a freedom from ideology. "Lack of freedom," I was told, "does not simply mean the lack of expression or a ban on dissent. It means that your life from the time you are born to the time you die is permeated with ideology." What they wanted most of all was the right to search for their own answers to the questions of existence and conscience. The Government in turn did not recognize them as political dissidents. Such a category does not exist in the Soviet Union; any dissent is tried under Articles 190 and 191 as "spreading falsehoods and slander derogatory to the Soviet State."

The year 1967 and the early part of 1968 were the most reassuring for the dissidents; this time is now called among them, "the feast of

3. See Anatoly Marchenko's book, *My Testimony*, about Vladimir Prison.
4. The offense is called "an attempt on life and property under the pretense of holding a religious ceremony."

democracy." At that time the protest letters were signed not by a few individuals but by hundreds. The news coming from Prague was also exhilarating; once more there was hope that, as Bukovsky had said at his trial, "Our society is still sick with fear that came to us from the times of Stalinsim, but the process of awakening has begun and it will be impossible to stop it."

In March of 1968, however, the authorities decided that the feast must be stopped. Several *podpisanty*—those who signed letters of protest—were dismissed from their jobs. In a country where there is one employer, the loss of a job is not a light matter. The harassments began and mass interrogations were initiated. Still, in April, 1968, a new and the most significant publication had appeared, *The Chronicle of Current Events.* Its function was to record all dissident activities and the activities of the courts, as well as to report, without any comments, all arrests and searches. The authorities designated the *Chronicle* as their main target, but apparently they first wanted to find out who was behind its publication.

The invasion of Czechoslovakia was another blow to the Russian dissidents. Litvinov, Bogoraz, Natasha Gorbanevskaya, the most talented poet now in Russia, and three others were arrested in Red Square for their demonstration against the invasion. The mood of despair set in among the Intelligentsia as the most inspiring activists were being sent to camps and exile. In May, 1969, two others were arrested, General Pyotr Grigorenko and the poet Ilya Gabai. They protested the decree by which the Crimean Tatars were not allowed to live on their own land and were exiled to Kazakhstan. Grigorenko was sent to an insane asylum and Gabai to a labor camp in Kazakhstan for three years. Though their arrests brought a sense of hopelessness, the physicists Andrei Sakharov and Chalidze, together with others, organized the Committee for the Rights of Man, probably as a counteraction to such a committee at the United Nations, whose members include the representatives of the Soviet Government. Dissident activities continued but on a much lesser scale.

In May of 1972 President Richard Nixon visited the Soviet Union. In preparation for his visit many dissidents were arrested and held for 15 days lest they should try to demonstrate or get in touch with one of his staff members. By negotiating with the Communist Party Secretary, Leonid Brezhnev, instead of with Premier Aleksei Kosygin, in whom the responsibility for conducting intergovernmental negotiations is vested by the Soviet Constitution,

Nixon lent support to the Communist Party, the de facto governing power, rather than to the constitutional State as represented by Kosygin. This legal abstraction carried a message to the dissidents as to whom the head of the American Government planned to support. The repercussions came quickly.

After Nixon's departure Pyotr Yakir and Viktor Krasin, at that time the most active dissidents, were arrested. Yakir's father, the legendary general Iona Yakir, was shot in 1937 during Stalin's purges. Consequently, at the age of 14 Yakir went to prison where he spent his next 16 years. Rehabilitated by Khrushchev in 1954, Yakir became an active campaigner for civil rights and later the main source of information for the foreign correspondents. He had a reputation for being fearless and tough, but many worried about his alcoholism and what the deprivation of alcohol might do to his determination.

As it was, both Yakir and Krasin confessed and testified against others. The authorities announced the names of all those who would be arrested if another issue of the *Chronicle* should appear. Thus, the KGB objectives were partly fulfilled. As one of them put it, "We will break some of you, buy the others, and throw the rest of you to the West." Unbroken were Bukovsky, Andrei Amalrik, General Grigorenko and many others, but they were all in prisons, in insane asylums and in labor camps. It was the women—the mothers and sisters and wives—who took up the fight, no longer with the hope of liberalization but simply to save the lives of these men. Meanwhile, many dissidents decided that emigration was the only course of action left for them.

It was at this time of doubt and despair that I decided to go to the Soviet Union. I wanted to see and feel for myself all that I had learned from the emigrants. In July, 1973, I went to Moscow. Though I have been to the Soviet Union several times, I knew no dissidents there. Two phone numbers and the mention of a few names of those who were already in the West opened the doors to several homes for me and to one of the most poignant experiences of my life. In terms of time my visit to Moscow lasted only two weeks; in terms of intensity and of transcending the confinements of time and space it will last forever. It bridged the gap between nineteenth-century Russia and my own time; it made alive the Russian fictional heroes who could not sit down to dinner before the question of the existence or nonexistence of God had been solved. Days and nights were only measured by impressions, by human faces. For a long time they will invade my memories, rob me of joy, and affirm Camus' words that in times of crisis and plagues there is more in men to admire than to despise.

We usually met during the day at someone's apartment and were together till the early morning hours. People came and went, bringing news of someone's arrest or interrogation, delivering a letter that had been smuggled out of prison, reading a message that had come from abroad. There was the all-night vigil by the foreign radio stations when, on July third, Garik Superfin, one of Solzhenitsyn's researchers, was arrested, and in the days that followed a collection for the food parcels to be sent to Lefortovo Prison and for his mother. At times a foreign student would drop in; a girl from Boston burst into tears after listening for an hour to the "usual" conversation of the dissidents. But there was also a lot of joy and music and vodka toasts.

Someone would pick up a guitar and reduce chaos to the healing communion and the shared misfortunes of their lives. Coming each day from a city hotel, I became immersed in that communion, and I shared it as one shares a mountain hut after a day of climbing alone and suddenly finding oneself in a company of strangers to whom one is bound by a hostile environment outside.

Because some of these friends came to see me off to the airport I still felt protected and safe until I crossed the line under the sign, "Passengers Only." Five KGB men were waiting there. They took me aside and searched my bags and checked every seam of every piece of my clothing. They looked inside the heels of my shoes and squeezed out my toothpaste, and when my plane left for Milan and I was still on the ground, three women took charge of me in a locked room.

They were polite, and one of them said she was sorry. She did what she had to do sadly and I was sad for her, because there was something in her face that showed the possibility of awakening. The other checked my hair, feeling my head and asked if anything was concealed there.

She was close, of course, but it was nothing she could touch or deliver to her superiors.

PROFILES IN RUSSIAN RESISTANCE

LEV NAVROZOV

Lev Navrozov was born in Moscow in 1928. He began to write in his teens, but knowing that he could never write anything within the framework of Socialist Realism he did not attempt to publish. Instead he became the best, the most skillful translator of English, and consequently a millionaire. Navrozov began to learn English at the age of 20 by memorizing the entire *Ballad of Reading Gaol* of Oscar Wilde. In learning the language, he says, he used two methods, "the Stanislavsky one when you have to feel that you are an American or an Englishman and the Meyerhold one when you must seem an American or an Englishman." The combination was so successful that Navrozov was considered the only person in the Soviet Union—"the one-man Trade Union"—who could translate certain complex Russian authors into English. Prior to him only foreigners were given the task of translating writers like Dostoevsky into English. Navrozov became so indispensable that he could name his own field of interest and his own price. He worked fast and was soon able to buy a summer mansion on the outskirts of Moscow, where only the Soviet elite lives. This gave the Navrozov family a safeguard from interference and supervision and freed them from certain rules. One of the rules they broke was in not sending their son to any school. The boy was educated at home by the parents. They bought him classics and a chemistry lab, and at the age of 12 he entered a competition in chemistry with high-school graduates and won the first prize.

In 1971 Navrozov applied for an exit visa and in 1972 the family arrived in New York. Here the Navrozovs live in Riverdale in an apartment like so many others of middle-class America. In the fall of 1974 Lev Navrozov's book, *The Education of Lev Navrozov*, was published by Harper & Row. It is the first of seven volumes he plans to write. He insisted that the interview be conducted in English. As he walked up and down my hotel room in New York, the words came tumbling out, and it seemed impossible that until two years ago Lev Navrozov had to keep this flow of elegant and adroit sentences to himself.

Q. Would you have left Russia earlier than you did if you had a chance?

I would have, at least 30 years ago. But there was just not a glimmer of hope in this respect since I was born. Please recall that before the mid-fifties the Soviet man was born into paradise. It was a shoddy kind of paradise, something like a carnival sideshow, jerry-built in a drab, miserable, hungry town. Still, it was a metaphysical absurdity to ask: "What if one wants to leave paradise?" If such a morbid fancy originated in the mind of a paradise dweller, it simply showed that he was not a paradise dweller at all but a spy, as described in those trashy spy novels turned out in quantity by a hack with the fat, oily face of an aging boy. At school we read about a spy named Trotsky who was so villainous that capital punishment seemed inadequate in his case, and so he was banished. However, this retribution was so inhuman that it had never been applied since, as our small, slovenly schoolmarm reassured us.

Q. Can you outline the reason for this persistent lifelong urge to leave?

Anywhere, whether in post-1917 Russia or in the best of democracies, life can be perceived as Tragedy. But in post-1917 Russia it remains Tragedy as long as you cannot get out. For if you can get out, yet remain and are made to suffer or die, this is no Tragedy. This is a self-imposed Farce. A clown's or a serf's Farce. In Russia I belonged to the richest 1 per cent of 1 per cent of the population. In the States I would perhaps always belong to the poorest one-fifth—even after my books have been published. But I regard my chance to leave Russia and go to the United States as the greatest miraculous, unbelievable success, gain, good luck of my life. My life will not be a serf's or a clown's farce. It will be life. That is, Tragedy. This is what was important to me as I left. As a writer I smuggled out my manuscripts, of course. But whether I would be a published author in the West or would mow lawns seemed to me as unimportant as the exact size of his or her retirement pension to a child yet unborn.

Q. From your pieces published in *Commentary* and the preliminary reviews of your forthcoming book, I conclude that there is not much danger of your mowing lawns here. Your English style amazed me. How could you, a Russian, develop it in a society where every individual style even in the Russian language has been suppressed at least for 40 years?

Yes, suppressed officially. But you forget that suppression can never be total. At least inside his own brain everyone has been free in Russia if he developed the self-defense mechanism of pretending that he is a "Soviet citizen infinitely devoted to our Party," et cetera. Outwardly, I was always an exemplary "Soviet citizen." Not a speck on my record, though not an atom of extra zeal either. Inwardly, I had at the age of nine no more illusions about the regime than, say, Winston Churchill had between the mid-thirties and mid-forties. Inwardly, I was certainly no more a "Soviet citizen" than Sir Winston was.

Q. Wasn't it rather precocious—to be able to grasp at the age of nine what some world-famous intellectuals could not understand?

You mean what some world-famous intellectuals did not want to understand. In order to understand something you must be free of motives that encourage you not to understand it, as William James showed long ago. If such motives are very strong, you may die still not understanding that two times two makes four. You may not know it after a lifetime at the Sorbonne. All my friends between the ages of 9 and 13 were rationalistic critics. Among writers' children those who were not sufficiently intelligent in this respect were called "degenerates." The truth of the matter was that they had read fewer "Soviet" books. This was merely the reaction of inquisitive, rational minds to a tangle of self-contradictory platitudes that claimed to represent perfect logic, to an irrational make-believe that called itself the science of sciences.

Q. Why do you indicate the age of 9? Why not the age of 15, for example?

Because it is at the age of 9—at least in boys—that there originates the ability to think in rational terms. Sometimes to the detriment of the more comprehensive ability to understand life in broader—mystic, emotional, humane—terms, which appears later, after the age of 13. Between the age of 9 and 13 we were "early teen-age rationalists," and oh boy, how we pulled to pieces the glaring irrationalism of everything called "soviet." A White Guard émigré magazine would turn green with envy. To begin with, there was the word "soviet" itself, an ordinary Russian word meaning "council"—specifically, the local council of self-government—which was the very thing that had been turned into fiction by "Soviet" power. The "Soviet" power was the most anti-Soviet force, to begin with, and yet it had been labeling anti-Soviet even the attempt to recall the story of its ruthless destruction of the soviets, the local councils of self-government.

Q. But how could you speak so freely in those years?

You could speak perfectly freely with your trusted friends. I always did. Of course once you took the wrong person for your trusted friend you were lost. But we never did. After some conditioning a lab assistant will never mistake strychnine for starch or sugar. As soon as there was a sign that your companion was not intelligent, congenial, or natural enough, you cut him adrift imperceptibly and automatically, as a kind of defensive reflex conditioned from early childhood, indeed transmitted by your elders. I doubt that even a highly competent agent provocateur could have tricked us into confiding in him.

Q. Why does Russia have such a long tradition of suppressing dissent? Do you believe this is something in the "Russian national character"?

Your question is rather typical of an American because you Americans tend to assume that your society is the rule, while Russia is an exception. Actually, the nineteenth- and twentieth-century democracies are rare islands of light after millennia of darkness, and still existing amid the darkness encompassing at least half of mankind, with other areas in precarious twilight. Having their eyes accommodated to strong light in their country, Americans, often including even leading experts on Russia, tend to forget that between 1861 and 1917 there developed constitutional monarchy in Russia, with the jury trial, freedom of the press, Parliament, and all that. In this respect, pre-1917 Russia was far better off than many countries today, more than half a century later!

Q. So you do not believe in the proposition that Russia has produced some of the world's greatest writers such as Gogol, Tolstoy, and Pasternak because of a limited human freedom?

Those who say so simply do not know Russian history well enough. Gogol lived when there was still pre-1861 serfdom. But *he* was a nobleman, not a serf. As a nobleman he was perfectly free to represent Russia as a horrible grotesque—and go to Italy and back whenever he wanted. All that with the pride or even arrogance that a free citizen of England of that day could well envy. Tolstoy was free to denounce publicly every social institution in Russia and the West, from medicine to religion, from court to marriage, from music to money, and every attempt to curb his unbridled anarchistic or even nihilistic iconoclasm, often entirely irresponsible, stupid or ignorant, was thwarted by the crowds of his admirers. Pasternak began to write in 1912, the freest year in the history of Russia, and lingered creatively throughout the twenties when the freedom of art still lingered. He could write his *Doctor Zhivago* only in the "thaw" of the fifties. But *Doctor Zhivago*, just as everything written in the fifties and since then, is, artistically, a big decline compared with the era that began several years before 1917 and was crushed completely by the mid-thirties.

Q. But what about you—were you as an underground writer affected unfavorably by the lack of freedom in Russia?

Of course I was. What was, for example, my notion of the culture of the West before I started studying English so as to be able even to *think* in English if necessary? The culture of the West was to me just what it had been to the traditional Russian intellectual of the beginning of the century. But what had been so new and alive then was musty and provincial decades later. I was steeped in provincialism, as is typical in closed, unfree societies, and Pasternak's *Doctor Zhivago* shows this too. To me the culture of the West was still German philosophy from Kant to Spengler (Bergson being a non-German exception), German music (Chopin a non-German exception), and French painting. However, while appreciating "austere German genius" and "lucid Gallic wit," the traditional Russian intellectual of the beginning of the century and his provincial epigone like myself conceived of Germans and French as vaudeville types, and a nobleman's knowledge of French and German did not prevent even Tolstoy from representing them as such, thus showing his readers once again that only the Russian has a *soul.* Even after the cultural elite migrated to France and Germany after 1917, many Russian intellectuals never rid themselves of these vaudeville images. Besides, they believed that Western (meaning French and German) culture was turning apocalyptically into what Spengler called "civilization," something "scientifically" soulless, cynical, lifeless—not unlike Huxley's brave new world.

Few Russian émigrés strayed to Britain. While the vaudeville German was an absurd pedant, ridiculously good-natured unless he was idiotically cruel, and the vaudeville Frenchman was vain, suave, sensuous, and superficial, the English were boring, cretinous clowns, [a viewpoint] traceable to Dickens, the only English author extensively read in Russia for a whole century and mistaken for a realist in the Russian tradition.

As for the United States, a Russian ex-Futurist poet who, to be paradoxical, "admired Americanism," wrote during his tour of the country: "The American will not greet you with our indifferent 'Good morning,' but will say instead his energetic 'Make money?' " Lowbrows in Russia liked their "America"—jazz, chewing gum, movies, et cetera—and the more they liked it the more this "America" appalled intellectuals. Not in Russia alone, it seems. A French architect's wife asked me huffily in Moscow in 1964: "What do you need a mastery of English for? You are not a businessman or engineer. You are a man of *culture.*" It is to break out of this musty provincialism of a closed society, fatal for real creativity, that I mastered English enough to *live* in the United States or Europe while remaining physically in Moscow.

Q. What is the main difference between the Stalin era and today?

Since 1918 and up to the mid-fifties the secret police could destroy anyone anywhere in any way without any proofs of his concrete action. Today, at least in the large cities, a secret police official must have proofs that the arrested person has really *done* something "criminal"—say, has distributed texts found "anti-Soviet," that is, running counter to the current official propaganda.

Q. I understand that you were all your life a "closed" dissident. But did you take part in any open dissidence that originated in the sixties?

No person of my spiritual vintage would have. Orwell's hero in *1984* tries to preserve his ego but perishes since the State is omnipotent and the individual is doomed. The goal of my life was to prove Orwell wrong, to prove that the individual can develop a defense mechanism matching the omnipotence of the state. I developed this defense mechanism. Why should I then disarm, let the secret police get at my real self and thus perhaps triumph over me, since my actions would be sufficient proof of "crime"? Suppose the situation would suddenly change and the old era would come back? Anyway, all my writings would have been confiscated in the very first house search, a common occurrence in the life of a democratic dissident. Yet without participating in their activity, I was friendly with many of the open dissidents. These people set the example of friendship in need, so essential in areas of marginal activity. They demonstrated that since the interpretation of what constituted proof of "crime" is often based on vague, ambiguous, contradictory instructions, and since no official wants to bear responsibility for the decision, rallying to the support of a friend often meant saving him.

Q. How did you begin writing?

Oh, as a writer's son I began writing since the time I remember myself, but it was in 1956 that my writing took a new turn. I realized that if I wanted to be a writer in the sense of Chekhov, and not in the sense of Beckett, who is not a writer but a poet, I must be a sociologist, psychologist, statistician, and so forth, otherwise social narratives turn to sentimental expositions of the author's social righteousness, usually based on his ignorance of the ABC of social knowledge.

Q. Is America very different from what you imagined it to be?

In Russia I studied the United States for many years. I knew that a democracy is vulnerable by definition—its survival among societies that are essentially war machines is open to doubt. However, it seemed to me that the weakness of the United States as a democracy is compensated by dynamism, vitality, efficiency, et cetera.

At close quarters these compensating qualities do not seem as impressive as they loomed from afar. Inside the U.S.A. one finds the U.S.A. more humanly weak, vulnerable, existing perhaps owing more to a lucky historic chance than to the will to survival. I find that U.S. bureaucracies may be as inefficient as their Soviet opposite numbers, but the latter cost next to nothing, while the former consume huge money. The overall resistance of democracy, even in the U.S.A., seems to be weaker under the effect of "détente" and other immobilizing peace drugs. But this impression could well be anticipated: a man who seemed to be ever exuberant with creative vitality from afar is bound to look more humanly weak if watched all the time at close quarters. Sometimes ineptness or absurdity or lethargy in the U.S.A. is curiously Soviet. When I found that in a home for chronically ill the upkeep costs the city or the state $1,000 per month per person or more, but the installation of an individual telephone (often solving the problem of loneliness) costing $20 is an impossible luxury, I could not help exclaiming: "Just as in the Soviet Union!"

Q. Can we do anything in the West to help the democratic processes in Russia?

Help? The democracies have been helping, on and off, the Soviet regime to consolidate and expand. Many of their businessmen have been helping the regime economically, and hence militarily. Many of their statesmen have been practically servile with respect to those in power in Russia. Many of their intellectuals have been approving of such regimes. The democracies can do a lot to help—by not helping those in power, for example, to strengthen, tighten, expand, their power.

Q. What is the single most important idea about the Soviet Union which you think Americans should know?

That the people of Russia are just human. Like Americans are. Except that the people of Russia are in a bad historic predicament, while the historic luck of Americans is in. Yet the survival of the lucky Americans depends on those who are now in a bad historic predicament, and this is the realization to which I hope to contribute by my books.

ANATOLY RADYGIN

The Russian psyche has conceived a folk hero who is at once solitary and gregarious, defiant and gentle, daring and soft-hearted. He is usually portrayed as having a certain awkwardness that is mercurially transformed into total alertness at the moment of danger, and his face is relaxed and watchful, ready to respond instantly to affection or a blow. His hair is rye-colored and windblown and his eyes have that special brilliant blueness by which the Russians claim to be able to recognize their own people. On seeing Anatoly Radygin, a Russian child would wonder if he had not materialized from one of the fairy tales.

As a child Radygin dreamt of a heroic life: to sail to the end of the earth, to fly a polar plane. But already in high school he had earned his first reprimand for having made a "political error." In his graduation term paper he compared Maxim Gorky's revolutionary hero, Pavel Korchagin, to his real-life prototype and concluded that the favorite Soviet writer had embellished him far above the call of duty. Later, when Radygin studied at the Soviet Naval Academy in Leningrad, which is equivalent to Annapolis, his superiors noted his defiant nature and he was thrown out a few months before graduation. But Radygin was also a poet, and for a time he was a trusted person in Leningrad's editorial offices. When Yuri Gagarin flew into space, it was Radygin whom the editors selected to write the first poem about this event.

When Radygin realized that he could no longer write to order and that as a seaman he would never be trusted, he decided to escape. As he prepared to dive into the sea and swim to Turkey from Batumi, he was apprehended by KGB agents and sent to prison. His sentence was ten years. At first he was sent to Potma, a strict regime camp, and later (for his attempt to escape) to Vladimir, Russia's most fearsome prison, where he spent six years. But even in prison Radygin continued to tell his jailers that he would never live in the Soviet Union. After serving his sentence, he was allowed to leave for Israel with his wife, Alla, and her mother. At present Radygin and his family are in the United States.

Q. Were you born in Leningrad?

I was born in Petersburg in July of 1934. For some time now it has been painful for me to say "Leningrad."

Q. As a child did you dream of a seaman's life?

Like most of the boys my age I wanted to be a polar pilot, a stratonaut, and lamented the fact that I was born too late to fly Chkalov's planes [Chkalov was the first Russian pilot to fly nonstop to the U.S.A.] or to drive Chapaev's *tachanki.* My childhood was during the time of the most horrendous repressions and purges, at the same time as revolutionary romanticism was being instilled among the children and youth with fanatical fervor. We were brought up on false history, on false geography, on pseudo-heroism as our parents, frightened into total silence, did not dare to interfere and simply watched helplessly as we were stuffed with lies and made into primitive stool pigeons.

Q. When did you first think of the sea?

During the Second World War my determination to have a naval career was strengthened by such books as Sobolev's *Sea Soul* and films like *Malakhov Kurgan.* I also, like every Russian boy, read all of Jack London and loved him. As soon as I finished a seven-year school I went to a technical school and during my free time I went to the Yacht Club to learn how to sail. After I graduated from the technical school I worked as a coal miner. I still believed in the "honorable mission of the Stalin workers' Vanguard." I was idiotically proud of my work as a mine electrician, and in the evenings went to night school in order to be accepted in the Military Institute of the Naval Academy at Leningrad. I entered the Academy in 1952.

Q. What are the most important qualifications required of the midshipmen?

Obedience, the ability to be a robot, marching, and parades. The cult of military discipline was first and foremost.

Q. When did you graduate and what did you do then?

I didn't graduate when I was supposed to. In 1956, several months before graduation, I was kicked out, demoted, and sent as a sailor to the Far North after a military court-martial. Later I found out that I would have been kicked out during my second year as "doubtful material" had it not been for the fact that they needed me as a propagandist. You see, I was writing poetry and prose then, and was published in the newspapers. I used to organize various shows, concerts, wall newspapers, and so on. The reprisals for not graduating were much more cruel than for a criminal act. And the years that one has to serve as a sailor in the Far North are not counted afterward.

Q. You mean that having served the punitive years a sailor may return to the regular navy?

He must return. But I was lucky. After six months there was a change in political weather, I was "rehabilitated" and was allowed to graduate in a different Naval Academy, in Sevastopol.

Q. What were the charges against you?

Twenty-three violations of military discipline.

Q. Could you defend yourself?

No. The military trial is not a court trial; it is an administrative trial and everything was decided ahead of time.

Q. When you were rehabilitated were you told why?

No, but I was having an affair with a girl who was working in the secret archives and she showed me a document in which it was said that in my case "diseiplinary overbending" was allowed.

Q. You graduated then as a first lieutenant?

Yes, but at the same time Khrushchev ordered the reduction of naval forces by 1,200,000, and the first ones to be discharged were those who had a record of a military trial. Therefore, I had to switch to the civilian fleet.

Q. Cargo ship?

I didn't like the idea of a cargo ship from the beginning. Very early in the Academy I understood that I wasn't trusted by the authorities in general and the KGB in particular, and I knew that I would therefore never be allowed to be on any ship that would go overseas. And those are the best-equipped ships. So from the beginning to the end of six years I sailed on fishing ships. And even then, even when I was a captain on one of those ships, as soon as the ship was due to sail somewhere where, according to the KGB, there was "border danger," I was taken off the ship. It happened six times in six years. When it happened for the sixth time I understood that I had to escape. I understood that I would never have an adequate ship to sail and that I would end up in prison, because I had a predilection for expressing loudly what I thought.

Q. Were your dissatisfactions personal?

No. From the point of view of an average Soviet citizen, I had unusual luck. Even during the time I was sailing those fishing ships I was still writing. I was being published and my chances in that field were indeed very good. I could have made a career as a writer except the return to a full-time pseudo-literary career had become ethically unacceptable to me. I began to be published in 1952. I made the decision never to write "in their way" again when I sailed for the last time.

Q. Where did you sail then?

To the Far East. When, during the interrogation after my arrest, I was asked what motivated me to sail to the Far East and I replied that I wanted to make some money, they laughed in my face. They realized that any "normal" Soviet man who had a choice between getting wet on deck and being a professional writer ["professional writer" is almost a ministerial title in the Soviet Union], who is free to get up when he wants to, work when he wants to, not to speak of an author's vanity, who can make money by writing, must really detest the regime in order to refuse all its benefits.

Q. Who took you off the ship for the sixth time?

The border guards. It's their duty. They get the list of the crew, their passport numbers, and other information, and if a border guard decides that someone is unreliable he takes that person off the ship. If it is a simple sailor or a mechanic, they just take him off. If it is a captain then the ship is grounded until the new captain is found, as it was in my case.

Q. How did you plan your escape?

First of all so that no one else would be involved at all, so that the responsibility would be solely mine. I planned to swim 23 kilometers from Batumi to Turkey and to ask for political asylum at the American Embassy. That is, if the Turkish bandits didn't catch me at the other end. They've done it to others.

Q. For what reason?

To sell an escapee back to the Soviets.

Q. Under what circumstances did your attempted escape occur?

I don't like to talk about it because I had bad experiences here with the newspapers. I feel I have a lot more to contribute than a sensational escape story, but all they printed is that suspense piece. I planned it for a long time. I calculated the direction and strength of the undercurrent in Batumi, the velocity of the wind on a stormy night, the height of the waves. It had to be a very stormy night so that the shore searchlights would have a difficult time picking up someone in the water. I planned to swim between two waves as much as possible for the same reason. I went from Leningrad to Batumi and waited for such a night. On September 11, 1972, the weather turned bad. It wasn't just raining, the rain came down as a massive wall. Just what I needed. The watch on the observation tower was at a minimum, the shore searchlights could pierce only a part of the wall of rain. I undressed in the bushes, spread a heavy coat of oil on my body (to protect myself from the chill), put on my fins, and waited for the electrodes to change in the lighthouse. When they do, for a moment everything is drowned in darkness. As soon as it happened I stepped into the water waiting for another second so that I could dive into a big wave. But suddenly I was surrounded by flashlights and drawn guns. They tied my hands and took me to prison. After three months of interrogation and psychiatric punitive wards, I was sentenced to ten years' imprisonment.

Q. Did you feel that you were being watched when you made your preparations in the bushes?

Yes. But I tried to tell myself that it was a feeling born out of fear and anxiety. Besides, had I obeyed that feeling I would have never forgiven myself for the "indecision."

Q. How did the KGB find out about your planned escape?

On my last night in Leningrad I had dinner with a friend of mine. Not exactly a friend, he was one of those miserable drunkards whom no one wanted for a friend. I befriended him out of pity. We had dinner and drinks and we talked all night, as is customary in Russia, and at 6 A.M. when I was saying good-bye to him, in a moment of weakness, I told him what I was going to do. I told no one else.

Q. Can you be sure that it was he who reported you?

Yes. When you sign the accusation they allow you to read all the testimony, and that is how I knew. I parted with him at 6 A.M. and at 6:30 he already was on the way to report me. He knew that if I was caught they would question him, or punish him for not reporting me.

Q. So he reported you to save his skin?

Of course, of course. Not just to rat on me. At the trial he was more persuasive than the prosecutor. For the same reason.

Q. What did you tell them at the trial?

I was honest enough. I said to them, "I'm alien to you. I wanted to leave. I can't live with you and your KGB in one bag, and I won't.

I told them I expected an arrest anyway. In short, I was open, even though I didn't have any friends or any movement behind me. It was out of despair that I didn't try to justify myself before them.

Q. At the time you conceived this escape were you exposed to any Samizdat literature or any anti-Soviet information?

Absolutely none. I was cut off from any Samizdat. I just understood, by reading the Soviet press between the lines that that nation is a Genghis Khan Empire. It is interested in unlimited expansion and in nothing else at all. What had Genghis Khan achieved? That he had the fastest moving horses and the most effective far-reaching arrows. Nothing else. And he marched all the way to Trieste. And all those noble Polish, French, and English knights were beaten by him to the ground. I understood that the aim of the Soviet Union was only one: not to produce Plymouths of the latest style, but to produce weapons for world conquest. All the best brains of the country are mobilized to that end alone. The West doesn't want to understand it.

Q. When you arrived at the labor camp did you find any hostility?

Depends from whom. I was expecting to find the elite there. I was expecting to find the diversionists there who would be able to teach me how to escape. But I found everything there. There were a few of those to whom I am obliged for my education. They freed me from the last illusions and fictions by which even a disloyal Soviet citizen lives. It is very difficult to part with a myth, and there were also those in camp who gave their lives to those myths. Because to part with those "sacred ideas" is to admit that one's life had been lived in vain. One can easily give up Stalin, but then one must give up one's love for the Party, and what's more difficult to renounce, the idea of equality. The fiction of equality is a delicious thing from the point of view of Christian and other doctrines. To admit that equality is unjust is very difficult. Because it gets transformed from a political into a religious category. But if you approach it philosophically the idea of equality is corruptive. In this sense the prison was my university. I don't think I could have had a better education elsewhere. And therefore I don't consider those ten years of my life a waste at all. If you look around in a labor camp, on the surface it is as though there are just ordinary people sitting all around you. But each life is an odyssey. You could find two people together, one of whom was defending Konigsberg 20 years ago and the other who was assaulting it at the same time. There were men literally from every kind of army of the Second World War. People who defended Tobruk and those who sabotaged Crete, those who took Paris and those who took Rome, members of various intelligences and counterintelligences. To see them together, to hear their stories as they sat next to each other was indeed an education one couldn't get elsewhere.

Q. It doesn't look as though you needed a library there.

We had an oral library. A new prisoner would come and bring with him the latest song of Galich. Or he would recite Samizdat poetry and prose by memory. My wife (whom I did not know at that time) was our biggest help in that. She wrote several letters a day, her assault on the prison walls with those letters was so powerful that neither censorship nor theft of letters could stop the stream. Thanks to her and her friends, we knew what was going on, who was arrested, who was on trial, and what was new. Her Aesopian language was so imaginative, so humorous, so inventive that we knew everything. (See the interview of Alla Tsvetopolskaya for her side of this story.) Thanks to these letters we often could prepare ourselves for an interrogation because if a friend was arrested we knew it immediately.

Q. In short, you became an ideological dissident in the prison camp?

Yes, unfortunately only in the camp. But perhaps it was fortunate. Prior to that I had no contact with any dissidents. Those who were in my "literary" circle, even if they were in opposition, were only flirting with dissidence. Though I was politically naïve I still sensed that their opposition wasn't serious. As for my naval colleagues, most of them were good people but hopelessly ignorant in civil-rights problems. So that in my own case I first made acquaintance with Ivan Denisoviches and only later read about them.

Q. What did you do in the evening in the camp?

Every evening there was a series of fireworks of arguments, lectures, and new discoveries. And it was especially intense if it was in a punitive (nonsolitary) dungeon; there always appeared an historian, like Osipov, who gave lectures, or a poet, like Valentin Sokolov, who read his poetry, and then the dungeon was transformed into a discussion club on the highest level. And in that dungeon, where we had nothing else, not even the regular "diet," all those arguments were of the purest essence and of the purest passion.

Q. I heard that in the prison camps the inmates are rather fanatical about belonging to certain groups or categories. Could you tell me about the main categories among them?

Yes, in prison, where people are deprived of everything, where they are deprived of even their own names, the questions and the search for categories is often maniacal. For example, they search for "scientific" proofs for the priority of their beliefs. With unbelievable erudition, with an incredible amount of quotes from archeology, literature, philosophy, and linguistics they try to prove that Adam and Eve spoke Ukrainian or Armenian, or whatever other national category they belong to. I would classify them roughly into five main groups. First, the Nationalists—all who oppose the Moscow Empire according to their nationality. Of those there are the "activists" who, arms in hand, tried to stand against the Soviet armies, and the nonviolent nationalists (teachers, professors, writers) who tried to preserve their national values ideologically. They opposed the Government's attempts to Russianize everything and attempted to preserve their cultural and religious traditions. The second group are the Revisionists—the average Intelligentsia, both technological and humanist, those who recognize the Soviet way of life for what it is, but still cling to Marxism. No matter where they've begun, whether with Marx, Plekhanov, Lenin, or Kautsky, they are still dreaming of going back to the purity of those doctrines that were "corrupted" by Soviet rule. Once, when some Russian nationalists tried to use Andrei Sinyavsky's name and authority by having him on their side, he replied, very friendly, but very firmly, that he preferred to be in the Soviet prisons than in theirs—that is, fanatically Orthodox and monarchistic. I would add to those words of Sinyavsky that I would rather be in both the Soviet prison and in the Orthodox-monarchistic ones than in the prisons of "renewed and purified Marxism and resurrected dictatorship of the proletariat."

The third category is VSKhSO [Vserossiiski Sotsial-Khristyanski Soyuz Osvobozhdeniya Naroda—Pan-Russian Social-Christian Union for the Liberation of the People]. It is not a big organization, but still they stand apart. These are conservative forces who are for the old orthodoxy and are anti-Semitic. Among the Russians there are no nationalistic problems. The Russian man, no matter how oppressed he is, does not suffer on the basis of his nationality. In any condition, under the worst circumstances he always remembers that he is a part of "the Great History." He never forgets that as a Russian he is either "an elder brother," a "Russian soldier," or a "Russian peasant." The first is beyond any argument, the second unconquerable, and the third was not only sung and lamented by the best minds of Russia, but still remains an enigma and a mystery to all his compatriots as well as Western philosophers and historians. The percentage of Russian political prisoners is nil in comparison with those of other nationalities and in contrast with the percentage of criminals. The best of those Russian apostles was Leonid Sitko, and I can state that it was very difficult to resist his charm and his erudition. He had a monstrous past, having been in the German concentration camps from the beginning of the war and then in the Soviet camps. He had an unending store of stories which he used with great artistry to prove his point: how the Russians could sacrifice themselves heroically for their "brothers." Of course, he never mentioned the other kind of deeds of the "elder brothers." Shortly after his arrival at the prison camp, all the Russian inmates became his disciples. They were mostly there on criminal charges. And these people, who only yesterday had nothing but militant contempt for anyone reading a book, all these bandits and thieves, were reverently dragging volumes of Soloviev under their arms and exchanging comments like, "You know, the Czar said to Count Voinovich . . ." or "I'm astounded, the Czarina wrote to Voltaire that . . ." It was all very amusing for many of us because it was for the first time that we found ourselves in a situation where the Russians were in the minority. Vladimir Osipov, of course, was also one of the leaders in that group. They had a single aim: to get rid of the Bolshevist ideologues at any price, but to keep Russia, also by any means, as a Great Empire, because a divided Russia would instantly become a third-rate power. Thus, while hating the Soviet regime they are obliged to place their hopes on its military might.

The fourth category were the "Polizei," those who worked for the Germans during World War II. Among those there are some ideological opponents of the regime, but en masse they are parasites who did not want to fight the Germans during the war, for which they received 25 years. Some of them cooperated with the Germans and in the camps they have analogous roles, that is, their "work" is of a police nature—they have to be informers.

Q. But if their sentences were for 25 years for the war crimes and it's been 28 years since the war ended, how is it that they are still there?

First of all, they weren't always caught at the time. Or the authorities knew about them but postponed their arrest until it was needed. The authorities know of a number of people who could either be considered guilty before the Government or who could be worthy of honor. Every KGB office in its own district knows a few in each category. And since it is necessary to raise the tension from time to time, they need a hero or a traitor. So at some moment the local KGB gets an order to produce a hero. The papers headline the event, meetings are held, the old guy is dragged to some tribune, a medal is hung around his neck, everybody cries, there is renewed enthusiasm, and all the veterans piss in their pants out of pure elation. They recall that they are also human and also heroes. In the same way they "discover" a traitor of whom they knew all along. There is an emergency trial, witnesses appear, and the 25-year sentence is given. At times when a certain district runs out of "traitors" they yank one out from some camp and present him with the new "previously undiscovered charges." Sometimes there is a death sentence.

Q. What does all this achieve?

It's all thought out. The after-the-war atmosphere of grief, hatred, and hostility is always maintained at a certain temperature.

Q. And what is the last category?

They are the Westernizers. They recognize that there is no chance of saving Russia, that the slogan "save Russia" or "Russia is being destroyed" is the most dangerous slogan there is. The West must be saved from Russia. Today Russia's "peaceful" invasions are much more dangerous than her military ones. We understood that beside our own national interests there is also humanity and that humanity is under the same threat as we were in the prison camps. Naturally, people who do not seek reforms, who long ago gave up hope for a good Soviet czar, who know that Communist religion is only a bait for nationalist expansion and the fight for world domination, these people are the real enemies of the regime. We understood that even though this power is invincible, even though we are doomed, a human being must still fight it though he will die in the battle. This is the smallest category, but it is strong precisely because of the absence of any disarming hope for a better tomorrow.

Q. Were there any Western inmates in camps and prisons?

Yes. You know the Western person doesn't make a very good inmate. No one has beaten him yet, he isn't yet hungry, or hasn't gone through any interrogation, and already he falls apart. Just from the humiliation alone that he's been locked up. The Russians are really hardened by their environment.

Q. Did you see any American prisoners?

Yes, Gary Powers. But, of course, he was in quite different circumstances from anyone else. He had a room to himself, with one cell mate, and plenty of food.

Q. Was the cell mate a Russian?

He was a Baltic republic, I believe. He was promised a reduced sentence for making sure that Powers would think that all Russian prisoners are in the same condition as he was. Once there was an incident. We were walking under his windows and one of the inmates saw Powers in the window. He yelled out to Powers, pointing to his stomach, indicating that he was hungry and asking Powers to drop him something. Powers threw down some margarine. The inmate sure got it from all of us later.

Q. Why? He was hungry.

Yes, sure, but he broke the prison ethics by asking for food from one who was better off than the rest.

Q. How is America regarded by the inmates?

My own pro-Americanism elicited a lot of hostility. The Zionists could not forget Eisenhower's betrayal of Israel in 1956. Most inmates, especially the nationalists, hate America no less than they hate the Soviet Government because the irresponsible Western journalists, senators, businessmen, and military men had promised help. They fought and died praying for America, and when Moscow triumphed and the help never arrived, and those who promised made a lot of money on it all, it resulted in hatred toward America. Now any kind of failure in America is met with joyful applause and is considered a revenge for that "betrayal." But I still believe that America is the last bastion.

Q. You were in the same camp as Andrei Sinyavsky—could you tell me about him?

He was loved by everyone, even by those who were totally opposed ideologically to him. He was a moral center that attracted everyone. All those who searched for warmth came to him; he could listen like no one else and even when he disagreed he objected so softly and wisely that the most furious opponents left him in a kindly mood. But despite all that he wasn't any kind of a priestly figure. No, he was one of us. He sang with us and drank with us and there was nothing in him of a tired wise man or a holy father, though everyone sensed his limitless erudition and his moral perfection. Once, when a large group was being transferred to different camps (in order to break up friendships formed in camps, inmates periodically get transferred to different camps), I was in BUR (barrack of strict regime). Two weeks before all such transfers all "unreliable elements" were placed in BURs. The transfers are usually painful. People part, perhaps forever; there is a lot of confusion, fear, and anxiety; and there isn't time to recall that someone has been absent for two weeks. Yet, though I was not Sinyavsky's personal friend but only one of his entourage, he came to the fence behind which I was locked up, to say good-bye. He had every right to forget and he didn't. And when I heard his voice calling me, I cried.

Q. Did you yourself write in the camp?

Yes, I wrote poetry. I didn't attempt to write prose there because it would have been confiscated. I wrote on strips of old newspapers.

Q. And the poems survived?

My comrades memorized them and took them out that way when they'd served their time. Then these poems appeared in Samizdat and in the West.

Q. How early were you interested in poetry?

As long as I can remember. My family loved poetry. My mother was a ballerina, my uncle a scholar, they knew the poetry of Akhmatova, Mandelstam, Tsvetayeva, but they could not open before me that forbidden world when I was a child. They watched helplessly while I was being stuffed with the hurrah poetry of Mayakovsky. My parents knew the poetry of Gumilev by heart, and they knew how a romantic lad like myself would have loved to know his poems, especially his travel poems, but all this they had to hide from me, so that in childhood, in my youth, I didn't even hear the names of those poets.

Q. When did you first get acquainted with the works of those poets?

In the labor camp, where people like Vagin, Sinyavsky, Aleksandr Ginzburg [tried and imprisoned in 1968] recited them for hours. And not only them, but others—hungry, persecuted, sick inmates—recited poetry often to themselves. In Margolin's book [Julius Margolin's *Journey to the ZEK Country*] there is a scene in which a Russian "Intelligent" is dying; he is lying on the ground of a concentration camp and with blue lips reciting *The Iliad.* So that in prison one paradoxically gains a freedom that one could never even dream of outside its walls.

Q. I read in Anatoly Marchenko's book, *My Testimony* [which describes his life in Vladimir Prison and labor camps] that you found your collection of poems, *Ocean Salt,* in the prison library and hid it.

Yes. Those were my early poems published in Leningrad. I didn't want anyone to see them, they are bad. I was ashamed of those poems.

Q. But not everyone in camp was interested in poetry and philosophy and in all-night discussions that took place, were they?

True, the others were bored. But for people who were interested in that mental tension it was an unequaled opportunity. They had formulations on which they spent years, polished arguments and counterarguments, quotes that they held dear for years and took around with them everywhere. And also music. The world of music opened up for me, as perhaps it never could elsewhere, because there in prison when you listen you listen totally, no mundane questions, no routine preoccupation can disturb you or divert your attention because these questions have no meaning. And again, there are always a few connoisseurs of music who would explain to you that Toscanini conducted this Beethoven symphony differently. Our minds were free, we were free of fear because there is nothing worse than prison, and our nerves were naked for the perception of music.

Q. Does that work for creative powers as well?

Well, as you know, Tupolev created his planes while he was in prison.

Q. Why was he arrested?

Because it was simpler, cheaper, and more effective. People could work without any administrative quarrels, and most of all, fear motivates better than encouragement. Ramzin produced his best trains in prison, Korolev began to invent his rockets while in prison.

Q. Did you have a chance to escape while you were still a captain of a ship?

I had. But it would have never occurred to me to escape when I was on duty and when the ship and people's lives were entrusted to me. I didn't want to be a deserter. When I did decide to escape I chose an individual method when I was not responsible for anyone but myself.

Q. You have found an intellectual brotherhood in camps and prisons, but was there any contact with nature, with animals, with the primitive world?

Of course, and again more acutely than in freedom. Among the animals there were also friends and monstrous enemies. The enemies were bedbugs and lice and worst of all, rats. God had pity on mankind when in creating rats he did not grant them technological civilization. Among our friends were the cats. They were loved by all inmates who gave them names and shared their rations with them. Dogs were, of course, forbidden since they could have been trained by us to perform certain tasks. During the times of mass concentration camps, once in a while a dog would manage to live among the inmates, and if it were a bitch it had often a mistress's function. Some people dislike dogs after the experience of prison convoys with German shepherds. I was escorted several times by such dogs, but I couldn't lose my affection for them. Once in a while there were horses; they were the ones given up by the farmers, but they still "worked" in the camps. They were loved especially by former peasants. I observed once how a peasant, thinking that no one was watching him, was hugging and kissing a small horse; he was crying and fed the horse his ration of bread. But that was all in camps, not in prison. When winter came we could not stand the sight of freezing birds. This was in Vladimir Prison. We didn't have enough bread, but many shared it with the birds. Blue jays can be saved with a little fat. If we weren't punished we received 200 grams of margarine a month. Though it was precious, we used to spread some of it on the windowbars and watch them peck it. We knew each bird, we named them and if one didn't show up for a day, we were anxious about its fate. Had it been eaten by a cat? In the Dungeon we were deprived of these joys.

Q. What could you do there?

I used to watch the cockroaches. They had steellike black suits of armor and reminded me of proud, distinguished knights, grand cavaliers of the Golden Fleece. Among them was a simple red-skinned relative, whom I called Don César de Bazan, Count de Garofa. The evil, black, powerful spider who lived in the corner was named Don Sallusty de Bazan, Count de Garofa. And I treated them accordingly. There was also an ant who used to come alone, having somehow lost his ant comrades—he had two names. Some considered that he was a spy from a foreign civilization, a traveler, and a missionary and called him Marco Polo. The others thought that he was a disappointed poet and a dreamer who was in conflict with the hypocritical morality of his ant heap and therefore exiled, and called him Lord Byron.

Q. When were you freed?

On September 11, 1972, I went to live in Tarusa where Marchenko and Ginzburg were living too. It is a place where many writers and poets live. As an ex-prisoner I had to remain under eight months' surveillance; that means not being able to leave the house after 8 P.M., not being able to go to a movie without their permission, and so on. At times they came late at night to check if I was home. However, I applied for a visa to Israel as soon as I could and nine months after I left the prison I received my visa.

Q. Do you remember your first impression of the West?

When we landed in Austria and entered the Vienna airport, we were left alone; the police did not surround us, there were no barricades in the halls; no certain "young men" sneaking around. There were escalators and there were advertising posters in German and we could literally go where we wanted to. The second impression struck me when we were taken for a ride through the town: all the windshield wipers were in place. In the Soviet Union every driver takes off his windshield wipers and hides them when he parks his car on a street.

Q. How do you picture your future?

I picture it in America. I've always felt myself an American. I'm glad I went to Israel first. Had I not done that I would have never forgiven myself that I wasn't here during the Yom Kippur war. I had to come here to find out where I really belong. When I was trying to escape I was thinking of eventually reaching the States. My ideal is still the American tolerance, the American Constitution, and that is why I, an atheist and a hater of all slogans, began and ended each day in prison with a prayer, "America, God bless thee from ocean to ocean."

Q. Why do you think you know America?

The Soviet authorities took care to acquaint us with all the "ulcers of capitalism," any weakness, any fault, any failure of America was instantly propagandized in the country. And even, believing every word, I still thought that there is no nation in the world that is better in both a material and moral sense. There are no ideal countries and there never will be, but all that mankind could achieve is in the New World. Look at the intolerance and nationalism in your neighboring Canada. And look how Kennedy, an Irishman, lives peacefully next to Monsieur DuPont, a Frenchman. I consider that nationalistic isolationism will give nothing to the world except hostility. I can forgive Israel because it is persecuted, and I can also forgive the Ukrainians. But any nation that wants to isolate itself to create its own, specific, the very best something or other, will end up in fascism or backwardness at best.

Q. What about American global expansion?

The expansion of capital, of building factories, roads, schools, which obediently "packs up" when the local government orders it, is not an expansion of tanks and military garrisons. It is not a forcible Russification of the population and the expansion of poverty and barbed wires.

Q. What about the Vietnam War?

I realize that you have one view of it and I another. My view is based not just on my personal experience but on what I was taught in the Naval Academy back in 1952. When the Soviet Navy was still pitiful, when the Soviet Union had barely gotten the atom bomb and it wasn't known whether it was transportable or not, that is when the Soviet Union was not really dangerous. Yet already at that time we were taught in very scholarly terms about Communist world domination. They named concrete places in the world that were potential revolutionary nodes. At that time Fidel Castro didn't know where he would be, and they told us: "We don't yet know which of the Caribbean islands will be our satellite, but we will have rockets close to the Panama Canal. We will block the delta of the Mississippi. We will be near Gibraltar. No ship will go by without our permission. We will reach Malta. Ushakov already tried this in the time of Nelson, but we will achieve it. We will mobilize the proletarians in the Arab countries who can learn to fire a gun in 20 minutes." They taught us that "only the preventive strike is just." And what is strange is that when they wanted to present to us a concrete example, they took a state that wasn't even a state but a French colony—Indochina. Our instructors used to take compasses and calculate the power of various planes, some of which were then only in the planning stage. In 1952 we had to figure out the potential losses, the potential fatigue of the crew, and we had to discuss all that very concretely. It seemed then that the instructor was a braggart, but now I watch in horror how those spots on the map have become targets. At that time it seemed boring and unreal because they had no means to concretize those plans. They have the means today. When the Soviet Union is in a position to strip the entire population in order to build any number of ships, while in the States every dollar must be begged from the Congress and every dollar must be accounted for, then it is difficult for even such a powerful nation as America to compete with the Soviet Union.

Q. How do you picture your life in America?

I hope to work in my own field. I know that at 39 I am too old for the Navy, but I hope to do something with the ships, the sea. If not, I wouldn't mind driving a truck, one of those heavy ones that crosses all the States. I will see America that way. And I hope to write a book. I have already begun.

Q. A book about your prison experiences?

About that too. But I also want to tell the West not to cry over us, not to defend us; the Soviet authorities have the means to destroy us. And indeed you have the right to ignore our pain and our tears and our blood. I want to describe all that I saw and experienced not as my yesterday, but as the possibility of tomorrow.

Q. And the name of your book?

S.Y.S—Save Your Souls.

ALLA TSVETOPOLSKAYA

As we walked along the beach in Nahariya, Israel, Alla Tsvetopolskaya suddenly stopped and pointed to a seagull standing in the sand on the edge of the water. "Look," she said, "look at the way the bird's wings match the white caps of the waves, how her image is reflected in the water. Were I back in Russia now I would have written about it to one of the prisoners."

Born and raised in Moscow, Alla followed the usual Soviet childhood, becoming a Pioneer and later a Komsomol. Then came the Twentieth Party Congress and the revelation of Stalin's deeds. Alla was shocked, but did not question the authenticity of these revelations any more than she had questioned the myth of Stalin's omniscience. Though she began to be disturbed at what she saw and heard, it was only 10 years later that she first dared to act, to sign a letter in defense of Aleksandr Ginzburg. Following this action she searched for a way to help others who were imprisoned. Someone suggested that she could write letters to the prisoners. She began to write to one; soon came the requests from others, and gradually it became for Alla not only a preoccupation but a way of looking at life. She no longer simply went home from work each day, she became aware of every little detail; as she passed through the streets, everything became a subject for description.

Among her many correspondents was Anatoly Radygin. Though she knew none of them, Anatoly seemed to her the closest in spirit. At some point it became clear to both of them that when Anatoly came out they would be married. The day he left the Vladimir Prison, Alla was at the gate, waiting. Ten months later they left Russia.

In their tiny room in the absorption center in Israel, we gathered one evening to hear Anatoly read his poetry. As he read for about an hour Alla watched his face. In her own expression were both joy and pain. The poems told of those who were still imprisoned, but at least for Anatoly it was all over. In Alla, as in Anatoly, one senses an immense strength; they can survive almost any inhuman condition or deprivation except separation from each other.

Q. When and how did you first begin writing letters to the prisoners?

When the KGB began the investigation of Aleksandr Ginzburg. I didn't know him nor any of his friends, but I signed a letter in his defense, since I didn't doubt for a minute that he was right. I understood that this letter wouldn't help him any and might harm me—because everyone who had signed the letter in defense of Yesenin-Volpin lost his job—but I had no hesitation. Soon someone took me to meet Ginzburg's mother, where I met the mother of another prisoner, Leonid Borodin. Borodin had no wife, and since all his friends were also imprisoned his mother was the only one who wrote him letters. She was a village teacher and was cut off from the city news and she asked me to write him.

Q. What was he in for?

He was in for belonging to an armed organization that intended to overthrow the existing system and reestablish Orthodoxy and the monarchy in Russia. He felt that the Russian people needed God and a czar.

Q. What did you write Borodin?

I found out that he needed excerpts from Nicholas Berdyaev and Vladimir Soloviëv, that he wanted to have the poems of Gumilev and Pasternak, and I began to write letters putting the quotes between the lines. He was also interested in the latest news, and I wrote him about what was happening in Moscow (in disguised form), who was arrested, and so on. Later, I began to write about my own life, about what I had seen in a theater, about people I loved, about poetry.

Q. Did he write you back?

Yes. He never wrote about the camp; that was strictly forbidden. But he wrote about Lake Baikal where he was born, and about the work he was trying to write in camp. This was a philosophical essay and it was confiscated from him when he finished his sentence so that the letters he wrote me were valuable for him later in that sense. We even had a discussion on what kind of puppy he would get once he was free. His ideology, based on faith in the Russian people and on a future Orthodox Russia, was not only alien to me, it was hostile to me. He thought for example that the Jews were always bad for Russia and their influence in Russia was always evil. But the fact that ideologically we were on opposite sides had no meaning to me, nor to him. While he was in that hell I just wanted to give him a bit of joy and if he, receiving my letters, could for a few minutes forget hunger, humiliation, and the lack of freedom it was enough for me. He could have become my enemy once he was free, but while he was in prison we had one enemy—the KGB and the Soviet Power. I knew that he read my letters to other prisoners and after a while Ginzburg's wife asked me to write to him too. Then came a similar request from Yuri Galanskov [young poet and activist who died in the prison camp in 1973 after delay in medical help for a bleeding ulcer]. In this way my circle of correspondents was getting wider and wider.

Q. If they read your letters to each other you had to write about different subjects to each.

Yes, I became inventive. I also drew pictures. Once I copied a portrait of Dostoevsky by the artist, Neizvestny. The censor who opened the letter and who was not used to modern art took it for a coded message and called in Borodin, to whom it was sent, showed it to him from a distance and asked him what that was. Borodin replied, "A portrait of Dostoevsky, done very originally." The censor said, "Tell her not to send you such nasty things anymore." For Christmas, I cut out paper animals and little men in hats (representing KGB agents) and sent it to Ginzburg, who had made a Christmas tree out of paper and my animals decorated it. They weren't allowed to have even a branch of a pine tree.

Q. Why not?

For the same reason Ginzburg wasn't allowed to accept the flowers that his wife brought him for their wedding anniversary: because it was joyful. Joy is outlawed in camps. The inmates still managed. For example, once in a while they were allowed to buy cheese in the prison store, and they peeled off the paraffin from it and saved it, hid it and made candles from it for Christmas. Until I began to write those letters, I was very far from any Democratic Movement. I knew about those courageous people and admired them from a distance. One has to be very noble and brave and totally selfless to express protest openly in the Soviet Union, knowing that society will never support it, that it would only mean loss of work, searches, arrests, and—the most frightening of all—the insane asylum. When I met these people it turned out that they were very simple, unpretentious people, at times weak and helpless. Take Natasha Gorbanevskaya [a poet]. She is small and very thin, with two little children. She has no steady work. Where did she have the strength to come out on Red Square to protest the invasion of Czechoslovakia? How could she then stand interrogation, arrest, prison, and insane asylum and not vacillate for a moment, not even for the sake of her mother? And Lyudmila Alekseyeva, who was an editor of a big publishing house and who lost her job the same day as her husband; or Yuri Gostev, who had finished his dissertation and had only to defend it, but was kicked out; and Larisa Bogoraz, who protested her husband's [Yuli Daniel's] imprisonment and went to prison, leaving her son alone. Then there was this old woman, blind, whose sons aged 27 and 34 were both in prison. She was called in by the KGB and advised to write a plea for forgiveness. "Considering your difficult situation," the KGB officer told her, "we'll then free one of your boys." "No," the woman replied, "I don't think any of my sons would want me to write such a plea." Knowing these people gave me strength.

Q. Was your own childhood and youth in any way unusual?

No, it was a standard, average childhood. My father, who understood what was going on, left his very responsible job—he was a director of a metallurgical factory in the Donbas—saying he wanted to study more, so he could have an even more responsible position in the future. In fact, he went to Moscow and took some small job. It saved his life, for all his colleagues were later shot during the 1937 purges. Nevertheless, having saved his own life and understanding the situation fully he did not tell me anything. He consciously isolated me from reality. In his opinion the Soviet Power was there to stay, and my life was going to be there and he wanted to spare me as much as he could. It was better, he thought, for me not to know anything, and anyway, "politics is not a woman's affair." And thus I lived, thinking that socialism is the only just system, that only in the Soviet Union everyone is equal. It didn't occur to me that we were living in poverty; everyone else lived that way, and the only thing we knew about the United States was that the Negroes were oppressed there. That every tenth person in the Soviet Union was in some slave-labor camp I did not know. How could I have known? My mother's brother was in prison, but no one ever mentioned it at all. It was this way until 1953.

Q. You mean until Stalin's death?

When Stalin died I couldn't imagine how we could live without him. In school we had uniforms with black aprons and I was heartbroken when, having announced Stalin's death, the teacher tore up another girl's apron for a mourning band around his portrait. In short, I was exactly the kind of Komsomol youth, thoughtless and trusting, that is needed there. For me the Twentieth Congress was the ruin of all my beliefs. And, strangely enough, I believed instantly in what Khrushchev said about Stalin. But I think Stalinism was in itself a good foundation for such a sudden switch of faith. When "our beloved Marshal Blucher" could be declared "an enemy of the people" in one day, then Stalin too could be declared the enemy. When I was in school, right after the war, there was a shortage of textbooks, and we had to use old ones and had to black out the pictures of old "leaders" who had become the enemies of the people.

Q. Where did you read Khrushchev's speech about Stalin?

It wasn't published anywhere. I didn't know anything; it was like a thunder from heaven. In the Technical Engineering Institute, where I was studying, they gathered us all in groups and read it to us. This is how it was done everywhere.

Q. All those things were still abstract notions; was there any concrete event that affected your attitude?

Yes, the people began to return from the labor camps and prisons. My girlfriend's father came back from a Kolyma camp. I listened to his stories avidly. Then the first Samizdat began to appear; poetry by Akhmatova and Mandelstam. We began to believe that the past would never return. Then Pasternak's case showed us that those promises were lies. At his funeral there were people from all over the country and the police as well as the KGB men in civilian clothes. All this was familiar, ominously so. But my soul was really shattered by the Sinyavsky and Daniel trial. It became clear that it was no longer possible to just feel, that something had to be *done*. If only to feel oneself human, not to be ashamed of oneself. That is why I so readily signed the letter in defense of Aleksandr Ginzburg. Until then I agonized in my own room, but was afraid to do anything. I think it was when I read *Into the Whirlwind* [by Yevgeniya Ginzburg, an account of her 25 years in a women's prison] that I began to step over my fear. But once I began writing letters to the prisoners, and especially when I met the mothers of those tormented men, I lost my fear altogether. This is when I decided that if they fire me, if they put me in prison, it's all right. But I won't be silent and inactive anymore. And if I hadn't left I don't know what would have become of me. I only know that no one could again transform me or my children—if there were to be any—or my friends into obedient cattle.

Q. How did your friends react to your signing the letter?

They tried to talk me out of it. And when I began to write letters and send parcels some very noble and loving people kept trying to convince me to stop doing it, because my return address and name would just attract the attention of the KGB. There were many people in Moscow who gave money and food for those parcels on condition that their help would remain anonymous.

Q. Were you able to send any books to prisons or camps?

Before 1969 it was allowed, but not afterward. Once the mother of Vladimir Bukovsky [then in prison for the first time, Bukovsky is again serving a 12-year sentence for having given a television interview to an American journalist about the punitive insane asylums in the Soviet Union] asked if I could send him *One Day in the Life of Ivan Denisovich*. I did, on condition that I would get it back because it had already become a rarity and it was impossible to get anywhere. You should have seen in what condition the book was returned to me. I found out that every inmate had read it; that they stood in line to get the book. And though I take care of my books, this book, old and dirty, was precious to me because it was in such an abused condition.

Q. Did you have any troubles in connection with your letter-writing campaign?

Yes. There was a scholar, Yevgeny Vagin, who was a co-editor of the last edition of the complete works of Dostoevsky. After his arrest his name was taken off those books. He looked like a young Russian prince, blue-eyed with a reddish beard, and he was in for his activities in the Pan-Russian Social-Christian Union for the Liberation of the People. I found out that he was left alone in the camp, that is, all his friends were transferred to different camps so that they wouldn't give each other moral support. So I decided to write him and, knowing that he was interested in Russian philosophers, I wrote him with long quotes from Shestov, Berdyaev and Soloviëv. I wrote him several letters and received no answers. But then one of the inmates who came from there told me that after the "re-educational" department received my three letters—all letters go there first—Vagin's "moral guide" called him in and without showing him my letters told him that a "nasty Zionist woman" wrote him shameful letters and that he should have nothing to do with me. Vagin said that he didn't know me but asked to see my letters in the presence of his "moral guide" so that he could himself see the content. He was told that in deference to his Russian nationalist feelings he was not able to show him the Zionist propaganda. It was, of course, a lie—I've never been a Zionist and my mother is pure Russian. But I don't know to this day if Vagin knows the truth. I think he had guessed.

Q. Did they generally write you back?

Since they are allowed to write only once a month, in some camps once in two months, I always told them not to bother answering my letters. I did not want to take those letters away from their mothers or wives or sisters. Most of them wrote back nevertheless. I was embarrassed about it because I truly didn't want to deprive their families of the letters, but also proud and happy.

Q. When I asked you if you had trouble in connection with writing letters, I meant trouble from the authorities.

Yes, I had a search. The KGB searched not my home, but my office where I kept a lot of poetry, essays and things like that. But by then I was already prepared by the Yesenin-Volpin "Memorandum."

Q. Was the "Memorandum" really helpful to you?

Yes, but I also understood that it wouldn't be to everyone. The line of conduct he recommends isn't easy and not too many people are capable of memorizing all the articles he cites. We simplified it to its main points so that everyone could understand it and I used to have rehearsals with my friends and my neighbors and even my colleagues on that subject. First of all if they find Samizdat in your house, they are mostly interested in the channel through which it is circulated. One must never name another person, but insist that "this is mine, I always had it and I never gave it to anyone else." Because only the circulation of Samizdat is a criminal offense. We had a friend who was called in for a talk with the KGB. He is an intelligent, educated man and he came back very surprised and said, "Listen, that KGB man wasn't some kind of a stooge, he has a university education. We discussed poetry." This is terrible. Not because you can't accept a KGB man for a worthy interlocutor, but because when you discuss anything with him in "a friendly manner" you relax and can drop something without realizing that it might be dangerous for another person. And they have it written down. So first of all, one must only answer questions—precisely, briefly—and under no circumstances "discuss" anything in a friendly manner.

Q. Can you give me a concrete example?

For example, they ask you how well you know so-and-so and what do you think of this person? You can say, "Oh, I know him real well and he is a great guy. We went to the theater the other day and he was telling me how much he loves his family." You may not know that this particular person is about to be interrogated or arrested. Then they'll say to him, "We have information that you have this good friend, that you went to the theater, and we know the nature of your discussion that evening. He told us." It can undermine that person's self-control. So the correct answer is: "You have no right to ask me about this person without explaining to me what relationship he has to the case." They have to tell you on which case you are being interrogated. If a person has 22 days vacation coming up and he or she gets 20, the person gets really upset and is ready to take this to court. But very few know their real, important rights, civil rights. So I used to go around asking people what would they do if they were asked various questions by the KGB. Because ignorance gives the KGB a free hand. And so when the KGB came to my place of work to interrogate me I saw in it an opportunity to test myself. I understood that it was a trick, an attempt on their part to frighten me or to make me "cooperate" later (they did a similar thing to a friend of mine), and I also knew that according to the Soviet law they had no right to question me at work without first sending me a *povestka* asking me to appear at the KGB. But I wanted to test my own knowledge.

Q. How did it happen?

I was sent out of the office at first in a horrible rain. Then the KGB men came in and began searching a few desks pretending they are checking classified material. Our office had nothing classified. Then they came to my desk and removed from my drawers five copies of Pomerants's essays. I didn't have a typewriter at home, so I used to type Samizdat material during my working hours. When I returned my colleagues told me about it and they also said that the KGB men told them, "We always knew she was a spy. She is connected with the underworld; her friends are criminals." I must say that my colleagues were honorable and didn't believe any of that. Then they called me into the office of my superior. There were three KGB agents there and two of my bosses who were helping them. When they were introduced to me as the KGB, they expected me to faint from fear, but I asked for their IDs. They weren't used to that, and it gave me a sense of strength. I was very nervous and I couldn't even read what was written on their IDs, but it calmed me down.

Q. What did the KGB agents ask you during the interrogation? Could you give me an example?

They asked me if I had read anything of Solzhenitsyn. I said I did. They asked me, "You read, no doubt, only *One Day in the Life of Ivan Denisovich*"?—the only novel of Solzhenitsyn that was published in the Soviet Union at the request of Khrushchev—and I replied, "No, I read *The First Circle* and *Cancer Ward* too." Their eyes lit up. "Who gave those books to you?" I answered, "Friends, but you understand that I won't name them and that I am only talking to you out of kindness because, according to Soviet law, I don't have to answer any questions without an official document designating me as a witness or a suspect. So this entire discussion is a favor on my part." Then they asked what did I like in particular in those two novels. In reply I asked them if they had read the two books. They said no. "Well, then," I said, "what's the use of discussing books with you that you haven't read? As for *Ivan Denisovich*, since you read it, I particularly like his aphorism (which I've made my motto), 'Don't knock and don't lick the bowl,'" meaning don't tell on anyone and don't be a sycophant. And I also said I liked the scene in which Ivan Denisovich works; he doesn't sit at a table interrogating people, he is working hard, and while he does he forgets where he is and those who interrogate him.

Q. What else did they ask you?

They asked me about the five copies of the Pomerants essays and I kept insisting for two hours that they were all for myself. I knew that typing and keeping Samizdat material is not a criminal offense.

Q. What about typing Solzhenitsyn?

That is different. Some of his works are considered criminal. Avtorkhanov [author of *Technology of Power*] is criminal; Djilas is; so is Amalrik and all the material on the Sinyavsky-Daniel trial. But so long as no one has been arrested for reading Pomerants, and there is no precedent, it isn't criminal to have his works so long as they are not circulated. The KBG men knew that I knew it, that my arrogance was supported by my knowledge of the laws, so when they were leaving they said, "Well, we see that there is nothing criminal in your activities. However, we don't like the tone in which you are speaking with us. Therefore, we will act through your administration. We will leave all those manuscripts with your superiors so that they can call a Party meeting in order to discuss your activities and your conduct here with us today, and your tone." I said that since I was not a member of the Communist Party, the decision of the Party members is invalid for me. Then they asked if I was a trade-union member. And, of course, I had to be. So they said it will be a union meeting which will decide about my situation and my conduct. At this point I turned to my superior and said, "How will you be able to discuss my situation with an audience that is not acquainted with the ideas of Pomerants? I am sure they don't know his works since I never circulated them." To which he replied, "It's all right, I'll quote him." And I said, "Well, fine, that will make you the circulator of his ideas." They threw me out. This minimal success reassured me. I understood that it is possible to behave that way with the authorities until they really want to arrest and imprison you. Then they will arrest you, no matter what you say or do. Until you are not so dangerous to them that they will openly break their own laws to put you away, they will stay within the framework of the law. And for that you must know the laws.

Q. How did all that affect you personally?

It affected me in two ways. I began to hate the Soviet system that represses any fresh thought, any fresh word, and I began to be contemptuous of the people who not only stand it all, but bless the hand that strangles them. I was this way myself until Stalin's death. I lost all faith in the Russian people, unrebellious, patient, unthinking, so that the possibility of leaving the country was for me a salvation both physical and spiritual. They tried to frighten me that I would never be able to return to Russia, that the "Motherland will never forgive" me, and I was happy to think that I'll never see these gray, frightened people. I left in order never to return, even as a tourist. I only think with horror of my friends who are still there.

Q. How did you leave?

I left with Radygin, as his wife.

Q. When did you first start writing to him?

A letter from prison or camp is an event not only for an inmate's relatives but for all the friends. Since an inmate is only allowed one letter per month he usually writes to his mother or wife, but includes messages for his friends and even friends of friends come to read those letters. In one of his letters to a Leningrad friend, Anatoly Radygin complained that Aleksàndr Ginzburg had been transferred to another cell in Vladimir Prison and that in his way he had not only lost the companionship of a friend, but was deprived of my letters, which Ginzburg used to let him read. He added that he was so used to those letters that he "would rather lose the bread ration, because I need them more than bread." This sentence was sent to Ginzburg's wife in Moscow and she told me about it. It was around New Year's and I wrote to Radygin wishing him a Happy New Year and to be in Jerusalem in the near future. I didn't realize that this wish would come true literally not only for him but for me. From Ginzburg's wife I found out that we are interested in the same things. Even my passion for ballet, unshared by my other correspondents, was understandable to him, because his mother was a ballerina. So I wrote to him with special pleasure. Once I got a 28-page answer from him; afterward we didn't count pages, only the days till we could meet.

Q. Did you ever try to visit him in prison?

Yes. He was supposed to come out the eleventh of September, 1972, and in July he was allowed the last visit from outside. This means a 30-minute meeting in the presence of a supervisor—no kissing allowed and the only approved topic is family affairs. July first was his birthday and he wrote me that no one was coming to see him. So I decided to go. In Vladimir that year there were the famous fires, so that in addition to the usual July heat there was a terrible smog. I asked for a date with him and was told to wait. I waited standing under the sun for an hour and a half. Then a man in military uniform called me in. He turned out to be Radygin's "moral guide," Fedotov, whose duty is to give political seminars to the inmates, read their mail, and try to reeducate them. Fedotov was courteous with me, said he was glad to meet a woman who stormed Vladimir Prison with her letters, and asked me what relation I am to Radygin. I said we were engaged. He then said that Radygin was rebellious and stubborn and that life with him would be difficult, that he would never get permission to live in Moscow and that I should think it over. Then he started questioning me about Daniel and Ginzburg—who had left prison four months before that—but I refused to discuss them with him. He then promised to arrange a visit with Radygin and left. I waited for two more hours and nothing happened. Then they took me to see Zlotov, an assistant director of the prison, a fat, dumb, dull military type. He said that since I had no official papers to prove that I was engaged to Radygin I could not see him. I left, but I sent him a congratulatory telegram from Vladimir's post office so that he would figure out that I was in the city to try and see him.

Q. So you met for the first time when he came out?

Yes, on September 11, 1972, 10 years to the day after that rainy Batumi night when he tried to escape, I was once more by the gate of Vladimir Prison, knowing that this time no one could prevent me from seeing my fiancé. I gave the guard a suitcase with clothes which we had collected from all kinds of people and while he was changing from his prison uniform I waited by the gate.

Q. What did you think about during those minutes?

It took some time. I repeated in my mind all the poems I knew, I sang in my head all the songs I knew. At times I thought what I would say when I saw him, but it was no use. I couldn't remember anything when I saw him. I don't know what I told him. I only remember his shattered eyes, his trembling lips. Then everything was like a high fever. We rode in a taxi for three hours. I brought sandwiches for him with all the special things that were difficult to get in Moscow, like caviar. He was eating all this mechanically. He kept looking out the window with those wild eyes. Anyone in Moscow can recognize an ex-prisoner by his eyes. At home my mother was waiting with all my friends, many of whom he knew from my letters.

Q. Did he meet any former inmates of Stalin's camps and did he compare notes with them?

Yes, I heard many such discussions. There were things that were worse then and those that are worse now, but one thing was indisputable. In Stalin's time a person who was imprisoned simply disappeared and was forgotten. Today, his family and friends, Western radio stations, protesters and courageous activists like Sakharov and Solzhenitsyn do not allow a prisoner to be forgotten.

All this gives strength to the inmate. It allows him to hold on, to withstand all that without this support he could not withstand.

Q. What were your first impressions of the West?

In Vienna it was the fact that we were escorted from the plane into the terminal by police and that this time the police was there to protect us. When we were approaching Israel it was at night, and the lights were below us, it was so beautiful. Then they said, "You are now approaching Israel," and the national anthem was played full force. We were all crying, my mother, who is Russian, more than anyone. So there was this exhilaration. But when we came off the plane there was so much bureaucratic confusion. And the first shock was when they asked Radygin, "What would you want to do in Israel?" and he said, "No matter, but I want to do anything that would prevent the Soviet Union from doing to others what they did to me." And the official said, "Not here you wouldn't do any such thing." Israel's policy is to remain neutral and cautious.

Q. How do you picture your future?

In America, where my husband wanted to go all his life. I love America beforehand, the country where a senator isn't forgiven for his vote for the Vietnam War, where there has never been any war and there never will be labor camps, where people don't even suspect how lucky they are. I'm sure that I'll look ridiculous with my sentimentality and my hysteria, which I brought from Russia, in that country. I wouldn't be able to look at self-respecting dogs without thinking about the psychiatric hospitals in Russia where patients are being beaten. I guess I'm hopeless in that sense. But I want my children to be born in America, to have children who will have a million conflicts with their parents, with their Government, with themselves, but will never be faced with the dilemma of whether to betray a friend or perish.

YURI GLAZOV

Born in 1929 in Moscow, Dr. Yuri Glazov graduated from the Moscow Oriental Institute in 1952 and went on to graduate work in Tamil. He wrote his dissertation on "The Morphological Analysis of Classical Tamil," and became one of the outstanding experts in his field. He was the senior editor for the State Publishing House of Foreign Dictionaries and in 1965 became a professor of Dravidian Linguistics at Moscow University. In 1968 Yuri Glazov was expelled from both the Academy of Sciences and Moscow University for having signed several protest letters, specifically the "Appeal of 12 Soviet Intellectuals against the Suppression of Human Rights in the Soviet Union." Forbidden to work, Glazov did free-lance translations, and worked on the subjects that interest him more than the exacting science of linguistics. He wrote two books, *Myths of the Eastern Peoples* and *The Narrow Gates.* The latter, a sociological study of the Democratic Movement, was published in London in 1973. His wife, Marina, a linguist in Vietnamese, says, "We both chose linguistics as a safe field; here in America I will study poetics." Glazov was one of the first to apply for an exit visa and in 1972 left Russia. At present he is teaching at Boston College and is a Harvard Research Fellow.

Yuri Glazov can be appealing, exasperating, charming, and infuriating. He can be utterly rational and logical and hold forth on some philosophical topic with finesse and erudition. He can also be gullible and naïve—as in asking a recent acquaintance with all the seriousness and eagerness of a child, "Do you like me?" In Moscow Yuri could stand in line for groceries for an hour and then ask a startled saleswoman, "What does a man live by?" With Americans he is soft-spoken, cool, reasonable. Among Russians he is excitable, dramatic, and argumentative.

On weekends his house is full of American students, who are getting an excellent education in what the Russian soul is. The table is always set for tea or food, the conversation is endless, and the mattresses are laid out in the playroom for those who might come up from another state and need to stay overnight. As yet another student appears at the door, Yuri Glazov greets him warmly and says to his wife, "Marina, feed our guest."

Q. The West admires the courage shown by the protest movement in the Soviet Union. But many of us wonder: do such people as Pyotr Grigorenko, the Medvedev brothers, Amalrik, and Litvinov risk so much *only* because they feel that there is some chance that their actions will bring about reforms or improvements in their country?

The fact that the West admires the courage of these people does not bring me any joy; what we need most is not praise or wonder but understanding. What is lacking is the understanding by the West of what is happening in the Soviet Union. As for the motives of these people, they speak out because they cannot keep silent—the atmosphere and the situation demand it. Before 1968 there was still a hope that some reforms or changes might be possible. After August, 1968, it became evident that any serious dialogue between the Soviet Government and the protest movement was impossible.

Q. So you think that their first motive was simply to speak out, without any hope for reforms?

There was no serious hope that the Soviet Government would respond to their protests. But after decades of repressions people came to the conclusion that a spiritual awakening was necessary. In the beginning many were shocked at these demonstrations and protests, but they later realized that what today was an isolated phenomenon would become the norm tomorrow. The point was not whether the Soviet Government would respond or not, but rather to express moral indignation and to focus public opinion, both in the West and in the Soviet Union, on the existing situation.

Q. Was the Government ever responsive to any of these protests?

Let me put it this way. If there had not been any serious protests in 1964 against the trial of Joseph Brodsky, we don't know whether Brodsky would have been released 18 months later. If there had been no serious protests against the sentencing of Andrei Sinyavsky, we do not know whether he would have survived prison, or whether he might have been shot as Mikhail Sholokhov had proposed.

Q. I meant whether the Soviet Government was ever concretely responsive to the protesters in terms of any enacted reforms?

Of course there were no reforms. On the contrary. But I understood responsiveness as concrete results in terms of softening of the official position in the case of the trials. The fact that Professor Duvakin—who defended Sinyavsky—was reinstated at Moscow University was a victory for us. Even the fact that the Government was silent in response to protests was a victory. The fact that people protested against the imprisonment of Zhores Medvedev is a victory. Any softening of the official position is a victory.

Q. Who are these dissenters?

They represent different layers of society. They come from various backgrounds and their intellectual approaches are different.

Q. What is the nature of their dissent?

In my opinion the West's understanding of the Democratic Movement or of the "dissent movement" in the Soviet Union in no way coincides with the reality of it. In the West the term "dissident" implies someone who has cut himself off from society. This is not the case in the Soviet Union; the dissenters in the Soviet Union are the only thinking members of society. They are people of very high moral and intellectual fiber. Their dissent can be defined as the anxiety of the Intelligentsia to change one model of government to another. In the 20 years since 1953, the Soviet Government tried to change from a system which was hermetically sealed off from the rest of the world, a system of naken power, to a more open system with limited connections with the outside world. As a result of this change a certain amount of freedom was allowed. But then there was a return to Stalinism. The Intelligentsia revolted against this fearful zigzagging in politics and intellectual life. So a great many individuals deemed it imperative to express their views, especially concerning the repressions and imprisonment of their comrades and in order to prevent future repressions. They also wanted to build bridges to the West, to establish a close contact with the public opinion of the West. This closeness with the West is felt much more intensely in Russia than it is in the West.

Q. What form does the dissent take? Does it express itself privately or publicly?

It's a public protest. By public protest I mean a declaration of solidarity with those who had already opposed the Government, whether they are already in prison or in the process of a trial or protesting the imprisonment of others.

Q. Do the dissenters know beforehand what risks they are taking?

Everyone in the Soviet Union understands that their every action is a sacrifice. And so everyone who is ready to act is also ready for repression. Very often the repressions have not been as severe as people expected. Many thought the measures taken against Amalrik—who was imprisoned for three years—were rather light. But his freedom depends on the authorities.

Q. What about Bukovsky, who was given 12 years?

Every period must be understood on its own terms. The trial of Bukovsky took place in the beginning of 1972. At that time the Government decided to stop the publication of *Chronicle of Current Events*, the most important underground publication, and the protest movement as a whole, and to make an example of Bukovsky.

Q. Does the Government sometimes allow dissent in order to identify the troublemakers?

The Soviet Government is in a very peculiar position. On the one hand it is quite capable of suppressing every movement inside the country. On the other hand it has its games with the West and tries to save face. That is why it isn't right to assume that the Soviet Government is absolutely free in its actions against the members of the moral protest movement. The movement at first was a shock to the Government. Later it was thoroughly investigated, especially by the KGB which, more than any other organization, understood the motives of the people in the movement. I think that the KGB wanted to see how the movement would develop. They didn't need to identify the people since the outstanding members of the movement had often been in trouble with the Government. It was kind of an experiment—to see if there would be a chain reaction. But to their great amazement they realized that the society they had created was rather stable and there was no chain reaction. The members of the moral protest movement are isolated not only from the authorities but also from the people and the other members of the Intelligentsia.

Q. Is "moral protest movement" an official name?

No, it's my name. I cannot use "Democratic Movement" because that is a Western term for it. Why call it anything? If you are a normal human being you express yourself and you defend your friends; you try to be a man after all those years when no one was allowed to be a man. But to call it a movement, I would refrain.

Q. You mean there isn't any movement?

If you mean by "movement" some structure with organizing principles and leaders, then there is no such movement. We are very cautious about using such words as "movement" or "organization" because these are precisely the words by which the KGB seeks to define us. Our wave of protest is based only on one principle: free will and challenging the Government's authority and actions. This is based on the movement of the heart, no other obligations.

Q. How do the dissenters communicate among themselves?

Like people do in everyday normal life. In their own homes. And if anyone is imprisoned then they try to address themselves to international public opinion. There is nothing hidden. Of course, there are at least two committees to defend human rights, one initiated by Pyotr Yakir and another by Valery Chalidze and Sakharov. You might say they are organized and they do meet. But there is nothing hidden; they act in the open.

Q. Do you think government agents penetrated the movement?

In the Soviet Union there is bilingualism and the Intelligentsia speaks it's own language, and, of course, the officials are interested in that other language and they send their agents to interpret it. But those who are in the movement are not afraid any more and they speak openly even if they suspect that someone is an agent.

Q. What role, if any, does the BBC, Radio Liberty, or the Voice of America play in influencing the dissenters and people in general?

They were once very influential, but their significance is now greatly diminished. I have a definite criticism about their work. When Pavel Litvinov and Larisa Daniel made their spectacular statement in January, 1968, all these stations broadcast it and various influential people—like Yehudi Menuhin or the widow of George Orwell—signed a letter of support. This was broadcast too, and there was an impression that the West was just waiting to help those people. I remember some of my friends relied very much on that help. It was a false impression that the broadcasts created, and when the repressions came there wasn't any help from the West. I see now that the positive reactions in the West are restricted to very narrow circles. People there should know this and not have any illusions.

Q. Has there been a shift in attitude toward America, then, among the dissidents?

Yes. After the crucial year of 1968, when the moral protest movement was mercilessly suppressed, when several outstanding scholars and scientists were dismissed from their jobs in April, 1968, and when Czechoslovakia was invaded, people understood that Americans had not raised a voice against all that, the voice they've been waiting to hear. Then came very strange rumors that Americans were afraid to raise their voices because they were afraid to damage the protesters in the Soviet Union. We thought these rumors might be inspired by the KGB, but now there is a very solid conviction that in America people simply don't understand what is happening in the Soviet Union, that Americans have their own problems and that the Russian protesters are alone. There are no more illusions about the West, although the public opinion in the West played a very positive role in the case of Solzhenitsyn and Andrei Sakharov.

Q. Did the Russians understand the nature of the dissent movement in America?

No, but they want to understand everything about America and the West. But this is my point about those radio stations. There is nothing in them about protest movements in America. There is nothing in the magazine *Amerika* about that. Why not? Another point is this: people who can read other sources don't understand American terminology. I don't mean they don't understand English, but American language. Even if these articles were to be translated into Russian, they wouldn't be understood. So it is necessary to find a mediatory language to explain what is going on in America to the Russians.

Q. Is there a viable comparison between Soviet dissenters and American dissenters as you personally now see it?

In the Soviet Union the dissent movement is characterized by either anti-Socialist or a neutral Socialist outlook. There is also a very evident religious background, a kind of human renaissance. Also, the obvious nonviolent approach. In American dissent there are elements of violence and a strict indifference toward religion, because in the West religion has been compromised by being indifferent to social affairs. The dissent here expresses pro-Socialist views, while in the Soviet Union people know the value of socialism, at least in the form in which it manifested itself in the Soviet Union. That is why there is a gap and a lack of understanding. In the eyes of the American dissenters, the Soviet dissenters are considered to be naïve, while in the eyes of the Soviet dissenters the American dissenters are considered to be crazy. The best way to deal with the dissidents in both countries is to send the American dissidents to Russia and the Russian dissidents to America. Of course, that's a joke, but here we see the whole drama.

Q. Is that your own opinion or a general opinion in the Soviet Union?

It is not my own opinion. There is often talk in the Soviet Union that American intellectuals are all leftists and therefore crazy.

Q. You don't see an analogy between yourself and Angela Davis?

I must say that part of our Intelligentsia supported Angela Davis. Academicians Pyotr Kapitsa and Andrei Sakharov wrote letters on her behalf. Other parts of the Intelligentsia can't take those who stand on a Communist platform seriously. Angela Davis is an ardent partisan in her defense of blacks; what worries me is how she is being used by Communist propaganda.

Q. What is the numerical strength of the dissident movement?

The number of those who have signed letters is about 1100 people. But one should take into account that behind each one we should see five or six who morally support him.

Q. Is there any religious orientation to the movement? To what degree do the Christian ethics play a part in it?

The religious orientation is obvious because the movement is closely connected with the literary movement, which was launched by Boris Pasternak's *Doctor Zhivago.* Such figures as Pasternak, Anna Akhmatova, Andrei Sinyavsky, Nadezhda Mandelstam, Vladimir Maksimov, all of these are religious people. Or people like Ogurtsov, the head of the so-called Berdyaev circle (who is now in prison) in Leningrad, and Levitin-Krasnov, another outspoken religious writer. Along with them were the two priests, Eshliman and Yakunin, who protested the discrimination against the churches and the KGB games with the churches. Yes, Christian ethics play a definite part in the movement—less in their Christian talk than in their Christian behavior. I agree with my friend, Levitin-Krasnov—who is also in prison now—that Bukovsky, who considers himself an atheist, is a thousand times more Christian than all those who consider themselves Christian but who refrain from any social action.

Q. To what degree is Solzhenitsyn accepted among the dissenters and for what reasons? For his writing or for his moral leadership?

Aleksandr Solzhenitsyn is acknowledged as the outstanding Russian writer of the century, and in the history of the movement he plays an outstanding role as a man of bright vision and remarkable bravery. The whole protest movement is the result of his literary activity. With his books Solzhenitsyn restructured the psychology of the Soviet Intelligentsia. He exerted a wonderful psychotherapeutic effect on society. His influence was extraordinary before the moral protest movement was born. His Nobel Prize is considered among the Moscow Intelligentsia as a prize to Samizdat. But his approach now is retrospective. He refrains from making a meaningful analysis of the present situation, and he is still concerned with the problems that one was confronted with in the prison camps. In *August 1914*, he deals with the causes of the October Revolution and his language there is archaic and obscure. What we need is to understand the society in which we find ourselves now. And I think that in this respect Vladimir Maksimov and Andrei Amalrik have made an enormous effort.

Q. In other words, Solzhenitsyn is not considered the moral leader?

There is no leader now. Solzhenitsyn is respected and even worshiped. As far as a moral authority is concerned, people like Sakharov are the more influential.

Q. But do you agree with the sentiments expressed in Solzhenitsyn's Nobel speech regarding "The World will be saved by beauty" and his attitude toward the importance of literature?

One thing is to agree with a sentiment, another is whether I believe it or not. His estimation of the importance of literature seems to be an exaggerated one. It just shows how difficult it is to judge the West from the Soviet Union. The role of literature in the Soviet Union is extraordinary. In the United States not all the problems can be expressed in literature. There are many other factors that shape society here: Women's Liberation, sexual revolution, new religious tendencies like the Jesus Freaks, and so forth.

Q. Are women liberated in the Soviet Union?

I don't think so. We have a different tendency there: the Russian women would like to be, so to speak, enslaved. They would like to live quietly in a family circle, with a husband who has an adequate salary that would allow them to raise their children quietly at home.

Q. Do they worry about being sexual objects for men?

They work so hard and their life is so miserable that they have not much chance to be a sexual object, because they are too exhausted.

Q. Do those dissatisfied with the conditions in the Soviet Union tend to identify the source or cause with one individual or group in the Government as we do so often here—for example, with the President or the Congress?

Not now. Twenty years ago the discontent was connected with Stalin and later with Khrushchev. Now the name of Brezhnev is seldom mentioned. And there is a growing tendency not to separate figures in the Government and hold them responsible for the situation, but to think of the whole Party apparatus and the Government body as responsible.

Q. Do members of the movement feel that there are people in the higher echelons of the Government and in the Party who are sympathetic or would like to be receptive to their demands?

In 1967 and in 1968, prior to the invasion of Czechoslovakia, there was an opinion among the Moscow Intelligentsia that there are such people in the higher echelons of the Government. But these people, who might still have such sympathies, are not free to express them. No one ever expressed any support for the protest movement, but we know from private conversations that there are sympathizers, say, toward Andrei Sakharov. Brezhnev personally awarded Sakharov the Lenin Jubilee medal in 1970 even though others were against it. But this can also be an expression of political rivalry between different groups in the Government.

Q. If the peaceful, lawful, and judicially constitutional protest of the past failed to prove effective, do you feel that it is likely that some other tactics will be tried? A more militant form of protest such as we have in this country?

I don't think it has failed to prove effective. There have been definite gains for the movement. People feel safer than they did before when the repressions went unnoticed. Though this is a period of exhaustion, it is also a period of reevaluation. As for militant protest, it is extremely unpopular because after the October Revolution and all the riots of the twenties and the fifties, people don't believe in riots or revolutions. I don't mean the minorities like the Lithuanians or the Uzbeks, and I don't mean the common people who out of despair may make some riots as they did in Dneprodzerzhinsk or Kemerovo. I'm not sure it's effective. It would be better to force the authorities to start a dialogue with us. After Brezhnev is dismissed or resigns—and it is natural that he would be dismissed in two or three years—then if the Government still does not respond to the Intelligentsia, I think the only position would be *aprè nous le déluge*.

Q. Why should Brezhnev be dismissed?

He is an old man. Brezhnev is not a dictator, he is controlled by other groups in the Government, conflicting groups. They dismissed Khrushchev. And after this year of hunger and many economic failures, they will use their traditional way of finding a scapegoat. Within two years we will see a new figure, more effective and more coordinated.

Q. How do you view the new accord between this country and the Soviet Union as exemplified by President Nixon's trips and the establishment of trade relations?

The Russian people, despite 30 years of anti-American propaganda, love the Americans very much. They remember the help during the Second World War and they like the idea of rapprochement with America. But there are several serious reservations. Let's look at the wheat sale. It is impossible to go on blaming the weather for the bad crops every year. Half of the Russian population is engaged in agriculture and yet there is always a crop failure. In America only 6 percent are engaged in agriculture and there is a food surplus. The Russian peasants don't like collectivization. There's a kind of strike. When the Americans sell them wheat they act as strikebreakers. On the one hand they are feeding the hungry, on the other they break the strikes and promote the position of the Soviet Government in agriculture. Another thing: J.F.K. was very much loved in the Soviet Union. But then Nixon comes and establishes personal relations with Brezhnev, after the 1968 repressions and the Czech invasion—and these questions are not even raised at all. The rapprochement should not be made at the expense of the Soviet Intelligentsia, which is what is happening right now. Don't play the KGB game when they ask you not to interfere in their affairs. Americans are sometimes afraid of contact with so-called dangerous circles, for fear that they will either harm their own careers or harm the Soviet Intelligentsia. That is an error. If the Russians want to meet the Americans, it means they are ready to take the consequences. Moreover, contacts with the West very often save people from arrests because it is much easier for the Soviets to arrest those whom no one in the West knows. One shouldn't help create the impression that the KGB games are successful, and one should remember that American public opinion is influential in the Soviet Union.

Q. Is the Soviet Government apprehensive about cultural exchanges?

Not so much any more. To their great surprise they realized that it is very difficult for a Russian to live in the West and that the majority of people who defect to the West end badly. They are cautious, of course. But every man who goes abroad is on some kind of a hook; he must do some service and his family is hostage back there.

Q. What about Americans who go to the Soviet Union—are they afraid of them?

Of course they are afraid of the CIA, but they also like to support any xenophobia among the people too. They aren't afraid of the average Americans because meetings between them and the Intelligentsia often prove disappointing.

Q. So the rapprochement is to the advantage of the Soviet Government?

Of course. The Soviet authorities appreciated Nixon's visit very much. Even special Nixon gardens were planted for his visit and squares were remade for his arrival. I would welcome the rapprochement if the best people would gain from that. Andrei Sakharov explains in the most unambiguous form that Nixon's visit didn't bring anything good for the moral protest movement. Of course he did something positive about the Jewish question, but as soon as the Presidential campaign was over, the slavery taxes were introduced for those wanting to leave, and with no objections from the American Government.

Q. What lessons did you learn from the Czech invasion?

They suppressed us several months before the invasion. They were afraid that the fire would spread to Russia. We understood that the Soviet authorities would keep their boundaries at any price—and they were ready for anything even though the suppression of Czechoslovakia occurred with fewer sacrifices than the one in Hungary in 1956. We also understood that the ideas of socialism are illusory, and that Dubcek, who wanted to introduce socialism with a human face, was a feeble man who finally was obliged to go back on his promises and to dismiss—even before his own downfall—his own partisans and followers like Kriegel and Smrkovsky. That is why faith in socialism was frustrated in Russia once again, and this time forever. It meant the end of any hopes for the transformation of the Party apparatus.

Q. Do you think that socialism does work in China?

After 90 flowers out of 100 have been exterminated, then for the rest it may be socialism. It is evident that the Chinese Government at least settled the problem of food and at least the people aren't hungry. Though I have no illusions about socialism, the Chinese experiment deserves serious investigation because they are not themselves cynical about it.

Q. Do you feel that Stalin subverted the original revolutionary ideals of Lenin?

Stalin was a real follower of Lenin, and he was as flexible with Lenin's ideas as Lenin himself was with Marx's ideas. On the one hand Lenin advocated a very patient approach toward the peasants, on the other he suppressed them mercilessly during the Tambov riots. Stalin was not a theoretician; he used many principles expressed by Leon Trotsky and took credit for these principles for himself. In 1937 he restored a new form of monarchy.

Q. Would the story have been different without Stalin?

There is a tendency to believe that if a person is bad his predecessor was good. I think that Stalin had to happen. We have no illusions about Lenin or Marx. Lenin himself did not understand what had happened in 1917 and to what extent he was a fatal force in these developments.

Q. Do you see any link between yourselves and the nineteenth-century Intelligentsia? Does the present Intelligentsia feel any links with the people? What are the myths of the present Intelligentsia?

The revival of the Intelligentsia in Russia is a real miracle. After all, it was exiled or wiped out during the Revolution, and wiped out again in the 1930s. And even though we don't have anyone on the level of Nicholas Berdyaev, Sergei Bulgakov, or Leo Shestov, we will. This reborn Intelligentsia is not the same as the Intelligentsia of the previous century, or that of the beginning of this century. These were very often infatuated with the people and were antireligious. The Intelligentsia now makes use of the lessons of the past and is trying a synthesized approach. Though they realize that the Russian people, in spite of everything, did not undergo any transformation and are basically very stable, there is no cult of the people as there was then. The Intelligentsia does not think that it is possible to communicate with the people, because there is a gap between them and they need a lot of education to understand things. So instead of *narodnichestvo* [populism] there is now *intelligentchestvo:* an appeal to Intelligentsia as a single class that may close this gap.

Q. Do the Soviet people take the Intelligentsia seriously?

The Soviet people do not know too much about the moral protest movement. They are preoccupied with the problems of livelihood, everyday problems. Also, there is the traditional mistrust and misconception of the Intelligentsia among the people. Perhaps they think the idea of establishing a dialogue between the Government and the Intelligentsia is not practical. For example, the common people weren't too interested in the trials of Sinyavsky and Daniel, nor in Solzhenitsyn's case. But when they heard that Ilyin tried in the beginning of 1969 to shoot Brezhnev, they were agitated for days. Maybe in the depths of their hearts they just want to overthrow the Government, not have a dialogue with it.

Q. Were the people indignant about the attempted assassination of Brezhnev?

It's hard to tell. They were agitated by the news—but they never showed whether they were indignant or sorry he wasn't killed. They know how not to express their wishes. The people are very ambivalent and peculiar; they are chauvinists and somewhere they might be dreaming of the overthrow of the Government to which they really never took, yet they act as though they are willing weapons in the hands of the Government.

Q. How does the passive Intelligentsia react to the activists?

The best of them respect and understand the motives of the dissidents and try to be helpful. There are others who hate the dissidents. They either enjoy the feeling of masochism, the feeling of hopelessness, or they don't want any challenges to the ideas that had been settled in their minds for 20 years. Also, there is always the suspicion that if the dissidents are speaking out so openly they might be KGB agents. If they speak out and are not thrown in prison immediately, something must be fishy. This is what I meant when I said that the society is sick, morally sick. When people try to be normal human beings and behave with dignity, the greatest problem for them is not Government opposition, but isolation from their own class.

Q. Does ideology always have priority today over scholarship in such institutions as the Academy of Sciences?

To be a scholar on the level of Albert Einstein or Nils Bohr, I think, is absolutely impossible. As far as a career of a scholar is concerned, if a scientist is not at all interested in politics and is interested exclusively in science, then he might achieve success. He will be supported by the Government and by the highest authorities. Yet, somehow it is still impossible to have this successful career without mixing into politics. Usually it is necessary to write an article that comes out, under the signature of another man; it is necessary to be ready to be used by the mechanism of Party propaganda, to belong to the Party. It's not really possible to remain within the sphere of the science alone.

Q. Isn't Andrei Sakharov a member of the Academy of Sciences?

Yes, he is. Andrei Sakharov is already a mythical figure.

Q. Do you foresee that he will be expelled?

They tried it two years ago. I think that he is relatively immune, but they might try to do something else. They have isolated him from his friends like Valery Chalidze and Yuri Shikhanovich.

Q. Who is Shikhanovich?

He is an outstanding mathematician who for several years had been teaching courses in mathematical linguistics at Moscow University. He is the author of a monograph on the theory of sets, and he made very significant contributions to the moral protest movement. He is now in prison and he is going to be tried for spreading Samizdat materials. [In July, 1973, Shikhanovich was declared insane and put in a punitive insane asylum. Sakharov made repeated public protests. Shikhanovich was released in July, 1974.]

Q. Does the fact that the Soviet Union allows dissidents to leave represent a shift in policy and if so, what are the reasons for such a shift?

It does represent a shift in policy, although it can also be understood as a logical continuation of the old policy toward the dissenters. The KGB showed caution in dealing with dissidents from the start. The previous methods proved ineffective; whether they were sent to Siberia or the insane asylums or dismissed from their jobs, they still remained members of society inside their own country. The KGB and the Government—being better informed—know exactly what problems menace a newcomer to the West and they figured out that it would be more effective to allow them to leave for the West.

Q. What are some of these menacing problems?

Just learning to understand the Western mentality is the first problem. Secondly, the organizations that take care of them here often dismiss them before they have a chance to adapt and adjust and they have to face the problem of taking care of themselves in a society they don't understand. The anti-Communist position of those who are victims of communism over there is not popular here. So they are not trusted by the Intelligentsia here. All this might cause a newcomer to perish or at least render him totally ineffective, which is what the Soviet authorities count on.

Q. What are the reasons for some Jews wishing to return to the Soviet Union?

I think that the main reasons are these: many Jews who want to leave the Soviet Union do not consider where they are going, but from where they are leaving. They go to Israel with many hopes—religious, nationalistic—and they think they at last have their own country to go to. But even though they are not free in the Soviet Union, at least the State takes care of them. In Israel they have to take care of themselves. Language is difficult too. Thirdly, in Russia they are considered as Jews and outside they are considered as Russians, so they get mixed up in their identity and they find out to what degree they are still Russians. Also, there is nostalgia and the close friends they left behind. Though it's a mistake for them to return and they will not be happy, it is better for them not to leave in the first place. The problem is not to help them leave, but to help them improve their situation in the Soviet Union.

Q. What do you think is the best course for those of you who came to the United States?

First of all, to understand the differences in the day-to-day life and not to make hasty conclusions about this country. One should not forget one's own country nor shed the sense of responsibility toward it, but rather to become ambidextrous in the sphere of both cultures. I think that the immigration will continue and in the next year we will see another dozen or two of the Russian Intelligentsia arriving here. For some it will be immensely difficult to live in the West. I personally would never ask any of my friends to come here.

Q. What about yourself, personally?

I don't want to forget my Russian substratum, and though I am trying to integrate into American society, I am still connected with Russia by an umbilical cord and I can't live without knowing what is going on there. But I understand how difficult it is to survive spiritually and intellectually in this other rebirth, in this new world.

Q. What are the main differences, as you see them, between the life-style here and in the Soviet Union?

In the Soviet Union there is a state-oriented society; this is a person-oriented society, though I sense now that there are growing tendencies of the State to increase its role in the country. Nevertheless, there is freedom here. I see that in the Soviet Union, despite the material deprivations and lack of freedom, there are good features like close friendships, a spirit of fraternity, and a very intense hunger for intellectual information. There is a very great value placed on literature. Poetry doesn't play any decisive role here at all. You see here scattered individuals and a very high value placed on personal space [privacy], where in Russia we have an overlapping of the souls. People feel each other better there than here where personalities are solitary and independent. Americans are so cautious that someone might interfere with their personal affairs, while in Russia usually people are more open with others.

Q. What is the greatest strength and the greatest weakness in America as you see it?

Strength is in the spirit of freedom and in equal opportunities for those who have lots of energy to realize their abilities. Of course, every society is restrictive in some ways. The weakness is in the absence of the intellectual and spiritual tension that is evident in some layers of the Russian society. In the spirit of freedom and in a pluralistic society, one has many choices, of course, and that is why the spirit of American society is characterized not by absolutes but by the refining of oneself relatively.

Q. What are the prospects of the moral protest movement in the immediate future?

The movement has now come to a standstill and frankly I am not surprised. There is a lot of disillusionment even though many things had been foreseen. I think that after two or three years of silence there will be other developments. Because if the Soviet authorities will not understand that it is necessary to change course, and to stop their spiritual genocide, then they will be opposed in at least four different ways. First by the underground—in some cases we have already seen the appeal for strikes in Moscow last year. Then there is a new revival of Slavophilism. I'm not a partisan of that, especially when it is connected with anti-Semitism or fascism, but I share their belief that the Russian people will finally gain their freedom. Another strange revival is neocommunism. The young people who do not want to learn from the lessons of Czechoslovakia think that Stalin did corrupt Lenin's ideals and that they could revive Lenin's teachings as put forth in his *What's to Be Done?* and try to realize a new approach to communism the way Dubcek tried. Lastly, there is the Christian revival, but one connected with social activities. The religious approach now demands action in the social sphere, as with Boris Talantov and Gleb Yakunin. That is why I am not pessimistic at all in regard to the future of Russia. We will witness all this in three or four years. I don't invite anyone to make another crusade against the Soviet Union. It is invalid to blame only the Party officials and the Government for what is going on. They are not more responsible than the people and the Intelligentsia. Finally, it is necessary to intensify everyone's feeling of responsibility for what goes on on this earth—whether it is happening in South Africa or Bangladesh or in Ireland or in the Soviet Union.

YELENA GLAZOV

This interview with 19-year-old Yelena Glazov took place in South Nyack, New York, five months after the Glazov family arrived in the United States. While her father and stepmother reminisced and worried about their Moscow friends, Yelena cooked, served, and took care of her two small stepbrothers. Though she seldom spoke, it was obvious that she was the strength and support of the family. It was to Yelena that her stepmother turned during the moments of intense homesickness.

Self-effacing and shy, Yelena is not unwilling to express her opinion when asked for it. From her answers it is obvious that she is self-questioning, aware, and alert to everything around her. She is also extremely well-read; one is constantly surprised by the contrast between her timid manner and the authority with which she is able to discuss Hegel, Faulkner, or Berdyaev.

"I've received my education while serving food at my father's table in Moscow," she says. "There were always people in our house and they talked far into the night, every night. They discussed Freud, Kierkegaard, Zen Buddhism, and various religions. I always hung around the table in order to hear them talk. I've learned all I know in this way. In school and in the University I was taught little outside of Marxism-Leninism, and I've forgotten that by now."

Born and raised in Moscow, Yelena is very nostalgic for her friends there and for the kind of friendship that existed among the children of the Intelligentsia. Though she certainly has no trouble in relating to American youth, it is obvious that she misses the intensity of relationships that characterized her Moscow life. In South Nyack Yelena went to work as a waitress to help pay for the house her father bought with the assistance of his American friends. The house was bought "so that our Moscow friends will always have a place to stay when they emigrate to America."

Q. What was the first Western city you saw on leaving the Soviet Union and what was your impression of it?

Rome. I was astounded. But at the same time it was a very strange feeling. We felt bereaved having left our homeland for good and there was this shatteringly beautiful city. It was laughter through tears. I thought I was on stage where everything was sets and decorations. It was in direct opposition to what I was used to. In the store windows there were pears, apples, melons, and everything was so beautifully displayed, so unbelievable. I felt I was walking around in a fairy tale. And the color of meat was very different, too, because in Russia meat is frozen and the color is not so bright.

Q. What was the most amazing thing to you?

Store windows. The incredible store windows—and they were everywhere. And then, when you enter the store they smile. I did not expect it. I came into the first store and they said, "Oh, signorina, que vuole?" and I was so shocked. Then all these young people so scantily dressed and walking around with their arms around each other. It was amazing.

Q. Did the young Italians bother you?

They had national elections at the time, so they were probably preoccupied with that. But some of my friends did get pinched nevertheless. I never did. I never walked alone.

Q. How long was it before the fairy-tale impression wore off?

It never did as far as Italy is concerned. All those narrow, little streets, the ancient monuments. . . . I still think of it as a fairy tale. The only thing that kept reminding me that I am still on earth was the way they push in the Roman buses, just like they do in Moscow.

Q. Would you tell me about your education in Moscow?

I received my education while serving food and tea at my father's table. There were always people at our house, and they talked far into the night about everything. They discussed Freud, Zen Buddhism, Jung, Kierkegaard with great passion. I always hung around the table in order to hear them talk. I've learned all I know that way. In the Soviet school I learned nothing except the theories of Marxism-Leninism.

Q. When you first saw the United States what did you think? Did your plane land at night or day?

It was during the day. The first thing I noticed, what made me very happy, was the similarity to Moscow, a big, modern city where everyone is busy. New York impressed me as an ugly city, but at the same time a familiar one and I felt very close to it. Some streets in New York look like Moscow's new district. And then the pine trees and birch trees outside of the city: I felt that I had come home.

Q. Do you find America different from what you were told it was like in the Soviet Union?

Yes. I like America very much, more than I expected. I like the absence of class here. In Moscow it is very easy to discern the circles among the young. The highest circles are those whose parents occupy high positions and are Party members. Those are called, *Sovetskiye Detki* [Soviet kids]. They can afford to wear Western clothes which are fashionable. Then there is the circle of the children of Intelligentsia, whose parents perhaps lost their jobs for their dissent or are under suspicion. If the children sympathize with their parents, they feel alienated from the other circles and even begin to exclude themselves, because they know that it will be difficult for them to enter any kind of society. Then there are the workers' children. However, this is changing now. The authorities, in an attempt to make the atmosphere healthier, are trying to bring more and more of the workers' children into the universities. Because the others begin to smart-talk about Pasternak and Akhmatova, they say that they don't like Sholokhov, so the idea is to mix them up with the working-class youth. What I like about this country is that there is no class consciousness. The young people form their own groups, according to their own interests and one group does not feel inferior to another. This is what I observe in college, anyway.

Q. At what age does a young person generally decide that he or she wants to go to college?

In high school everyone wants to go to college. Boys, of course, want to go to any college to avoid the two years' army service. So they try to go wherever it's easier to get into.

Q. How does one get into a university? Are there any tests like we have in high schools here, SATs?

No, nothing like that. There are the entrance examinations and only when a case is doubtful do they look at high school records.

Q. When is a case doubtful?

When the entrance exam grades are half passing. Although in most institutions, for example in the Institute of Oriental Languages, the passing grade for a boy is a C, for a girl it must be an A.

Q. When does a student decide on his or her major?

It must be declared right away and it's not very comfortable. I did not know what I wanted to be when I finished high school, and I still don't. Yet one must decide right after high school to follow a particular specialization, and it is very difficult to change the major later.

Q. Are the relations between students and professors different from what you've observed here?

There is always a war between students and professors back in Moscow. It starts in elementary school. Teachers, because they have huge classes, are irritable and nervous and often scream at the pupils. Everybody dreams of going to a university, but when they get there they find the same kind of boredom and stupidity. Professors are not loved as a rule. However, if there is a good teacher, his fame spreads very fast and then he gets incredible love and devotion from the students. I was very surprised at the mutual respect I found here between students and professors. A lot of things were very shocking at first. I've forgotten already how shocking. First of all, I was shocked that the students did not stand up when the professor entered and left the room. In Russia it's the first thing a child is taught on his first day in an elementary school and then it continues in a university.

Q. Do you think this teaches respect for authority?

I doubt it. It just develops a meaningless habit.

Q. What was your first experience in a Western school?

That was in Rome in an American Overseas School. My entire time there was one of amazement and I felt completely lost. First of all in Russia there is no high school and elementary school division; it's all in one building, one big boxlike school. Here there are small houses and pupils spend a lot of time outside. In Russia there is a person who watches the students all the time so that they won't go outside.

Q. Why aren't the pupils allowed to go outside?

So they won't skip classes.

Q. The school in Rome, was it high school or college?

High school. I was very surprised that no one was scared of the teacher or that he would ask a question. In Moscow everything was built on the fear that a teacher would call on you to answer and you wouldn't know. And the atmosphere of informality, everyone is walking around like they are on vacation all the time, except during the exams.

Q. Is there much of a difference in relations between the young people and their parents?

Here, students, if they want to, can make money and begin to be independent very early. In Russia, if a student goes to college, he is financially dependent on his parents for a long time. It is actually impossible to study and work at the same time except for those who go to night school. So people between the ages of 20 and 30 are very immature, unindependent. They are better educated than my father's generation, more aware, but they are like boys. Maybe . . . it's because they don't feel in charge of anything.

Q. What do the Soviet young people think of our youth?

They think that life is much easier in America but at the same time that the young people don't have so much fun and gaiety and excitement when they get together as in Moscow. In Russia, friendship is very, very important. For everyone. I wrote my friends there and told them that everyone here is . . . not for himself . . . but in himself. They wrote back saying how sad that must be, although we already had an inkling of that from reading Salinger's *Catcher in the Rye*. Everyone loved the book and everyone got depressed about it. They said how lonely it must be to live in America.

Q. Is Salinger the most popular American author?

He and Hemingway. And William Faulkner among the children of the Intelligentsia.

Q. Whom do they like among the Russian authors?

The anti-establishment youth like Pasternak, Akhmatova, Mandelstam, and Tsvetayeva. These four are their idols. Also Zosychenko and Babel of the prose writers. The establishment youth like Yuri Kazakov and Nagibin—those whom Galich [songwriter] defines as "romanticism about nights by the fire."

Q. And Brodsky, Solzhenitsyn?

They are very controversial. Some people think that Solzhenitsyn is a very good writer, others think that he writes about very interesting things but is a bad writer. Still others of the establishment youth think he is a scoundrel.

Q. What about music? Is there a cult among the young?

They are mad about the Western music. But the records are almost impossible to get. They are very expensive and difficult to find.

Q. What are the most popular artists there?

The Beatles.

Q. Any Americans? Bob Dylan, Joan Baez? Any groups?

No, we didn't know those. We know the Beatles. It's a very courageous thing to know the Beatles. The older people think they are silly and the dances are silly.

Q. How do the young people entertain themselves?

Since no one dreams about a car and there is no possibility of going anywhere, they often walk the streets or in the parks. They can go to a movie or a café. Only it's not easy to get into any café. The saying goes, "We've spent the whole night last night trying to get into different cafés and we came home with nothing." The best form of entertainment is to get together in someone's house when the parents are gone, dance to records and drink wine.

Q. Is wine the most popular drink?

Wine and vodka. Sometimes when people run out of everything they drink eau de cologne.

Q. Do they know about the drug situation here in the United States? What is their attitude toward it?

There are two attitudes. One is to believe whatever the Soviet press says about it: that every second young person is a drug addict, that there are murders on every city corner because of the drugs. The other attitude is that the whole thing is Soviet propaganda. So many stories are invented, it's hard to know what to believe. But then there is addiction in Russia, too. I know some cases.

Q. Addiction to hard drugs?

To hashish.

Q. That's considered a drug addiction? By whom?

By students. By smokers themselves.

Q. I meant heroin, LSD, speed.

I've never heard about those.

Q. Are there any young rebels in the Soviet Union?

Yes, there are hippies.

Q. They are called hippies? What do they mean by that?

Yes, hippies. They mean long hair and independence.

Q. What do they do that is hip?

They imitate Americans. We even had two hippie demonstrations in Moscow.

Q. Against what?

Against the Vietnam War. They don't care about the war, and it wasn't really about the war. They just wanted to imitate Americans, to present a picture totally unfamiliar to Russia. So they sat down with placards in the Square and they were dispersed by the police; some were arrested and beaten. They told me that they were beaten; I don't know if that was true. I don't know that circle well.

Q. What did they really think about the Vietnam War?

Some think that it isn't a bad idea to give it to the Communists wherever they are, and others that it would be good if America could hold out and beat them. But things look different there than here. It's very complex here.

Q. Did you hear about the protest movements in this country while you were there? What did your friends think about that?

In the first place everyone was very interested in the possibility of protest. The content wasn't interesting to anyone. They think that if a protest is possible, then it follows that there is nothing to protest about.

Q. What was the official attitude toward the protests, the press attitude?

They were dual. On the one hand they wrote how nice it was that the young Americans were protesting and trying to break away from their fathers' values. Then, parallel to this, there was always the position that these Americans are fat, spoiled, and disobedient. I don't think they have worked out the final attitude toward this question.

Q. You know that the American youth didn't protest only about the war. They protested against their parents' values, against their preoccupation with material things. Is there anything like that in the Soviet Union?

I'd say it's the opposite there. The past generation did live by ideas and ideals. At least they played that game. Now, the present generation values material success because they consider that their parents were too concerned with the ideas and ideologies and they don't like the results. So the young people in general want a simpler life, with simpler goals, cozy and warm.

Q. To what extent do you think the Soviet young people are convinced that such accepted institutions as socialism are good for the country?

Socialism is not in vogue among the young. It's in vogue to talk contemptuously about it. They understand now the difference between life in Russia and in the West. When they hear that some people in the West treat the question of socialism seriously, they can't understand how that could be.

Q. What percentage of young people do you think look forward to becoming Party members?

I don't know the statistics, but all those who want to succeed in any way do not exclude the possibility that they would have to join the Communist Party. Very few people aspire to that, but many think of it in practical terms. They are quite cynical about it.

Q. Do you think American youth is more politically aware?

It's a complicated issue. How does one compare the American youth with the Soviet youth who have no access to any information about the rest of the world? I would say this: that those who are aware and those who do speak up are perhaps more seriously aware than the youth here, because the risks and responsibilities are much greater. But I also know a lot of young people there who are simply afraid to talk about such things; they know the consequences. So it's difficult to estimate anyone's awareness. The openly aware, though, are only concerned with Russia. They are not interested in any other country—Ireland or Bangladesh, or Vietnam.

Q. Have you heard about the attempts of some of our young people to live in communes? What is your opinion of communal living?

It seems to be a beautiful idea, but I am always afraid that a communal life inevitably gets transformed into a communal psychology. It narrows a human being in some respects. It seems to me, though I'm not sure that I'm right, that if a person is searching for something, he must go from person to person, from idea to idea, from one thing to another. It seems to me that those who search are loners. I don't think it's possible to search in a group. That is why I am afraid of group psychology. It keeps one back from passing the stages necessary to a search. I always want relationships between people to be like the relationships between stars so that when people gather together it would be like each coming from a different world, bringing something of one's own, but never enclosed in just his own.

Q. What about people who are not searching at all? Would it not be better for them to live in a commune and share responsibilities?

That would be very frightening. In a communal life if there are all those people devoid of spiritual dimensions, one with such dimensions would be like a white crow. I'm always afraid . . . I'm most of all afraid of social condemnation. When people with spiritual dimensions judge you, it is possible to get over it. But when people devoid of any spirituality are in judgment over you by virtue of a group, then it's best to avoid such situations. But I realize that I'm thinking in terms of the Russian communal life that I knew. Perhaps a communal life here could be different, if only because you have this word in the English language which doesn't exist in the Russian language, is it personal space?

Q. Do you mean privacy?

Yes, privacy. The fact that this concept exists here and not there may make the communal life here different.

Q. Is there anything like the American sexual revolution in the Soviet Union?

Well, of course, the older generation thinks that ours is a fallen one, a more corrupt one. Anyway, no one talks about it; it's not a popular subject there.

Q. What is your opinion about it from what you observed in this country?

I think it means that people stop being pharisees here. They can understand and forgive and even consider it none of their business. In Russia, when a girl has fallen, she has a very traumatic experience just from the attitude of those around her.

Q. What do you think about the availability of the Pill to teenage girls?

I think it's good. There are no [birth control] pills in Russia, but there are a lot of abortions and they must cause very big traumas.

Q. When you were in Moscow, did you ever hear about the Women's Liberation Movement in America? What do you think about it?

I only heard of it here. I think that it is a very interesting movement in terms of future results. What they are striving for is correct. But I disagree with the position that there aren't any psychological differences between men and women. And I don't like an overly serious attitude toward that subject, as though it was the most important one. It seems to me that when they discuss it too intensely, it looks a little ridiculous.

Q. Does the fact that many women in the Soviet Union are doctors, engineers, judges, demonstrate that the women are more liberated there?

They are less liberated. They carry the responsibilities of these professions in addition to housework and children. And they are expected to be very feminine. It is not in the Russian man's character to help around the house.

Q. Do women follow our fashions in the Soviet Union?

They'd like to, but few can afford to. They wouldn't walk around with patches like the young do here. You see, for a long time they tried to imitate the West, learn to use makeup and curl their hair. Finally, when they got there, it turned out that styles had changed in the West and they are late again. The girls finally won the battle of miniskirts, and now it's passé in the West.

Q. What are the most negative aspects of this country to you?

I don't know if I can explain. It's complicated. When I left Russia, I left many very good people there. Very rare people. People in whom something new, something very important has been forged. And from what I see, it will be very difficult for the people here to understand those Russians. I don't mean the relations between Russia and America. Those people in Russia . . . would seem very foreign to people here. Their incredible strength and courage are only possible to understand if you live there. I don't know how else to put it. It's just too difficult to understand all this from here.

Q. How do you picture your future?

I want to study very much. I want to find out what I want to study most. Then I dream that one day I will have close friends like I had in Russia. Because being Russian, I can't live without that. I think that whatever I'll be doing it'll be tied up with Russia. I don't think I could ever forget it, nor do I need to. I feel responsibility toward it.

Q. Are you used to the idea that your life will be here from now on?

Yes. I would want to be an American, too.

Q. What does American mean to you?

Americans are free. To be an American means to feel free, personally. And so first of all I want to learn how to feel free in this American way. Then it wouldn't matter where I lived once I learned that. I have a very strong inferiority complex. I usually feel ashamed about expressing my ideas. I'm surprised at how Americans can calmly say what they think. I think it must be the spirit of the country. I don't think they were taught to be that way. It's just the spirit of the country.

Q. What do you write your friends back in Russia about America?

I tried to describe this little town we are living in. It's very different from our towns. It's similar to the vacation places near Moscow. But to this day I do not write my friends about this house we live in, this staircase. They wouldn't understand; they might think that we are rich. And in Russia, among our friends, to be rich is always associated with a spiritual decline, with a fall even. They would think that I no longer understood them and it would be perceived, even by my very closest friends, as a sort of . . . betrayal.

YURI KUPER

When asked by an earnest art lover if he would have sold out as an artist, Yuri Kuper replied, "For 300 rubles it's not worth it, and they don't pay any more than that over there. For 1000 I would have considered it. But one must keep in mind the local conditions; one is never sure that the client will pay up in the Soviet Union."

This self-deprecating lightness and irony is typical of what seems to be Kuper's revulsion against any kind of romanticism. This might well pass for cynicism, but in his paintings one can see a search for beauty untarnished by sentimentality, a softness and melancholy. This gentleness is also felt in Yuri's relationship with people. While cynical in his speech he is not simply tolerant, but kind and warm to others. The incongruity is not surprising. Above all Kuper seems to have a profound distaste for the cliché image of the artist and for maudlin attitudes toward art. Both his cynicism and his friendliness are shields against any invasion of a very private world.

Born and raised in Moscow, Yuri Kuper did not feel any early calling as an artist. It happened accidentally. Or so he says. He was never a dissident, unless one thinks of dissent as a refusal to comply with prescribed standards. Yuri always followed his own path. In 1972 he and his wife, Mila, a fashion model, emigrated to Israel. In 1973 they moved to London where they presently live. Last year Kuper began to write a novel, to preserve the memory of his bohemian friends in Moscow. A friend read part of the manuscript, liked it, and it was sold before it was finished. His novel, *Holy Fools in Moscow,* is marked by a unique voice, as his paintings are by a unique vision. Life for Yuri Kuper seems to be a succession of moments, each distinguished by a particular state. What interests him most is to be able to capture that particular state, either on canvas or in words.

Q. What was the impression or event that made you realize that you wanted to be an artist?

It came about accidentally and relatively late. I mean it wasn't as some people say, "I always loved to draw as a child." When I finished high school, and the question of my future came up, I didn't have any special attachments. I knew I didn't like math or science, but I had no specific inclinations. I had a friend, one of those who stands out in a faceless crowd, a poet, and he said that I should apply to the Stroganov Institute, an art school. I asked him, "What for? I can't draw," and he replied, "The people on the selection committee will know whether you can hold a pencil or not. They'll figure out whether you have talent or not." So I went. The procedure required submitting some drawings; of course I had none, so I wasn't even allowed to take the entrance exams. But for some reason, from that day on, I decided that I must study art.

Q. So how did you begin?

There was in Moscow a famous woman, Vera Tarasova, who was rumored to have some connections with educational institutes, and to whom the so-called Intelligentsia brought their children to study art. I prepared with her for the entrance to an art institute. It was there that I first came in contact with the concept of what an Intelligentsia is. It was a children's salon.

Q. In what sense?

The classes were conducted while music was playing. She loved French chansonettes. The children were brought up to be melomanes. They went to concerts and I felt awkward there because I grew up otherwise, in the streets, so to speak, and had never been an Intelligentsia child.

Q. What do you mean you grew up in the streets?

Well, I ran around with a certain group of boys, it's called *shpana* in Russian, a sort of street gang. We wore white scarves and caps, that was the highest chic.

Q. What kind of chic?

A prison chic. Naturally, we weren't thieves, but we dressed and behaved like thieves. Later, as you know, came the *stilyagi*, those who imitated the styles of the West, but we just imitated the brigands. We were required to wear ties in school, but as soon as we'd leave school the ties were pocketed and we'd put on our caps and scarves.

Q. When did you feel an irreversible conviction that you could only be an artist and nothing else? Was there such a point?

This was much later, when I was already in the Art Institute.

Q. How did you get accepted there?

I studied with Vera Tarasova for a year without much enthusiasm. Nevertheless, she did give me something; she taught me how to imitate professional apprenticeship. To be accepted in a Moscow art school doesn't take much. For example, I could now prepare anyone for any art institute by knowing what style of drawing this particular institute prefers.

Q. Is there an entrance exam?

Yes. One must draw a landscape, a still life. In short, a primitive approach.

Q. What did the Institute give you in terms of art?

Communion with other students; we learned from each other.

Q. How many years did you study there?

Five years. I finished the Potëmkin Institute with a major in graphics. This entitles a graduate to be an art teacher. They taught me to be an artist in the sense that I stopped trying to learn art from teachers, and became an artist myself.

Q. What was your curriculum like?

The history of art and Marxist-Leninist aesthetics.

Q. What did that mean?

Aesthetics from the position of Marxism. It's a required subject. It's like the usual subject of political economy, only it's tied up with art. To understand it one must live in the Soviet Union. It's just an abracadabra. Absurd. It's an attempt to take one more subject and sew it onto Marxism.

Q. What other subjects did you have to study?

Geometrical drawing, landscape, and other subjects like political economy.

Q. Did your parents approve of your desire to be an artist?

I only had my mother. She wanted me to be an artist very much.

Q. While studying art history did you have to visit museums?

Yes, we did. There was a very interesting old woman, Shileiko. She was one of those old Intelligentsia women and she couldn't understand what was happening around her. She looked at the students as though they were some kind of strange animals; she spoke very quietly, gently, and no one listened. She could not understand this generation of ill-mannered, ignorant people. It was enough to put on a clean shirt and a tie for an exam to raise your chances for a good grade. She liked gentility.

Q. Was she politically aware?

Absolutely not. But she did work very hard and was an excellent specialist in the art of ancient Rome. She had a lot of works published on that subject.

Q. Did she influence you at all?

No art teacher influenced me. My most significant influence was literature. Not Russian or Soviet literature. The first time I felt something very close to me, something I wanted to develop in myself or aim toward, was when I first read Marcel Proust. His soft contemplation, the stream of consciousness, gentle, yet very sharply delineated, very deep yet not heavy, but light.

Q. One can get Proust in Russia? I understand homosexual writers are forbidden?

The 1928 edition.

Q. And did Joyce impress you?

Joyce is a great writer, but he preaches; I don't like preachers, even if they are great. He is deliberate and I don't like deliberateness, or those who carry their "I" around, like the films of Antonioni. He is obvious as though he puts too much pressure on being closed up. Proust is more subtle.

Q. But isn't it strange that none of the artists impressed or influenced you?

When we studied in the Institute we didn't see much; our education ended with the French Impressionists.

Q. Did you use slides?

We saw reproductions, books of modern art. As for slides, we were shown the ancient art, French, Italian, and Russian. Afterward, when I finished the art school, I saw other things, and I liked Delvaux, Magritte, the Surrealists, and I liked them very much. I also liked Morandi; he isn't a pure Surrealist, he is different.

Q. When you were an art student, did you have a chance to see Malevich or Kandinsky?

We tried to see them, but, of course, in vain. In the Institute they didn't show them to us. I saw them by accident. Some Bulgarian artists came to Moscow and I was showing them around Tretyakov Gallery. They wanted to see the closed archives and with great difficulty, through the Ministry of Culture, we finally succeeded.

Q. And what did you think when you saw those works?

That they were very interesting, that it was most unfortunate that they weren't being shown, but at that time I was already formed—the way I am now. That is, I wasn't outraged. I and my friends, you understand, are passive Intelligentsia, we are nonparticipants, we don't want to take part in anything. The demonstrations in

Red Square, the books people write that are dissident, these are fantastically courageous people, as democrats, as publicists, but their artistic achievements don't interest me.

Q. And Solzhenitsyn?

The same. I am astounded at his heroism, his honesty, his courage, but he could never be the writer to me that he is for the West. Joseph Brodsky, for example, who never participated in any movement, is a much greater writer to me.

Q. And what is the passive Intelligentsia? Do you mean the silent one?

Yes, I do.

Q. But the people who demonstrated on Red Square, Litvinov and others, they were not silent?

Right. This is the more open way. But there is another way; don't get up in order to say half-truths; don't go at all. Or if you do get up on the tribune, then say exactly what you think, that all of you are worthless, that you have sold out. Either one should be like Sinyavsky, like Galanskov, like those democrats who went all the way, or else don't participate at all. Take the popular film director, Khutsiyev, one of the pillars of the so-called left Intelligentsia. He puts a film together where there is a hero, a taciturn guitarist, whom he keeps in the background throughout the film in order to reveal him at the end. So the implication is that though the hero is silent, something goes on inside him. Then comes the time to show the audience who this idol is. There is a picnic and each person tells some frightening tale about his life. Then the hero's turn comes. He tells how he was lying down in the bushes of lilacs, behind him was a mined field, ahead of him was a mined field; in short, he relates without a smile, seriously, what a good man he is. It doesn't enter the director's mentality that a genuine, delicate bright person will never serve himself up like that. It speaks of the fact that Khutsiyev himself is a half-Intelligentsia, he doesn't understand such things, he hasn't read good books, doesn't know what a real person is. But he will tell you how he was censored, how he was obliged to cut scenes out of his films, and indeed he was obliged, but it's not the point. He makes half-truth.

Q. And a half-truth is worse than a lie?

It is worse. First of all the people know so much now that the propaganda is no longer dangerous. Everyone understands that it's a lie, even those workers who don't understand anything else. The propaganda has become antipropaganda. The jokes in *Krokodil*, Soviet songs—everyone laughs at those now. But things like the films of Khutsiyev, the poems of Yevtushenko, students' theaters, these deceive the youth. The students, when they go to the theater and when they hear some little needling against the Soviet Government, the so-called showing the finger in the pocket, they applaud wildly like children, and they leave the theater with the feeling they were told the truth. They don't understand that they've been taken in. That the most dangerous thing is half-truth which appears as truth.

Q. And if it is impossible to tell the truth?

Then one shouldn't participate at all. These pseudo-Intelligentsia support half-truths. They are the cannon fodder that is needed by the Government organizations; they are being used, that's all. The young ones go to the theater and applaud those fingers in the pockets, and then they go to the virgin lands, sing songs, build, participate in life, in the system, normally. And those theaters of half-truths are just so they can let out the air. You see, during the Czechoslovak invasion, some came out on the Square and spoke the truth openly. And some were saying, as I heard one such "liberal," "Listen, I can't understand this. How can our Government bring troops into Prague?" And he was asked, "And the rest, you understand?" They know it is possible to shoot people there, and the liberal would ask, "I can't understand, how can that be? What horror." Doesn't he know that horrors go on there every day? I'm also anxious about Czechoslovakia, though I'm not at all interested in politics. But to discuss it in a homespun way, over a cup of tea, is like wearing a satin vest. It's a social chatter, a foam. Not even the Komsomol workers know how to speak like Intelligentsia. Only when you listen carefully can you see the ignorance. One of those said to me, "We'll buy all of you." And I said, "What do you mean, buy us?" He said, "You need a studio to work in? You want to go for a trip, we'll finance your trip to the Far East." And I said, "But I'll still draw the way I want to," and he replied, "Then next time you won't go anywhere." Then he named some artists and said, "They'll have studios and trips." They don't even buy them outright; they give them so many commissions so that the artists don't have time to do anything else. And gradually they become the way the system wants them to be.

Q. And if a person doesn't want to be bought?

Then they don't participate at all. Because you know how everyone wants to arrange everything? They want to be in the Artists' Union or in the Writers' Union and to remain human beings at the same time. So that their friends could say you have talent, but that you are not a scum, that you haven't sold out. So such a person sits on two chairs; at times when it's not dangerous he'll say the truth, and at times when it's really needed that one should speak up, he doesn't. When they expelled Okudzhava from the Writers' Union, the others should have left too in protest. Instead they say, "What good will it do? It won't help anything." The people who walked out on Red Square also knew that it wouldn't help anything. They knew that the Soviets thereby would not take their troops out of Czechoslovakia, but they came out in order to tell themselves, "We did not participate."

Q. How did you find your own painting style?

It came to me accidentally. You know, the young beginning painters usually go to the so-called beautiful places to work on landscapes. So did I. I was on the White Sea. It didn't give me much, but it's true that I saw the sea and liked the landscape. Then I went to Shikotan—it's in the Kuril Islands—and there I was struck by a condition which I've never seen before. And later I only saw it in Antonioni films. It is a condition when everything seems to be immersed in a fog, in milk, and all the objects lose their contours. Later, when I walked in town early in the morning, with no one in the streets, the most usual objects—water pipes, windows, garbage cans—each of those appears in the landscape alone, by itself, diluted in this morning fog. And then it fills up with a different content.

Q. As in Claude Monet?

Not exactly. Impressionism is colorful and I'm not moved by color. With Monet even light is given through color, and for me this is a bit sweetish. What I am talking about is an ascetic state; you don't notice the color but the state of an object.

Q. When you talk about the state of an object, do you personify the object?

No, I don't, and at times I am making it dead, but it is filled with some strange sense. I don't know how to express it. For example, take a fishing boat in a harbor—a banal picture that was drawn a thousand times by many artists. But when everything is dissolved in this milky fog, you don't see the ship, you simply see in the sky some thin webs, carcasses, some little circles, little hooks, and all this is dissolving. Or a child is riding a bike on the beach; you don't see the bike, it's dissolved in the fog; you see half a figure of the child moving in space. Of course, later I saw it in the Surrealists, in reproductions, but at that time I saw it for the first time in nature, in life. So this state which I caught there I made my own, my bag, so to speak, which I'm carrying with me.

Q. Do you think that your style belongs to some school or movement?

It's the job of art critics to define styles of artists. But mine is probably close to Surrealism, gentle Surrealism, with the elements of ironic romanticism.

Q. Have you had any shows in the Soviet Union?

Yes, and also a group exhibit. There was a group exhibit of illustrations for Sholem Aleichem and Isaac Babel. Jewish writers.

Q. What does one need to have a show in the Soviet Union?

Well, first one must be a member of the Union of Soviet Artists in order to participate in an official exhibit. Then the works must be approved.

Q. And who approves what can be shown?

Before it was only the art council of the Kombinat, the artists themselves. The Kombinat is a commercial organization which is subordinate to the Union of Artists and which collects 20 percent of the sales. The members of the Art Council were Party and non-Party people, but they themselves make the decisions. The director of this Kombinat was a Party member, and had some instruction of the Raikon, but when my exhibit opened for some reason the Party bureau got involved, and not just the Party bureau on graphics but an enlarged Party committee, and they argued and argued. But there was really no excuse to close my exhibit.

Q. Were you well known then?

Yes, of course; this was more recently, just before I left Russia. And then because of someone's denunciation, the OBKhSS [*Otdel bor'by s Khishcheniyem sotsialisticheskoi sobstvennosti*] people came, the branch that occupies itself with the theft of Socialist property, with speculators and sellers of stolen merchandise. They sealed the exhibit and began a search. They found one etching that didn't have a signature and closed the exhibit. They called me for questioning and accused the salesgirl who worked there of selling stolen merchandise.

Q. There is such an article?

Yes. It was explained to me later that had I left some paintings on the way to town because they were too heavy to carry around and they had been found there, I wouldn't be able to prove that I just left them there because they were cumbersome to lug around. It would already have been "selling stolen merchandise." It's the same if the OBKhSS would find an unlisted 200-pound bag of potatoes in a grocery store, the salespeople would be responsible for the crime.

Q. So the exhibit was closed because of you personally?

Yes.

Q. Did they have anything against you?

Well, when I was young I used to speak out at meetings, tell the truth, struggle against lawlessness. Then I stopped attending any meetings.

Q. Which meetings?

The meetings at which it is customary to speak about "partial defects" within the framework of permitted criticism. And besides, they didn't like it that I placed emphasis on the Jewish themes.

Q. Did you?

Yes, precisely, in the Moscow Union of Artists.

Q. I don't see any Jewish themes here.

Oh, these paintings I couldn't even exhibit ever.

Q. Were the Jewish themes realistic?

More or less. They are tied with literature.

Q. What brought you to those themes?

Nothing special. I needed to have shows and to do that one I had to make illustrations. And since I had no favorite among the Soviet writers, except for Babel, I was pleased to draw illustrations to his works. Sholem Aleichem is an officially allowed writer, so I chose those two writers. Besides, there was a spirit of defiance: you don't want those themes, so I'll work on them. These are not my favorite writers.

Q. How did you become known? Was your case typical or atypical?

In the first place I, like many others, sat on two chairs. The moment came to make a decision, but then I left. I was considered an honest artist, and I didn't make compromises. I was not working to my full capacity, like everyone else, though I thought I was freer than most. I only now feel I am beginning to loosen up.

Q. How is that?

It's difficult for me to analyze my inner state, but I thought that I didn't allow myself to be led into doing the themes which they ordered. I offered my own and they agreed. I worked for the graphic arts Kombinat and made four prints a year. Many artists worked on the ordered themes; for school, for Raikoms, for the military, for the soldiers' recreation rooms, for the parachutists' schools.

Q. You refused to do those projects?

I didn't do that. Once I did the Song of Songs, another time Pinocchio, and a doll in a window. Neutral things, and they always took them from me because they knew they would sell.

Q. Who is they? And to whom did they sell your work?

The Art Council members. They sold it in the Salon for foreigners, on Gorky Street.

Q. Have they ever sent your works to the Biennale or the Documenta?

No, my works weren't exportable.

Q. When you finished your studies, how did you begin to work?

It was in a funny way. When I finished the art school there was no work assignment. I didn't want to teach, so I went to work as a loader in a factory and at the same time I showed my work to Burov at the publishing house, the Soviet Writer. Burov was an art editor and he promised me a book to illustrate. So I worked in a factory until he gave me the first book. It was by Gladilin and was called *The First Day of the New Year*. In this way I began as an illustrator.

Q. Does it pay? Can one live on it?

If you work for one publisher only, then the answer is no.

Q. How does an artist make a living? Is there a difference, in terms of earning, between a mediocre artist and a good one?

It depends. There is a very good pop artist, Kabakov, and he doesn't live badly. Not because he sells his paintings—he doesn't sell many—but because he is a rather well-known illustrator of children's books. So he lives well while remaining a good artist. But there are some who try very hard to do the right thing and they still are not doing too well. Rabin, for example, lives better than those who do what is asked of them.

Q. But Rabin sells to forcigners doesn't he; he is well known abroad?

Yes. Times have changed.

Q. But I mean an ordinary artist, how does he make a living if he doesn't sell to foreigners, doesn't do what is required? Where would he take his works, for example?

Nowhere. He has to stay home and paint if he is a saint. Become an in-the-drawer artist.

Q. What does that mean economically?

I suppose death from hunger.

Q. What about the artist who is ready and willing to do what is needed? How does he begin?

He begins with the youth section of the Union of Artists. That is, those artists who haven't yet joined the Union, but who wish to do so.

Q. Must one belong to the Union of Artists?

It's better if one does. The youth section subsidizes them, at times their works are exhibited, the more promising artists are noted, and it is in this way that they progress. And if such an artist justifies the hopes of the Union and the Komsomol, because the youth exhibits are financed by the Union and the Komsomol together, he is on the way. But he must also know the demand. Now there are different demands. One can't simply draw Lenin and the building of communism and be assured of acceptance as one used to be. Now there is a different tendency; one must do such a painting that it would be impossible to say that it was calculated for a sale. A painting must have an element of originality and at the same time have a Soviet content. If, for example, one is painting a landscape, it must affirm the Soviet way of life.

Q. How can a landscape affirm a Soviet way of life?

It's possible.

Q. Perhaps one can affirm life by a landscape, but how can one affirm a specific way of life by a landscape?

I understand that. But in their understanding it is possible. If you take any of my paintings it wouldn't suit them not only because it isn't realistic, but because I use gray colors. And in their mind gray is associated with pessimism. If I draw a garbage can, the question would be why do I draw a garbage can and not a summer landscape with sun and flowers, something "life-affirming." It used to be worse. Now, I know a young man who painted Lenin by the fire. He is a young fellow, has a family, wanted to make money fast, I understand him. It wasn't well done; he didn't know the demand. And the youth committee is composed of young artists and they treated him with contempt: "Do you want to go to paradise riding Lenin?" So they rejected the painting saying it was technically imperfect.

Q. They didn't tell him the real reason? Served it under technical sauce?

Yes. Now, had they accepted it, naturally the next step is that the Party commission would have to pass it, of course. But it didn't pass the first step.

Q. So youth has some influence?

In this sense, yes. But on the other hand, very often paintings that are approved and chosen by the youth committee are later rejected by the Party committee, which always has the last word.

Q. How was it in your case?

I decided to make my way by doing what I wanted. But it was an erroneous impression that I had, and later I understood that in this way I wouldn't go too far, that the time had passed for the kind of works I did for myself and that they weren't bought anymore. And with time they began to be more nasty. And knowing myself, I decided that if I remained in Moscow, but was not able to do what was unpleasant for me to do, I could count only on sales to foreigners, and that in time I would have troubles with the authorities. The troubles were already beginning.

Q. Is that why you left?

Not only—there were many reasons.

Q. Is there such a thing as an underground artists' movement?

Not anymore. It was Rabin who began as an underground artist 10 years ago, but now he is trying to get into the Union of Artists. I don't know if he got in or not, probably not. But he works for the publishing house, the Soviet Writer. Kabakov was an underground artist and now he is in the open.

Q. How did that happen?

They became known as illustrators inside the country and the foreigners bought their paintings.

Q. And if an artist sells only to foreigners, is it possible to become as well known as Solzhenitsyn, so that one would be immune from arrest?

No. No one is that well known. Rabin, Glazunov—but they aren't the best artists either.

Q. Who are the best?

Kabakov. There are others. But you know what aspect the West is interested in as far as Russia is concerned? It is even painful for me to talk about it. There is an exhibit right now being organized in Paris, an exhibit of Soviet artists. The organizer is sending for an old painting of Rabin's, *The Soviet Passport*, to give the exhibit a political tinge. People aren't interested in the art itself, but in the fact of "those poor, miserable Russian artists . . ." But there are real artists over there.

Q. Is there a feeling of solidarity between those artists who are not being exhibited?

No. Each lives his own life; there aren't any groups. The artist in the Intelligentsia is in a state of quiet contemplation.

Q. Do you have a feeling of belonging to some kind of an international brotherhood of artists?

No. I don't like artists in general as a class. I have very few friends who are artists. Generally, I prefer to socialize with people of other professions. With an artist I can understand from the first words whether I want to see his work or not. It must be the same for yourself with writers.

Q. How did you decide to write a novel?

I began like a graphomaniac. Not being a professional, I didn't know whether it was good or bad. I simply felt that there was something in it, in those people whom I knew in Moscow. So I was just doing it for myself, beginning and then dropping it and beginning again. But once someone liked it, I began to work on it as a professional, with the proverbial torments of creativity and all that.

Q. But how did you conceive of the idea at all?

Back in Moscow, but there it was impossible. I lived among the characters. When you see the people every day it's difficult to write about them. For me this world of holy fools was my prison. That is, I perceived my life there, normal life in the city, among my friends, as a prison. And my friends were my cell mates. My freedom seemed to me a cell situation. That is why my characters as well as myself felt that the reality is this way and that it is no use trying to achieve something. And those people who tried to do something, achieve something, seemed to us a little abnormal. Didn't they realize that they were behind bars? The life of my friends was more conscious because they understood the prison situation they were in. But nevertheless, they tried to enjoy themselves. I didn't feel the so-called bearing of the cross. If I felt like working, I worked, and if not, I didn't do anything. It was a game. If I felt like sleeping with a woman I did. But to talk to her seriously about life's problems was ridiculous. Because first I'd have to explain to her that we are in prison, which would take too long and would be too boring. And there was no guarantee that she would understand it. So I just played the game.

Q. Didn't you, at one point, have to serve in the army?

Yes, I was 22 then. I had some personal hassles and decided to volunteer before they called me. You know how people enjoy the feeling of loneliness and self-pity. So, in this frame of mind, I decided to go. But when I came to the recruiting office, I saw those army magazines on the tables, heard those army anecdotes about sergeants, all those posters and slogans on the walls . . . I began to feel nauseous. And I decided that I wouldn't serve.

Q. Could you have refused?

No, we have universal military training. But there was a lucky coincidence: the doctor didn't like the way my heart worked. The night before I drank a lot of vodka and that was probably why. So the doctor sent me to have an electrocardiogram. It was normal, of course, but having already made up my mind that I would do something to avoid the military service I took ephedrin in order to up my blood pressure.

Q. Could you get it in a drugstore?

At that time, yes. Now one needs a prescription. But in order to declare me sick and unfit for service, the doctors had to make sure that it was not accidental or temporary. So they sent me to a hospital for a month.

Q. In order to check you every day?

Yes, by way of excluding various possibilities. And every day at 10 A.M. a doctor on duty checked my blood pressure. So I had to be "ready" by that hour. So I woke up, went to the toilet and swallowed 20 pills, the entire package. After a while I had to swallow two packages, because one ceased to affect me. Friends smuggled them to me during visits.

Q. What effect did they have on you besides raising your blood pressure?

A state of severe hypertension. That is, after the doctor would leave, I would still feel sick for about three hours. I guess it would be like having a good dose of narcotics. After a month, they gave me a certificate to the effect that I was not fit for military service.

Q. Do many people practice such tricks?

Yes, and on all levels, some very primitive. They swallow objects so that the X-ray will show a shadow. Or they tie a piece of iron on a string to a tooth and then swallow it so that later they can pull it out again. But the doctors caught on; they look for that first of all. I have described a variety of those practices in my novel, *Holy Fools in Moscow*.

Q. But did you feel yourself a writer? You are an artist, after all.

No, I just wanted to write about those people. I love those people, the ones I describe in the book, and I consider them to be very interesting. The real intellectuals are less interesting to me. For me those people were the intellectual elite, from whom I could learn something new. They were self-aware and yet they lived by an imagined life, as people do in prison. It seemed to me that very few people knew this aspect of the Soviet life and few had observed it. I wanted to write about those who had never been in prisons or labor camps, yet nevertheless felt themselves imprisoned.

Q. How did you come to your style of a montage in your novel?

It is somewhat like I paint. I wanted to convey a condition, a state, without going deeply into it—not to tear up the situation as a whole, because one could break a lot of trees this way and make mistakes. I just wanted to express the sensations of these people I knew. It didn't matter what we did or where we did it, so long as we were together. We didn't care if it was a football match or a movie theater, we just went to various places to be together. And the women were there for decorative purposes only. By the way, they liked it too.

Q. Were any of those people considered "parasites" and tried for it?

No, we weren't parasites in the legal sense. We were members of the elite, if you will, the show people. We had one professional parasite among us though, but he earned himself an official designation. That is, he simulated a mental illness and received an appropriate certificate, and a pension of 30 rubles a month. He earned this privilege of not working by going and spending time in an insane asylum. The 30 rubles pension allows him not to die of hunger. By the way, in Russia one can manage without 30 rubles a month. You can go to your friends' to eat. In that sense it's a fantastic country for idlers. But I noticed many times that if one simulates mental illness long enough, it gradually becomes real, and as this one person progressed he became less and less interesting. When he first began he was very interesting.

Q. How did it express itself, his illness?

With him you are always at a theater. He plays the role for you, for himself, for others. He read poetry endlessly, seemingly not paying attention to your reaction while he did. He had various games with different people. With Yezhov [screenwriter, author of *Ballad of a Soldier*] he played a serf. Yezhov was the master and he the serf. He would say, "Would you like me to read you Yesenin's poetry?" If Yezhov was in the mood, he would say, "Go ahead," and pay him for the performance. Yezhov would then tell him to read it quietly or loudly or to whisper, and he, like a serf-actor, performed. He could play this role for 48 hours straight.

Q. How did the KGB take to him?

These types do not interest the KGB. Also he changed all the time. At one time he was obsessed with cool jazz. He prayed to Dave Brubeck; he would to to a café, the Blue Bird, and sit there for hours, head in his hands, and listen to music. For a year he was an expert on cool jazz. Then he began to write poetry, which was terrible. Then he decided to paint. He borrowed the materials from me and painted three paintings. Not bad. Primitive, but not bad at all. One especially was good, a scene from an insane asylum. He did have some depth. And what he had previously told me about that scene did come out clearly in the painting. It was a normal creative process. Then he was infatuated with Futurism. He had many periods. Then he wanted "to go into nature," to go to the village, buy a horse, drink new milk, and, as he put it, "fuck his mother-in-law." The mother-in-law was a myth of wealth to him; she owned a little wineshop, and he thought that she wanted to sleep with him. So she was like a material base in his imagination and he would live in nature. He came to that without reading Faulkner or Thoreau.

Q. What did the mother-in-law think of that?

She was scared to death of him. He was in an imagined world, the way we all lived by an imagined world. Only his was the most naïve, the most primitive. There were all different levels, because in Moscow there aren't any whorehouses or nightclubs where one can relax, so that's the way to relax. But still, it's their real life, and work is only a material base that provides these escapes. And another thing, it's a way of letting go among your own kind of people; it's not like going somewhere among strangers to relax.

Q. I think you will miss all this in the West.

I think that what was good in one period of life, some particular place, particular people, should not be repeated elsewhere. Here I must live a certain way, meet the English bourgeois, and maintain good relationships with them. I could probably find similar types of people here, but I can't afford the time. Besides, I don't feel any need for it. As I said, one shouldn't seek to repeat experiences. It was wonderful, while it lasted, but it doesn't mean that I can't exist without it. I can recall it, I can miss it all, I can feel nostalgic about it, but it doesn't mean I have to seek a similar situation here. I wrote that book in order to remember it all.

IGOR GOLOMSHTOK

Igor Golomshtok was born in Kalinin in 1929. His mother was a physician; his father, though from a rich family, was miraculously spared during the Civil War. He was, however, imprisoned in 1934. When Igor's mother remarried, they went to Kolyma, a region of labor camps, where they lived until 1943. Later they moved to Moscow, and Igor worked in a bank and studied at Moscow University. He then worked in a restoration workshop until 1953, when he was thrown out as a "Cosmopolite."

One of Golomshtok's closest friends was Andrei Sinyavsky, and in 1960 they co-authored a book on Picasso. During the Sinyavsky-Daniel trial in 1966, Golomshtok was one of the witnesses. He refused to give evidence in court against his friends and was sentenced to six months of forced labor. Afterward he worked in the Institute of Technical Aesthetics, gave lectures, and wrote books. During his last year in the Soviet Union Golomshtok worked in a museum. When he applied for an exit visa he resigned in order not to put his director in the embarrassing position of having to fire him. In November, 1972, Igor Golomshtok, his wife, and their three-year-old son emigrated from Russia. The interview took place four months after their arrival in London, where they now live. Though at the moment we met their circumstances were still very difficult, Igor was completely preoccupied with the fate of Sinyavsky, who, at that time, was still in Moscow.

Igor "had a remarkable relationship with his students," I was told in Moscow. "When Golomshtok left Russia, the students truly suffered an irreplaceable loss." Soft-spoken and self-effacing, but intense, Golomshtok reminds one of a priest temporarily defrocked and separated from his flock.

Q. What is the nature of professional training for art historians in the Soviet Union?

At Moscow University there is the Department of the Theory of Art. It's very difficult to get in because of the great competition. If a person gets in he studies five years and gets a diploma as an art historian.

Q. How many get into graduate school?

Of the undergraduates each year only one or two can get into graduate work.

Q. What does one need to get in?

One must have a political face; be active, like being a leader of a Komsomol; and be recommended by a Party member. Of course, that is in addition to ability and excellent grades. But for art historians graduate work at a university is not the only possibility; one can go to the Institute of Art History at the Academy of Arts, or one can go to the Institute of the Theory and History of Art at the Ministry of Culture. So if one is recommended for graduate work, and one fails to pass examinations at, say, Moscow University, one has those other two chances. One can also work for several years and then reapply.

Q. Do they have art schools in Moscow?

Yes, they train artists there.

Q. How early do children get art training in schools?

Singing and art have the lowest priority. However, in Moscow there are so-called art high schools, where children get emphasis on art from the beginning and then go on to art schools. But in general the subject is neglected in schools.

Q. Is there a curatorial training for those who want to work in the art museums?

No. They get their apprenticeship on the job. There is no strict specialization. This is true of all professional institutions. The specialization begins with the job. At the University and the institutes a lot of time is spent on the subjects that have nothing to do with one's specialty: history of the Communist Party, political-economic history, atheism. The specialization is determined by one's choice of a thesis.

Q. What about art schools for practical drawing, sculpture, et cetera? Do they also have to study those subjects?

Of course, of course. Going back to your question about specialization, if I want to specialize, for example, in American art or Roman art, then I choose this particular topic for my diploma work [thesis]. That is the only thing that determines my specialization.

Q. Are there any forbidden subjects?

Of course. But this changes from time to time. Now it is a little freer than when I was a student in 1955. When I was a student it was impossible to specialize in post mid-nineteenth-century art. It was difficult altogether to write about Western art or about El Greco or about medieval art. Now it is permitted.

Q. What isn't permitted now?

It's not that it is officially "not permitted"; it is that no one would approve a thesis on the Russian avant-garde, on Melevich, Kandinsky—absolutely not. Also one can't write about contemporary Western art. Unless you write something like "Critique of the Reactionary Tendencies in Western Art" or "Formalism of Matisse," formalism being a derogatory term. This you can write.

Q. But you and Andrei Sinyavsky wrote a book on Picasso?

It was one of those miracles that happens once in a great while in Russia. Ilya Ehrenburg pushed it through by various illegal means. I was given a few weeks to do it and since Sinyavsky and I often spoke of Picasso we decided to do it together. We just risked it. Usually it has to be pointed out that Picasso has degenerate bourgeois tendencies and so on. We didn't, but it was somehow pushed through with the assistance of various people. But after the publication they stopped publishing my works altogether because in that book I "presented myself as a formalist and an ideological 'diversant.' "

Q. I would have thought that Picasso would be favored there.
Picasso's works of the blue and pink period are favored. Nothing after 1907.

Q. What is the main direction in Soviet art education?

It is ideological, with a historical twist. The emphasis is on content.

Q. But your museums, in particular the Hermitage, has one of the best collections of the Impressionists. How can one look at Monet, for example, from the point of view of content? Take his lilies or the cathedrals and his interest in light and the disintegration of form?

It's possible. You can look at it as a cultural phenomenon. Impressionism can be looked at not as a stylistic movement, but as an event. Because behind the preoccupation with light, behind the disintegration of forms, stands some sort of development of a human spirit. You can look at it that way.

Q. Are there those who write about Impressionism or light from the ideological point of view alone?

Most write from that point of view. The mass literature is exactly that way. And if the official creed is to look at art from the point of view of historical materialism, then among the serious art critics this decree transforms itself into a kind of philosophical sociology.

Q. How did you personally get interested in American art?

I was always interested in American culture in general, in its literature and art. Then there was a youth festival in 1957—this was a period of liberalism—and before the festival there was a campaign and we were given permission to explain to the public about contemporary Western art, about which until then nothing was known. But, of course, it was demanded that we explain its reactionary essence. Then there was the American National Exhibition in 1959, and there you had an exhibit of contemporary American art.

Q. But the foreign art magazines were available to you before?

Yes, but only in special places in the Lenin Library and only for art specialists. You have to have a paper from your place of work that you are working on a certain subject and then you can go and read those materials in that special hall.

Q. Is Camille Gray's *Russian Experiment in Art* [1962, the only book on Russian avant-garde art written in the Soviet Union by a foreign scholar] available there?

I'm not sure. I read it privately. Usually books of that sort are available only for special people with special permissions.

Q. How did she happen to write this book in Russia?

She is an Englishwoman who came to Russia to study art, married Oleg Prokofiev, son of the composer, and collected all this material. She was given quite a bit of help unofficially. The museum workers helped her. Then it was simpler because it was possible to see the closed archives. Everyone was helping her collect reproductions, some people took photographs of what she couldn't see. She got acquainted with the relatives, with widows, children of those artists, went to their homes, saw the originals there. She spoke to them, did all she could for research and her book was a kind of revelation for the West.

Q. Do people still have private collections of those artists?

They weren't private collections exactly; the paintings were just around the houses of the relatives. No one knew what to do with them, since in Russia they didn't represent any value at all. People used to throw them in the garbage; there was poverty, no place to keep the "worthless" paintings.

Q. Did they know they could sell them in the West?

There were no contacts with the West; it's only in the last 15 years that some contact has been established.

Q. To what extent are educated people in Russia now familiar with the Russian avant-garde paintings of 1916–1918?

There is a great interest in that subject among the Intelligentsia. They are acquainted with those artists through Western art books, through occasional articles and through oral tradition.

Q. But can they see the originals?

No. No one can. Even the museum workers cannot see them; they are in closed archives. If a foreigner comes and gets a special permission from Miss Furtseva, then he is taken there.

Q. What is the official motive for such a refusal? Suppose I were to ask for a permission to see those paintings, would they let me?

They wouldn't give you an outright refusal. They would send you to the Ministry of Culture and there you would be sent to some other organization and so on. By the way, it happened because (I think it was in 1962) the director of the São Paulo Museum, a very famous art historian, was given permission to see this collection. Afterward, he went to Furtseva and said, "You are not showing this collection publicly anyway. You don't consider these valuable. I will buy them from you for a big price." In short, he placed her in an embarrassing position. After that there came an order to close all reserves and not allow anyone there. At about the same time an American journalist wrote an article—in *Life* magazine, I think—about these painters and published some photographs of the paintings that he had been allowed to see just before the São Paulo director. These two incidents resulted in the prohibition.

Q. Was there any parallel in art to the liberalization of literature when Solzhenitsyn's *One Day in the Life of Ivan Denisovich* was published?

No. Literature and art in Russia are in different circumstances. There is no Academy of Literature, while there is an Academy of Art. The Academy of Art was organized in 1947 during Stalin, and it assimilated all the reactionary forces—they still hold the politics of art in their hands. Tomsky, the president of that Academy, used to be a court portrait painter of Stalin. The Academy of Art usurped art education—that is, all the art institutes are subordinated to the Academy. The exhibition halls are in their hands; so is the main art magazine. And the members of the Academy do these gigantic patriotic canvases that are distributed throughout the country. Every year there are exhibitions usually in connection with special jubilee dates: 50 years of the Soviet Union, 42 years of the Soviet Army, Lenin's birthday. Then there are various annual exhibits of different Soviet Republics.

Q. Are the artists then obliged to produce works on those specific themes in connection with the jubilees?

Not necessarily on the one theme. Many people do landscapes, for example. But the landscapes will be then called "Volga-Russian River" or "Here Such-and-Such Battle Took Place 50 Years Ago." The landscapes have to have thematic titles.

Q. Can one paint something pessimistic?

Yes, but on a single plane only. Several years ago, for example, there was an All-Union (meaning all republics participated) exhibition. It was a horrible sight. Two pessimistic themes are allowed: the Civil War or the Fascist invasion. So this exhibit had pictures of different executions, shooting, fighting, dying. It was a horror show. It was all very ideological.

Q. I meant pessimistic in a philosophical sense?

No, that isn't allowed.

Q. Well, when they need to send works of art to the Biennale or Documenta exhibits, what do they send?

Well, here they understand that hurrah-patriotic art wouldn't go in the West. They usually choose neutral things—salon art, landscapes.

Q. What does the general public think of American art?

The Intelligentsia is interested in every aspect of American culture and loves America a priori. Officially, the only American artist that was widely publicized was Rockwell Kent. He gave all his works to the Soviet Union; he was a "friend of the Soviet Union." He is not a bad illustrator, but in America he wasn't as popular as he was in the Soviet Union where he had one exhibit after another. His exhibits were always packed. He had a fantastic success among the masses.

Q. By masses you mean what?

Those who attend the art exhibitions. Not the Intelligentsia, just those who like to go see the pictures in museums. Here you have pubs, cinemas, dozens of places to go after work. In Russia there is not much to do, so people go to museums much more than in the West.

Q. And how do these masses react to modern Western art? Surrealism for example?

Surrealism they like, because they look at it as a riddle to be solved. Since they always look for the content first of all, Surrealism gives them a chance to find some kind of content, even if it's their own. Abstract art, of course, is very foreign to them.

Q. What aspect of the American contemporary art influenced the present-day Russian artists?

Tachism; they began to look to Jackson Pollock at some point.

Q. So is it possible to have a private exhibit for any artist under some special circumstances?

No, no, absolutely not. Well, there is a kind of exception: in recent years the Physics Institute has been permitted to hold exhibits of so-called left artists. There are two institutes, those of Kurchatov and Kapitsa, and sometimes they do that. But these exhibits are usually closed, in the sense that not everyone is allowed there. It's rather difficult for the authorities to argue with the physicists, and the authorities probably think, "So what. It'll last for two days, their friends and colleagues will attend, and that'll be that. Better not to make an argument over that."

Q. So the physicists are influential in many spheres of life. Speaking of that, what do you think of the Democratic Movement in Russia?

I think that the Democratic Movement which had its peak during and after the trial of Sinyavsky and Daniel, is now at its end. Or rather certain forms of it are over. When the people in it had to face arrest, they overcame that danger; but when unemployment is the danger, then people got scared.

Q. Is prison easier than unemployment?

No, but unemployment is more real than a prison. Prison was a risk: maybe one will get arrested and maybe not. But the loss of work is certain in such cases.

Q. What happens to a person when he does lose his job? Is there unemployment insurance of any kind, or food stamps?

No, there is nothing. Friends help.

Q. Did you ever lose your job?

Yes. I lived by writing books that were published under the names of my friends. Many *intelligenty* do that.

Q. Doesn't the publisher know who wrote a book?

The bosses don't. It's all done through friends who are below.

Q. Well what if a person cannot write books—suppose he is an engineer—then what will he do?

His position is very bad then. But it's not just that he is deprived of a livelihood. He can be hauled to court as a parasite and tried and sent out of Moscow as a freeloader.

Q. Did you lose your job once, after Sinyavsky's trial?

No, several times. The first time in 1953, during the anti-Semitic campaign. I was out of work for a year; it was a hopeless situation.

Q. Is there still a quota on accepting Jews at universities and at work? And if so, how is it officially rationalized?

Yes there is a percentage norm. But it isn't rationalized by anything because officially it doesn't exist. It exists on the level of oral instructions and every director of an organization knows it. And he also knows that if he went over the quota he would be called in to the Party organs and given a scolding.

Q. But it doesn't exist on paper anywhere?

No, and you are never told officially about it. But if a director is a good person, or likes you or is a friend, he'll tell you. Suppose this director is someone you went to school with. He'd say to you,

"Look, I took Shteinberg yesterday, so I can't take you today. I'd like to, but you know I'll get it if I go over the quota." And if he doesn't know you, he'll just say, "Your qualifications are not suitable for this position."

Q. Is leaving the Soviet Union still considered treason?

It used to be considered so, but now it isn't formally considered so. However, I was told that when at a Party instruction session one of the main secretaries was asked how to regard those who leave Russia, he answered, "As traitors, naturally." That isn't an official but a moral attitude.

Q. I notice that those Russians who come to the West often have a feeling of guilt; an American expatriate seldom has such feelings. What about yourself?

I personally have no such feelings. There is a feeling of guilt only for those who are left behind. As for a sense of indebtedness toward the Motherland, I feel none. On the contrary, I feel that the Motherland owes me a lot.

Q. How long have you been here?

Four months.

Q. Is the West as you had imagined it to be?

No, even though the difference isn't great. I always knew that my conception of the West was very relative. There are more difficulties here than I expected. Material difficulties.

Q. Was there anything that astounded you in a positive or negative way?

I was astounded at the Home Office, the local Ministry of Internal Affairs. After one hour of talk, I was given all the documents, congratulated on my arrival to London, wished a happy life, given a work permit, and that was all. In Russia that would have taken years.

Q. You mean you were astounded by the swiftness?

By the swiftness, the well-meaningness, and simplicity.

Q. And visually?

Visually the city of London astonished me. It's a gigantic city with a gigantic motion and it seems with a very tense life, and at the same time there is this absolute calm. It's a city with a measured rhythm, full of dignity. That is, from the very first day here, and without knowing English, I felt here much more comfortable than in Moscow, more tranquil. From the first moment I felt the absence of Moscow's hostility, Moscow's anger.

Q. Did you feel that the English people are isolated from one another, that there isn't a sense of friendship as there is in Moscow?

I feel that the English have a different way of life and a different way of communication. I think it's meaningless for a newcomer to expect the kind of friendship he had in Moscow, to expect to have it here with the English.

Q. What I mean is that it is usually said that the English among themselves aren't warm.

I don't think it's our right to judge how the English relate among themselves. Although the English themselves say that. But the point is that this Russian soulfulness in human relations is also relative. The Americans, English, or other foreigners who come to Moscow are in exceptional circumstances. They take the friendly, warm attitude toward themselves as typical for Moscow. And it isn't typical. When the foreigners come, they socialize with the dissidents who accept them instantly, or else they socialize with the officials who pretend—feed them caviar, pat their backs—and they don't seem to see the difference between this false friendliness and real warmth. Or else they take the real, rare human attitude for a typical one. I could never explain to the foreigners that what they see among us dissidents isn't Russia, but exists in spite of Russia, in spite of the system.

Q. Are these soulful relationships in these small groups based on adversity?

When a person lives under the threat of arrest, there appear certain friends on whom he can rely and whom he can trust. It's tested by life then. But we must ask, is it natural? A soldier also always remembers war as his best time, but it doesn't follow that it is a natural state and that in order to have true friends one needs war or camps. Are the relationships brought about by unnatural circumstances natural?

Q. But in your system, from childhood on, there is a stress on group values. The Soviet child is told that he must work for the good of society, his country, and so on. In our system what is stressed is personal advancement. The child is not told that he must live and work for the good of the State, but that America gives him unheard-of opportunities for self-advancement and a career. It's the word "you" that he hears, not "we." Isn't there something in your system that gives a sense of unity to people from the beginning?

No, I'm absolutely sure of that. The official upbringing of people in Russia plays on disunity. Those of us who lived outside the system, who disagreed with the system, had a great advantage over those who lived within the system. We really had friends, we really had close relationships, we had human values that a person living in an official society cannot have. And the higher a person stands on an official staircase the more isolated he is and lonely. He has no friends he can trust; he trusts no one; he is obliged to lie and no one believes him and he believes no one. I'm sure that the degree of disunity and loneliness as it exists there exists nowhere else. And in this is their tragedy. For that they have brandy and caviar and don't have the most important things.

And those people who accept the system from the beginning develop a conflict, because the proclaimed values are so opposite to reality. We didn't accept the system from the beginning—all those speeches about the collectives, Komsomols, and Communist communal life were meaningless to us. I've seen those collectives since childhood. I was a part of them and emerged with nothing but horror of them. True, my case was exceptional, since at the age of nine I lived in the Kolyma and lived among the labor camps. I saw things there that would last me a lifetime. The fact that my father was imprisoned when I was five, of course, wasn't exceptional; people of my generation were mostly fatherless. Only many of them used their defense mechanisms to cut themselves off from that reality and made a career by closing their eyes to it. These people are morally destroyed, they are as lonely as wolves, and I wouldn't change my beggarly life there for their high positions.

Q. Was your life beggarly as an art historian?

I worked in a museum and earned 90 rubles [$120] a month. I and my wife—who also worked, she is a microbiologist—rented a room of seven square meters and paid 30 rubles a month rent because this room was not from the Government.

Q. Wait a minute, I was present when Khrushchev told Nixon that every Soviet citizen had the right to *zhilploshchad*, that it's his birthright.

In the same way every American has the right to become President of the United States. Of course there is the right. But people wait for years, for decades to get a place to live.

Q. So you lived in a room that you found yourself, a private room?

Yes, when we got married we found this room, we had a communal bathroom, and a communal kitchen for five other families. Before that I lived with my family (mother, stepfather, grandmother, grandfather) in a room of fourteen square meters.

Q. When did you decide to leave Russia?

I always wanted to leave.

Q. Would you have left illegally if the legal possibilities did not arise?

No, I couldn't do that.

Q. Why did you choose England?

It was by accident. But if I had the choice I would have chosen England. The Anglo-Saxon culture and life-style were always close to me.

Q. How do you picture your future in the West?

Ideally or actually?

Q. Ideally.

I would want to do what I did there; I would also want to teach, but there is the language problem.

Q. What would you want to write about now that you are here?

I always wanted to write about Bosch, about symbolism and space in medieval art. But that would be very difficult here, I see that now. And I began to be interested in a subject that never interested me before, Soviet art. Because in the Soviet Union all the books are about official art. That's very uninteresting. In the West they write about the Russian avant-garde art. I'd like to write the history of Soviet art from1917 on in all its aspects. Of avant-garde, of the underground, of the official one. Of how they interact. I would like to show this as a part of a universal process. Because it didn't happen only in the Soviet Union—it was in Germany. In the 1930s something similar happened in America, and you can even see it to a degree in Picasso. This is a more realistic desire. I have a family to support and there are hundreds of books about Bosch here.

Q. How long did it take you to get an exit visa?

We applied in May and in August we paid 26,000 rubles for our education tax.

Q. That much? I heard Joseph Brodsky paid only 500.

They were so anxious to get rid of him he could have paid nothing.

Q. Why?

Because he is an excellent poet, and they don't need an excellent poet in the country when he isn't working for them. Just the way those in the Academy of Art were not interested in having someone like Picasso around. Because Picasso is a great artist, and they couldn't allow him to be seen by the public. Because Picasso, by the fact of his existence, nullified them.

ALEXANDER YESENIN-VOLPIN

Several years before the Russian Revolution a young poet from Ryazan, Sergei Yesenin, arrived in Saint Petersburg and straight from the railroad station went to the home of Alexander Blok, Russia's most important symbolist poet. The aristocratic Blok, whom he didn't know, and later other literati, embraced Yesenin's village naïveté, the fresh lyricism and vivid imagery of his poems, and he gradually became one of the most popular poets in the country. Yesenin lived intensely, was married several times (once to Isadora Duncan), traveled abroad, fell in and out of love with the Revolution. In 1925 he checked into a Leningrad hotel, cut his veins, wrote his last poem on the tablecloth with his blood, and hung himself. Today he is still in great esteem among the Russians.

A year before the suicide, Yesenin and Nadezhda Volpin had a son, Alexander. Though he became a mathematician, Alexander also wrote poetry and in 1949 was arrested for his poems. He was placed in an insane asylum and was later exiled. Yesenin-Volpin had apparently become fascinated with the psychic processes that take place during interrogation, with the game of the interrogator trying to trap the prisoner. On being released, he learned the law, and when he was arrested for the second time he was prepared. Law and forcing the authorities to comply with their own laws had become an obsession with Yesenin-Volpin. In February, 1969, he wrote a "Juridical Memorandum" for those who are facing interrogation or arrest (see Introduction). The authorities were rather anxious to be rid of Yesenin-Volpin, and when he applied for an exit visa, there was no delay.

At present Yesenin-Volpin lives in Boston and teaches at Boston University. Though logic is uppermost in his mind, he can also be emotional, agitated, or melancholy. He can talk animatedly for hours, his great blue eyes blazing, and be the life of the party, and he can also be silent all evening, withdrawn from the company into his own private world. At a gathering in Boston, one very similar to the kind the dissidents used to have in Moscow, Yesenin-Volpin read the following poem. It was a poem he had written back in 1952, in a labor camp. At that time its contents seemed fantastic; Stalin was alive and no one could ever dream of surviving imprisonment. The poem is strangely prophetic:

. . .
If I manage to live through war and hunger,
Maybe I'll wait another year,
Staring at those unsightly places
I grew up in and so feared the whip,
Talking with left-over friends
From the camps of Ukhta and Ust-Vym . . .
And then, when the trains are running freely,
I'll take myself out of Russia forever!
I'll go to Byzantium and Algiers;
Though penniless, I'll stop in Cairo,
And I'll see across the water white steam
By a jagged rock, and over it Gibraltar!
. . . And I will remain so much a child
That my joy in the Louvre will have no sadness!
And I will remain so much an ascetic
That I'll still hope for something at the age of forty,
And I will remain so much myself
That I'll call all the Catholics out to battle!
. . . But it will turn out that the West is old and callous,
And that to oppose faith is merely foolish,
And it will turn out that too long a winter
Had burnt the rage out of a hopeless mind,
And it will turn out that far from Russian places
My protest has no soul or purpose! . . .
. . . What will I do? Of course, not go back!
But get desperately drunk and shoot myself,
So that I will not see the merciless simplicity,
The general wretched vanity,
So that I will not spoil someone's young life
With a gloomy and sacred exasperation,

And furthermore, so that of my ashes
Nothing will be left for Russia!

Yesenin-Volpin
Karaganda—Moscow
April, 1952—October, 1958
(*Translated by Richard Pevear*)

Q. You are considered to be the father of the Democratic Movement. Do you consider yourself as such?

I consider myself less than anything the "father" of something. I know that I am thus identified and it seems to me that I recall this alias as being slightly humorous. But I can say that in the 1960s, and particularly in 1965, I accomplished one vital, very vital action in this movement. I demanded, after the arrests of Sinyavsky and Daniel that the trial be public. I declared that since people wanted to act, one decisive action was needed: the demand for the publicity of that trial.

Q. Where did you call for such an action?

In Moscow. At first among friends, then later in the organization of the demonstration. I called it "the meeting of *glasnost'*." Later it was renamed the "demonstration." There was no procession whatsoever—we simply arrived. When I suggested the idea of a battle to publicize legal proceedings among the Moscow Intelligentsia in which I circulated, they initially reacted to it as though I was ignorant, as though I didn't understand or had forgotten that Russia is an illegal State. I knew very well what was involved, and I decided to take the fight as far as possible. I stood for the juridical point of view. By definition, the State is a legal institution—a contradiction in terms. But I didn't attach much significance to the idea that Russia is an illegal State. I know our historical circumstances as well as anyone—I have already managed to spend time in mental hospitals on several occasions. I became aware of many injustices and developed several ideas on how they could be fought.

Q. So you think that it is possible to fight?

I consider that it is always possible to fight if there is legislation that makes formal provision for democratic freedoms. The people can then get those provisions observed, although they need patience, knowledge, and a purposeful attitude toward the problem, particularly to its formal aspect. It helps that I am a professional logician, and that I easily become obsessed with understanding the ideal maintenance of legal norms. It is difficult for me to take things as they come. I even describe defects in terms of rules—that's the way I think.

Q. Do you believe that the root of these problems lies in the nonobservance of the laws which exist, or in the system itself?

In what system? The system of laws?

Q. No, in the system of State.

But the State is a legal institution. Let's differentiate between the terms "state" and "country." Surely we see what kind of country the Soviet Union is. It is a country where one political party has seized control over the State. People speak ironically about the power clique, saying that they falsely promised a "withering away" of the State—but, forgive me, in my opinion there *is* a "withering away" and a "death" of the State. The Party has succeeded in destroying some 90 percent of the Government. Russia is not a State. The Party commands the State as it wishes. What kind of Government is it when there are no well-defined rights and responsibilities? However, I must underline, especially as I live abroad, that I am in no way a partisan of the pre-Revolutionary regime. Had I lived before the Revolution, undoubtedly I would have fought not for socialism, but for notions of an anarchic order, in the spirit of Kropotkin and Bakunin. Only I would have occupied an independent position—I would not have identified anarchism with socialism. I would not have divided the world into the right and the left—the stupidest of divisions, losing any meaning after a 180-degree turn: then the right becomes the left. This is the turn that Russia took in the course of the Revolution. But the Revolution didn't take place here, and so it is understandable that people speaking in various different languages still use the terms "right" and "left."

Q. And is that Party which seized power Marxist-Leninist?

The relationship between this Party and Marxism has never deeply interested me. I don't particularly recognize Marxism. I can recognize Marx's economic achievements, especially in the province of nineteenth-century economics. But Marxism is one thing—it is an economic doctrine, or, if you like, an economic, political, and sociological doctrine. But societal life is simply a different thing. It cannot be reduced to economics. And if a conversation with Marx were possible now, in all likelihood he would not object to the proposition that, all told, the economic oppression of the people is not the most cruel. To imprison a man by placing him in a mental institution is worse. If you say to a Westerner that he can be imprisoned, he will assume that he might be jailed for two or three months. If that was the problem, then perhaps we wouldn't have to worry so much about it. However, it's different in Russia. A man is imprisoned not for three months, but for three years, and even that is liberal. The authorities toyed with this liberalism for several years, but now, for instance, they are not releasing Amalrik, who has already served his three years. They want to give him three more years.

Q. And in what cases do they prefer to commit a man to a mental hospital instead of prison?

There is one answer. They prefer to place someone in a hospital in those cases where it is hard to use legal proceedings. Sometimes a man is able to resist.

Q. How?

Well, to make the problem of conviction difficult. Some glasnost' has been achieved. I had to insert the question of glasnost' into the conversation. Glasnost' is a matter of principle, especially the kind that encourages action. I perceived the mood of the Moscow Intelligentsia in the autumn of 1965 after the arrests of Sinyavsky and Daniel. I would like to remind you, what sort of time that was. A year before, in October, 1964, Khrushchev was deposed, and there emerged a new leadership, pro-Stalinist. That was clear to me on the very first day, when I heard about it—I remember, I was riding on the trolley bus. I saw the newspaper with photographs of the new Premier and Brezhnev, names which not long ago had been of minor significance, although known. There was a short explanation of how Khrushchev had resigned from his duties. I understood right then that this forebode no good. When I heard, either right then or on the following day, that Suslov was conducting the plenary session, then I needed no further explanations. And when after yet another day I read their editorial, I was amazed: there was an exultation, though it could not be expressed openly.

Q. What sort of exultation?

Well, the editorial in *Pravda* described the plenary session which had taken place with the expression, "The Party is free from conceit and idle talk." "Idle talk." In the next few months, with every mention of the phrase "idle talk," I understood what they were talking about. There was nothing more definite.

Q. And what did they have in mind?

They meant Khrushchev. Of all the statesmen of the Soviet Union, I personally regard Khrushchev as the best. This is in spite of the occupation of Hungary—that was a terrible evil. In general, from the human point of view, he merited removal. By the way, his removal was unconstitutional; dismissal from the office of First Secretary of the Party is not governed by the constitution. According to Article 70 of the constitution, the Chairman of the Council of Ministers is elected by the Supreme Soviet, and not by the Party Presidium. In theory that procedure would have allowed Khrushchev to speak to a meeting of the Supreme Soviet—and who knows how that would have turned out.

Q. Did his reforms achieve something in the country?

His achievements were not in reforms so much as in the 10-year policy of releasing people from the camps, and, of course, the criticism of Stalin. But if the present Government grants permission to emigrate more frequently, that might have a more significant meaning for the liberation of Russia than all the reforms of Khrushchev.

Q. That is to say?

The climate of the country is changing. A man who finds himself in Russia now is forced to accept the conditions there because he has nowhere to go. If a man accommodates himself to conditions; if he thinks more highly of his own life than of cardinal problems related to truth, history, the people; if, as most men, he is primarily interested in his own well-being, then he can solve his problems under any circumstances. But if he is interested in questions higher than his own well-being, he must analyze the conditions of the regime as it exists. If a man tries to do something independent of the spirit of the Party, he will simply be denied. So he must realize himself in the realm of abstract thought, where he needs no help—as long as he doesn't feel the need to publish. Such a man can operate in any regime up to a certain point. The impossibility of publishing is one of the vital problems for thinking people in Russia. I have been published abroad but I couldn't be published in Russia, in spite of the formal absence of a censor. But while there is no legal censor, the "noncensor" is more cruel. I would prefer censorship to what is a more exacting "freedom of the press."

Q. Formally there is no censor?

Strictly speaking, no. Formally, there is "freedom of the press."

Q. Very well. You say that if the climate changes. . . .

That's just it. There comes a time in a man's life—at least such a time arose in my life and that of many of my friends—when a singular desire occurs to him: to leave the country. "Let the others live as they are able to—but that is not for me. I am different." In such a situation in any "normal" country, a man would get a passport and leave, and his country would be all the happier for it. If the State enforces conditions with which a man disagrees, then it should be glad if such a man leaves, even if only for a time. But that's not the issue. The issue is that there should be a right to leave. That is critical because the Soviet rulers can tolerate the departure of one man, or even ten men; but in no way can it tolerate the departure of the whole Intelligentsia—or the best flower of the Intelligentsia. That would rather quickly precipitate a crisis for the Government or the Party leadership—it would be forced to make some compromises. But if people cannot leave, then they can be forced to accept any conditions, even if they don't want to. This is especially true if they have no access to publicity, for then they can be put away in prison, and no one will know about it.

Q. And what forced the Government to change its policy?

That is an interesting question; there are many factors. For instance, the Soviets have signed a pact concerning the rights of man. It has not been ratified because many nations have still not signed; they have been splitting hairs over minor points. The Soviets have simply hushed up this problem. Nevertheless, the Government has never taken the position on the international level that they are against this right, that its citizens are slaves. No, they admit the right to emigrate; they assert that simply no one wants to leave. The Soviet State in practice absolutely refuses to recognize legal rights, which means that a man can decide nothing for himself. The State as it actually operates is confused with the State as a purely formal legal institution.

Q. And if they did begin to let these people leave, then would the climate become clearer?

New dissidents will constantly be appearing, don't worry.

Q. They will?

This is inevitable. A man holds ideas, and whether they exist or not is not unimportant. The main thing is that he believes that these ideas exist in him. But they don't permit him to express these ideas, they don't let him publish them. Of course, half of such people give up in the end, but an appreciable number will keep striving. This is a State where everything is held in custody, where the uniformity of thought is supported by constant surveillance—a rather hazy surveillance, but a surveillance with definite consequences if one behaves freely: it will result, although not always immediately, in one's being placed in prison or a mental institution—to say nothing of losing one's job.

Q. And they don't worry that people who emigrate here might organize something?

Most likely they have been worrying about this for a long time, but in the final analysis they considered that danger to be less than if these people remained in the Soviet Union.

Q. Do you think that in some instances execution is better than committing a man to a mental institution for life?

I wouldn't say that. A man can, in spite of everything, be released from a mental hospital. The right to suicide might be conceded, if you think that a man would prefer to die rather than undergo such treatment. Perhaps give him a revolver, poison—whatever he wants—that I can allow, but why shoot? First and foremost, one must distinguish between the concepts of the voluntary and the forced. People constantly act without knowing that strictly speaking they are not bound to do the things they do. However, they are not free to the extent that they can refuse to do that which is prescribed in the given societal situation. Acting according to the herd instinct is not, of course, peculiar to the Soviet Union. But the issue lies in the character of the compulsion. There are compulsions in the West. Having lived here a year, I see that in the Western countries this is not immediately noticeable. But in the West I see that it is common for people to accept stagnation, banality, a standardization as part of the order of things. A man can have a free, independent, individualistic viewpoint. However, it is as though there exists a sort of social prescription for common sense that doesn't permit original thoughts. One or two perhaps, but at any given time, only one or two. This is a serious limitation. Of course, this restriction is not binding. One won't be placed in a mental institution if one has not followed the prescription. In Russia, however, a man also won't be imprisoned for his originality alone. It is much more subtle and complex.

Q. I am always asked how a man survives all these prisons and mental institutions. Is there a method?

I ask you to remember that a great number of people have already perished. Of course there is a method. Every Philistine knows it: to become a Philistine, or at least to get into that state of mind through one's own timidity. However, in my opinion, there is little difference between these two, though in Russia people mark some sort of distinction. They don't want to call everyone who adapts out of timidity a Philistine, although in my opinion that wouldn't be a bad idea. Of course, if a man only wants to extend his life up to the moment of his natural death, if he wants to avoid a sharp conflict with the authorities, it's more than easy to resolve.

Q. I am speaking of those who are already in prisons or mental hospitals. How do they survive?

In prison or in mental institutions? Imprisonment has a term that will pass, though a man doesn't necessarily survive that term. As for mental institutions, I remember very well when they were considered a salvation from a more awful punishment. Now mental hospitals inspire terror in us. However, when I myself was arrested for the first time in 1949, I preferred the mental institution.

Q. You preferred it?

Of course. I knew that after a year—let's say three years—one is released and besides there one does not have to do physical labor. I ended up in a mental institution. I could tell the doctors to go to the devil's grandmother. In any case, I risked that my sojourn in the mental hospital would be extended for another six months—which, by the way, didn't happen. As it turned out, I was exiled.

Q. For what?

I was arrested for my poetry in 1949. At that time I was by no means an active defender of legal rights: that is simply because I was a mathematician and had no cause to be concerned with rights. However, that experience in a very fundamental way confronted me with this problem. I had a certain propensity for this in that when they arrested me, I tried to somehow make use of a formal method to deal with the legal proceedings. Though at that time I was unable to do anything effective, I gradually understood that that was the gist of it. The chief problem was not what they might do to you—that, strictly speaking, was not your affair. The point was to consider that one was finished, and that the question lay in the "quality" of such an end. And it was there that the question arose about how one should react to that. Of course, physically one might be alive, or perhaps one might not be—that was not the point. The point is this: that one single phrase that turns out to be treachery is much worse than 10 years in camp.

Q. Elaborate.

It is thus: When they speak with me, I don't want to say that my friend said such and such—but they force me to talk. *Not* to say what the authorities require of you during questioning is not only a question of courage, firmness, and so on, because the authorities can force even a very courageous man to say what they want him to by gradually sucking him into the conversation.

Q. Even without drugs?

Without anything. It is not very complicated. A professional interrogator can do much. He knows how to gradually draw you into conversation. Generally, the interrogator will speak with you about a different subject. You will not understand why he is talking on this theme. He will pretend that he is just tired of his work, and that he wants to have a little heart-to-heart talk with you. "Well fine. Of course, you are arrested, but that is not necessarily a very serious punishment." He would say that generally there is no punishment. But he knows you won't believe him. At least a year ago he could have said that, and, of course, there are still those who hold such illusions. If the interrogator perceives that a man holds such illusions, he plays upon them. If a man doesn't have them, then he doesn't. It means nothing if the interrogator promises release, and the court gives you 10 years. The investigator doesn't concern himself that his words should necessarily be truthful. Once I had had the experience, I reacted to it differently. One must simply ask what the evidence is. This is simple: every criminal knows if there is material for evidence. I could simply say that all of this happened, but I would not sign my name to it. I could say, "Let's agree that you are right. But I am still not a fool. Why should I help you? You have procedural difficulties, I agree, but of course it's better for me that you have them. And you can say anything to me that you like. But the important thing is that you have procedural difficulties. Too bad for you, but all the better for me."

Q. But can they force you to sign something?

Nothing. If a man has stubbornly decided not to sign, there is nothing they can do. How can they force you to sign?

Q. Can they administer drugs?

Forgive me, they can give you drugs; however, why should drugs act upon you so selectively, that you would sign precisely what the interrogator requires, and not what you want to yourself? Drugs can act upon you in a general sense—you will want to sleep, but nevertheless you still have some sort of control. "Aha," you will say, "I want to sleep. I can't continue to give testimony." The investigator will say something to you, and you will answer, "I am tired. I can't speak objectively, which means you are receiving nonobjective evidence."

Q. A man can know those things if he's been through them once, but the first time it must be difficult?

I know it's hard. The first time that I was in prison, I admit, I committed several mistakes. Fortunately, nothing deplorable for others came of it. However, if the investigators had wanted . . . I allow that if they had increased the pressure a little, they could have made use of my arrest. But at the time I understood what was going on before it was too late and chose the means of a fictional suicide in order to be placed in a mental hospital. It ended the questioning—I had no other thought but this. I committed an elementary action; it was an elementary calculation. I wanted to be placed in a hospital because for me personally that meant the most expedient release. I didn't know, of course, for how many months or years. I only knew that it was the most expedient means.

Q. Did they give you paper and pencils there?

No, they don't always distribute them. In the investigative chamber there in Lubyanka, it was absolutely impossible to obtain them.

Q. Do you know why I ask? Once I saw two prisoners of war who had been released after the Korean War. They were rather young, healthy lads. They were completely shattered by prison; they had spent three years there. With them was a rather elderly woman from Vienna. How she ended up there I don't know, but anyway she had been there. And she looked as if she had just left a hotel. She said, "We didn't have paper, or pencils." She had been there for three years in solitude. She said that she occupied herself with translating Shakespeare from one language into the other in her head. She knew five languages and she had memorized Shakespeare. And in contrast to the Americans, who were totally broken and destroyed, she seemed untouched by the imprisonment.

This has a secondary significance. Prison by itself is not the most fearful place that a man can end up in; it depends on what sort of prison it is and how those in charge treat a man. I would like to spend a little time in an American prison, simply out of curiosity—for a comparison. I'm not interested in a showplace; in principle, I am not against spending a short time in such places.

Q. And so they didn't actually give you paper and pencil?

They did not give me paper and pencil in the investigative chamber. Although in one case they brought ink: when I disclosed that I wanted to write a complaint. I carped about the infringement of legal procedure. I wrote out several pages. I didn't want to write anything else. I gave it to them, but it had no effect.

Q. Did any officials see it?

What officials? In prison they saw it, the interrogator saw it, but who else could have seen it? I simply felt I should make a formal accusation on this, and then, when I was convicted, I could say that I had written such a document, that I disagreed. But in actual fact they placed me in the Serbsky [mental institution]. The trial formally took place, but behind closed doors, and even I didn't know what was taking place.

Q. The trial took place without your being present?

Yes. That is precisely the goal. The main goal consists in pronouncing us as mentally irresponsible so that the court can be rid of the accused. The more complex question is, Why was it that way under Stalin? Because there was then a system of trials conducted in the absence of the defendant. It wasn't even called a trial! After all, a trial requires the presence of the accused. But the right to conduct such trials was given to special boards of the MGB, the Ministry of State Security.

Q. The troikas?

Troikas. Slthough they were called "special councils." However, immediately after the death of Stalin these troikas were halted almost immediately, in 1953. But there were still secret trials, and when a trial is secret the situation, generally speaking, is not much better.

Q. Does this mean that a man had no conception when a trial was being conducted against him?

Under Stalin, under the troikas, a man did not receive a decision, but rather an excerpt in which the character of his indictment was defined in a couple of words. When the matter was political, then they tried to put it into the category of a "counter-revolutionary agitation" or something of that kind. There were several such terms to denote a "member of the family of traitors to Russia." There were many others, written in abbreviations. If you didn't understand those abbreviations, then they explained them to you verbally. Thus a man might present you with a scrap of paper with the letters CRG (counter-revolutionary group), or ASA (anti-Soviet agitation). Sometimes, instead of that, there would be the 58–10 Article of the code. When I was arrested the first time they used Article 58.

Q. You were starting to speak of how people survive this.

Well, how do people generally live through prison? They live through it because the danger is after all not a mortal one. It is an unpleasant situation, of course. But the physical conditions are not necessarily extremely severe. Sometimes they are severe—sometimes people are maimed. Often, but not always. And then, things always depend on one's ability to accommodate oneself to circumstances. Unfortunately, in the Soviet Union this doesn't always work. Much depends upon luck—a man often finds himself in situations where if he doesn't make certain compromises, then he won't be able to save himself. One can make compromises in a variety of ways—not necessarily with a loss of personal dignity.

Q. But you had an opportunity to write poetry in prison?

If there is the desire, then there is an opportunity. Those conditions can only increase such opportunities—they never lessen them.

Q. Were you able to note your poems down?

Generally a poet doesn't have to. A poet memorizes verses by heart. Actually, I couldn't write them on paper—but I didn't have to. I simply memorized them. For me it didn't matter if there was paper or not. But, in truth, I didn't consider myself essentially a poet. I wrote, and considered that I wrote poorly. It was more important to me that I was a philosopher, that I had become involved in philosophy and logic. Actually, I had unlearned how to write.

Q. Do you consider yourself a mathematician now?

A mathematician? No. My work is essentially related to theories of proof with a foundation in math. For me math is vital—I am still a good logician, and I understand the logical aspect of rights—the vulnerability of my opponents' formulations, the necessity of choosing the most invulnerable formulation possible. This is a verbal battle. It's quite possible to find the formulations. This started to intrigue me in my maturity, not from the very beginning, though from the very beginning I became familiar with the law, with the legal controversies in 1950. In 1949 I was too young; but in 1959—the interrogator probably had a hard time with me then.

Q. That was the second time you were arrested?

Yes, it was the second time. I was 35 years old, but even then I was a good logician and mathematician. And because of this I was able to preserve a sufficient degree of calm before the interrogator I had to deal with. I perceived the elementary rule: when you are arrested and they threaten to detain you longer (as I was threatened) it is in your favor and not in theirs. I had to defend myself, and from that point of view, I had to prepare for the trial, so that in giving me a long period of detainment they gave me a long period for preparation. And the rest is not significant.

Q. This means that you consider that trial to have been legal?

I consider that there exist certain articles that must be upheld. If they are violated, then it is my business to react, to write exposures of these infringements.

Q. And does anything come of this?

What comes of it is not insignificant. If I am arrested, the investigator wants me to give evidence. But instead of speaking about a man, I speak about the infringement of procedural rights. Thus I remind him: "I am an accused, and I am not obliged to speak with you. However, if you should like to talk to me, then if you please, here are the subjects. You have transgressed this, this, and this."

Q. Instead of accepting the negative, you take the positive point of view?

That is how it should be.

Q. What interests me is that, to a certain extent, this play of two intellects begins to concern you more than the legal proceedings themselves—than the trial itself.

But for me this is one and the same thing. In my opinion the trial consists of this. Yes, I understand what the power people are saying, but I don't want to help them convict me. And furthermore, this game gives me a mission. It is still an open question which mission is more important from the moral point of view. To evade the punishment, or to stand up to ordeals with regard to not becoming a traitor. And if at my first arrest I could be satisfied with what is by no means an extremely lofty achievement—that is, that no one suffered because of my testimony, then the next time I could attain significantly more: that no one could manipulate my testimony. If no one suffered the first time, perhaps that was because the authorities blundered. But had they wanted to make me say something the second time, they couldn't. I solved this problem in a new way, though there is actually nothing complicated about it. Before it is too late I simply say "Forgive me, I refuse to answer this question"—or even without the "Forgive me"! And further on I can just pronounce, "I refuse to answer this question." Like a parrot. I play my own game: "You might perhaps be in a weak position Everything here is ideological and political. However, you are accusing me of a criminal offense, and I will speak of politics and ideology elsewhere. But now I'm accused and am making use of my procedural rights." After a month this will end in a psychiatric investigation. The experts will conduct it, and I will continue the same process.

Q. Does this mean that when they arrested you the first time you wanted to fight the issue from a legal point of view?

Yes. I understood very well then that I must know the procedural laws.

Q. But did you know them?

Not very well. The first time the investigation lasted from three to four weeks. They questioned me about 10 times. However, the second arrest was simply an entertainment for me. And when they interrogated me the third time (I was not kept in custody) the investigator simply called me for questioning—then his legs were jelly and I was simply having fun. If they had questioned no one else, then they would have only written down those things that I wanted to disclose. However, because they had questioned others as well as myself, I felt it necessary to amend their errors. Sometimes I felt forced to speak on those subjects that I had wanted to avoid—simply because otherwise it would have been worse. It was still hard for them, because I didn't give a damn about them!

Q. Does this mean that you had rid yourself of fear?

There was no fear. In fact, they would often trap us at that very moment when we were no longer under the influence of fear. When you fear the person you are talking to, you will not say a lot, you will invent ways to avoid talk. They needed us not to be afraid. They wanted us to think that we were not being questioned by the KGB, that it was not a formal interrogation. People often committed treachery—not while speaking with the interrogator, but with someone else. This treachery is not even "official"—it is not used in the trial. However, the information is received by the KGB. A man simply does not guard himself against this. For example, you could go to the Soviet Embassy tomorrow and give them what I have said here today—and I am speaking with you openly. This method is vital to them, because they are unable to talk with us openly. They don't have the opportunity of talking to us in such a way, and when they find a way, it is much more important to them. I will not say that they don't employ torture. However, clearly you already understand that your signature means something by the time they question you. But if they need to learn something from you, rather than simply to obtain your signature, then a more reliable means is to place someone else in your cell, in order that you should come to consider him your friend. In any case you will tell him more than you will the interrogator. There is no torture as effective in making you tell more to your executioner than your friend.

Q. And if they feel they need to put you away, you personally . . . ?

If they need to put you away it is because some other person gave some sort of information about you; otherwise they wouldn't have to. The existence of any sort of non-Party organization is impossible in Russia. I understood this when I was imprisoned the second time. As early as in Khrushchev's rule, such organizations were springing up. I have been told that some sort of Social Democratic Party arose—truly Menshevik. It considered itself as such. What it actually was, I don't know. You understand, these large-scale revolutionary parties were never formally and legally dissolved. The people were liquidated; that's all there was to it. There are still those there who are living. They will tell you what I am saying.

Q. Who?

Well, for example, the SRs, the survivors of the SRs. There was never a meeting of the SR Party to declare that the Party ceased its existence. So it exists.

Q. Do you consider that the Democratic Movement has a future, or has it all ended?

In the Democratic Movement the issue was the transformation of Russia into a legal government guaranteeing people their rights.

Q. Without destroying the system?

It is not necessary to legally destroy the system, because it will suffice simply to erase the many shortcomings in the laws if the triumph of elemental democratic principles is possible. To change the law into a dead letter, and then to demand its repeal—that is a long process. This is because the tragedy of Russia is not in the fact that she is under a Communist regime. Let the regime alone. It is the Party—a Party of 14 million people. However, why should 14 million people have power over 250 million: that is the question. By law? This is also not written in the law. This means that if the law is upheld . . . yet the very concept of law in the Soviet Union is extremely vague. The commands of the authorities (not only in the Soviet Union, but in other places too) enforce the law. In fact, these commands are in the interests of the authorities, rather than in the interest of the laws. I think the error lies in this: Even if our fate depends on the authorities and not on the laws, our rights are determined by law, and not by the authorities. I have said this very thing to everyone I have spoken with: that our rights are defined by the law, and not by the authorities. The authorities can control our fate, but deviating from the law, they do this illegally. Indeed, in Russia we have no tradition of insisting upon legal procedures, but that is the principle upon which we must make our battle. Everything else is secondary. If you replace the Communist Party with something else, if you install a church or something of this sort, then everything will be under different slogans, in a different ideological mold. I agree—but I'm not interested in that. I am concerned that this element of our system should be obliterated—whatever the ideological or political pretexts. I suggest that questions pertaining to anything other than legality, procedure, and civil liberties should be considered secondary.

Q. Tell me, did you dress up your reasons for leaving the Soviet Union?

The authorities wanted me "to leave for Israel." I didn't give my word that I'd be going there; I didn't use cunning. I didn't answer the question "Why do you want to leave?" with the usual "I want to go to my national Motherland." I wrote, "Because it is the first time that such an opportunity arose."

Q. And what was the first country you arrived in?

Poland, Czechoslovakia, then Austria and Italy.

Q. And what was your first impression of the West?

I had an impression of having slept through the Czech border, then I woke up in the territory of Austria, on the train, to the word, "Passport?" I handed him my visa, waiting for him to stamp and return it to me. But instead this frontier guard disappeared and I saw that it was a conspiracy. The conductor laughed and I received my visa only in Italy. And in Austria I lived with no documents at all, without any proof of my identity. And this was done by an Austrian border guard.

Q. How long did you stay in Austria?

One week, although my visa was for three months. I didn't particularly hold on to my right to be in Austria. To this day it continues to outrage me, this conspiracy, a triple conspiracy between the Soviet Union, Austria, and Israel. But Israel by itself would not have resorted to such a rude device—even though it may be advantageous for Israel—to deprive a man of his document so that he wouldn't have any confirmation of his identity. It's indecent to take a man's document and to disappear, and then to return the document to me in another country. What is that? They did that with all emigrants who were on the train. It's a general system, but the fact that an Austrian border guard took part in it was, to say the least, unpleasant.

BORIS SEGAL

Boris Segal was born in Tashkent in 1926. Both his parents were medical doctors. When Boris was nine years old his father was arrested as "an enemy of the people." When his mother inquired about his fate she was told that he was in a faraway labor camp "without the right to correspondence." It was a euphemism for a death sentence. Indeed, several days after his arrest Doctor Segal was shot and Boris's mother was arrested as "the wife of an enemy of the people." She was later exiled.

As a child and youth Boris did not like medicine. He was very interested in philosophy, in literature, in politics, psychology, and foreign languages. But when he expressed his intention to pursue these subjects, his mother begged him to become a medical doctor. She told him that as a doctor he would have a better chance to survive in prison or a labor camp. In 1946 Boris entered the Moscow First Medical Institute and later became an M.D. with a specialty in psychiatry. He was almost arrested in 1953, but was saved by Stalin's death. From 1954 to 1956 Segal was the head of the department for alcoholics in the Moscow Psychiatric Hospital and for the next five years a research fellow at the Institute of Psychiatry of the Academy of Medical Sciences. From 1966 to 1970 he directed the Department of Clinical Psychology and Psychotherapy of the Moscow Institute of Psychiatry and from 1970 to 1972 he was the director of the Department of Psycho-Hygiene and Psychotherapy at the Moscow Central Institute of Physical Culture. In this capacity he was a consultant to the many famous athletes during their preparation for the Olympics in Munich. Segal is the author of about 100 articles and monographs on alcoholism, psychosomatic disorders, and the role of personality in mental illnesses. At present he is interested in the problems of personality under the conditions of a totalitarian society and is a research fellow at Harvard.

Boris and his wife emigrated to the United States in 1973. The interview took place several months after their arrival in Boston, in the living room of their apartment where a portrait of Sigmund Freud dominates the wall.

Segal is soft-spoken and cautious. He thinks out his answers carefully. Stalinism is not an abstract notion to him; he knew it personally from childhood. "When I received my visa," he said, "I did not tell a single soul that I was leaving the country."

Q. How many years did you study to become a psychiatrist?

The specialization is within the program of the medical school, not beyond it. In the United States a doctor who graduates receives the title of a general practitioner, and then goes into specialization. In Russia you simply choose a specialty in the final, sixth year of the medical school.

Q. How did you become interested in psychiatry?

I wasn't interested in medicine at all. In 1937, my father was arrested and shot along with millions of other honest people. I never knew why. Perhaps the reason for the accusation against him was that his brother lived in the United States. And perhaps the reason was that my father studied in Berlin before the Revolution, and thus maintained friendly relations with many German doctors who escaped from Hitler to Russia and who were later arrested as German spies. Finally, there didn't have to be any reason at all since at the same time almost all the people working for the Ukrainian Ministry of Health were arrested. This is where my father worked at that time. We didn't know about his fate. My mother was arrested and spent two years in prison; then she was exiled. When she came back she persuaded me to enter medical school. She said, "If you'll be in the humanities with your mood and your tongue they'll soon commit you, whereas in the medical school it is less dangerous." Besides, she had an idea that there would be a new campaign of terror and she thought I would have a chance to remain alive if I were a doctor. She said doctors had some privileges in camps. Many of my friends who were children of persecuted parents entered medical studies for the same reason.

Q. So you entered medical school solely for that reason?

I was always interested in psychology and in psychiatry, so I decided to specialize in psychiatry. Nevertheless, during my third year of medical school I attempted to enter the Institute of Oriental Studies. I was not admitted because of my Jewish nationality. After that I began independently to read psychiatric literature, before I took any courses, and became infatuated with it and never regretted having become a psychiatrist.

Q. Where were you sent after graduation?

At that time we were living in Moscow. My mother was very seriously ill and according to the law I was allowed to remain in Moscow. But in spite of the fact that I finished medical school with a gold medal I could not get work because that was the time [1951] of a strong anti-Semitic campaign. With great difficulty I managed to get a job in a suburban hospital for the chronically ill. A month after I left my mother died.

Q. What did you learn in that hospital?

Not much. The building was an old, dilapidated factory. Russian hospitals in general are converted from former factories or camps, except for Moscow where they do build hospitals. It was packed to overflowing with patients.

Q. How long did you work there?

I worked there about a year, and then, everywhere, the arrests of doctors began. This was the time of the famous Doctors' Plot. The Jewish doctors were persecuted and harassed. There was another Jewish psychiatrist in the hospital where I worked. The KGB called our nurses in and ordered them to sign a document stating that we were killing and torturing the Russian people with electric current. Of course, we did use electric-shock treatments. Some of them, being afraid, signed it. Then an order was given for our arrest. It was the beginning of spring, 1953. Our hospital was 30 miles outside the regional town. The KGB car came twice for us, but because of the horrible Russian roads, which during spring floods become absolutely impassable, the car could not reach our hospital. Then, in March, Stalin died and we were saved. But we were still scared and did not use electric-shock treatments any more.

Q. What did you give the patients by way of treatment?

When I was there insulin was in use. At the present time there is a widespread use of psychopharmacological drugs.

Q. Does it help the chronically ill?

Sometimes, yes. You know the condition of a chronically ill person can at times improve spontaneously, without any treatment. Chronic psychiatric illness is very conditional. Even the most helpless can suddenly show improvement. But all those hospitals are very depressing.

Q. Like Chekhov's *Ward Number Six*?

No, it's worse. *Ward Number Six* was just one ward. There are huge hospitals like that. Of course, both the patients and the doctors themselves are in a fearful position. Among the doctors there are also many sick ones, schizophrenics, alcoholics, psychopaths. You will never meet such doctors in big cities. One could write a novel just about the doctors in the provincial mental hospitals.

Q. How is the medical help organized in the psychiatric hospitals in general?

Everything depends on the particular organization. For example in 1954–1956 I was working in Moscow, in Hospital Number One. This hospital is the chief medical center of the whole Moscow region. About eight million people live beyond Moscow itself. Every district has its hospital. The hospitals are for the severely ill and for the chronically ill. There are 20 such hospitals, but they surely need 200 in order to place all those who need it. Doctors often have to sign out those who still need hospitalization. Where I worked they used to send us about 25 people a week from the city, whether we could take them or not. As a result some lay on the floors; some had to lie two to one bed. If a patient had relatives we tried to give them to those relatives.

Q. How did they get sent to your hospital?

A patient is driven to Moscow and there he receives authorization to go to some district hospital. The relatives on whom we had unloaded a patient would drive him to Moscow and he would receive authorization to go to some other hospital. In this way a circle of unloading was created.

Q. What is the system of committing one to a psychiatric hospital?

The system varies. It is organized best in Moscow. The relatives come to a psychiatric clinic with or without the patient. His condition is discussed and then he is either invited to the clinic or the doctor visits him at home. But in the country, if someone becomes mentally ill, he is simply bound and driven to the district center. If he has no relatives, the neighbors gather and tie his hands and bring him in. The doctor gives him a pass to some hospital. It is very hard to transport a patient there. The suburban trains won't take you, so it is necessary to hire a car. If, for example, they bring such a patient to us and we can't accommodate the patient, we give him a pass to some province. And he must be somehow taken at night, because it is impossible to spend a night in Moscow. It is very complicated.

Q. When you studied psychiatry were you taught Sigmund Freud?

No, of course not. Freud is considered "reactionary."

Q. How about Jung? And did you have a chance to read something on your own?

I did read. But it is not easy to get those books. One has a lot of trouble obtaining them. At present the situation is a little better, but to get the contemporary Western psychiatric literature is still difficult.

Q. On what premises is the theory of psychiatry built there?

There isn't any theory. The Pavlovian theories are dated. The so-called clinical direction dominates, which is based on the old German psychiatry of the nineteenth century and the beginning of the twentieth century. On the other hand, there is a widespread belief that psychosis depends on the chemical processes in the brain. In most scientific papers the psychiatrists attempt to establish "parallelism" between a psychopathological syndrome and a biochemical or electrophysiological deviation.

Q. So the therapy is mainly pharmacological?

Yes, as a rule. Soviet psychiatry maintains the Marxist point of view that the psyche depends on somatic causes. In order to understand a psychological illness one must understand the workings of the brain and its mechanisms.

Q. But the word "subconscious," does exist in the Russian language?

In general no kind of subconscious was recognized until recently. About eight years ago they began to speak of the subconscious, or rather of the unconscious, but with great reservations. It is discussed in the materialistic sense, not in the psychoanalytic. Several works appeared—for example, the works of I. Bassin, which try to place a different interpretation on that word. But the official directors of Soviet psychiatry still refer to psychoanalysis as "bourgeois ideology." Psychoanalysis and psychodynamics are not known in Russia at all. I think that will not change soon.

Q. But take your case. You have read Freud. Perhaps you have a patient and you see that according to Freud he is sick in such and such a way and he can be helped by Freudian methods. But officially you are forbidden to use those methods. What can you do?

This situation does not exist only in the psychiatric sphere. It exists in all spheres in Soviet life and work—double-think. You think one thing and say another.

Q. For instance, does a theory of repression and its consequences exist?

No. You see, the Soviet psychiatrists are not interested in those things. The problem for a Soviet psychiatrist is to give a descriptive picture of a psychopathological syndrome and, as far as possible, suggest a pharmacological cure for it. The psychological interpretation with diverse psychological theories is first, unknown; secondly, it is condemned; and thirdly, it is not only condemned, because it is not allowed, but because there is a general hostility toward it. They don't know any of those theories and don't want to know them. The large psychoses—schizophrenia and so forth—are studied in the Soviet Union; the little ones, such as neurosis, sexual deviations, alcoholism are neglected.

Q. In American universities there are psychiatrists in the students' clinics. Is there a comparable service in Soviet universities?

No. In America the psychiatrists specialize in various spheres of life. In Russia they have narrow specialization, involved mainly with the insane. An ordinary Soviet person wouldn't go to a psychiatrist anyway, for many reasons. In his imagination a psychiatrist is associated with being tied up hands and feet. He is scared of a psychiatrist. Moreover, it is formally dangerous to go to a psychiatrist, because one is then registered. He is "on account," and it can prevent him from getting into an educational institute, from traveling abroad, from getting a driver's license. And even if he does go, he won't get any help, because the psychiatrists are conditioned not to pay attention to such problems. A psychiatrist doesn't have either time or knowledge for anything but the "major" mental diseases.

Q. Are there any private psychiatrists?

Yes, but unofficially and only a limited number.

Q. What about the very highest echelon, people like Brezhnev and the like?

First of all, they go to the Kremlin Hospital. There, there is a totally different arrangement and everything that is necessary is available. The elite has everything.

Q. Do Soviet psychiatrists admit the existence of sexuality and sexuality in childhood?

No Freudian terminology is accepted. The word "sexual" has an obscene connotation there, and the problems connected with sex are ignored. Not only sexual problems, but even alcoholism is ignored even though it is of fantastic proportions. One can see drunks everywhere, at any time, in the villages and in the cities. They are lying around everywhere. Their number is simply overwhelming. When we made a survey of the factories we found that every third worker was an alcoholic. Even among women and youth alcoholism is on the increase. But statistics are unknown.

Q. To what do you attribute it?

Before the Revolution, Engels wrote that alcoholism is the consequence of capitalist exploitation. But the fact is that those who drink among the workers are the more prosperous ones. But it is not so simple. The economic factors are influential, but it's not the main reason. It is a problem not only in the Soviet Union. In Sweden, one of the most prosperous countries, alcoholism is very high. In the U.S.A. and Germany too. This is the very proof of the inauthenticity of the economic theory.

Q. And what do you think are the causes of alcoholism?

There are many factors. Hippocrates said that no sickness has only one cause. A lot depends on tradition, national and cultural customs, and on the kind of alcohol different people drink. In Russia vodka is the national drink. In the wine countries, such as Italy, Spain, the Caucasus, they drink wine regularly and you won't see drunks there very often. That's because alcohol has been gradually distributed through the whole biological system so there is no loss of control in the drinking situation. Exploitation, poor living conditions, the absence of spiritual interests and of amusements may also be motives for drinking. Alcohol takes the place of what is lacking in life. But the motivation could also be interpersonal, subjective, from inner conflicts. Impotence or latent homosexuality can also cause alcoholism. A widow can become an alcoholic as a result of the trauma caused by her husband's death. In this case alcohol acts as a strong tranquilizer. But there is also drunkenness, to be distinguished from alcoholism. In Russia there was always drunkenness. In a pre-Revolutionary Russian village during holidays, people drank themselves to death. But on working time peasants didn't usually drink. That was when the village was patriarchal. With urbanization and proletarization, especially after the creation of collective farms, and as the peasants went to towns and cities, they began to drink regularly. The growth of alcoholism in the Soviet Union and in the United States stems not only from urbanization and industrialization, but also from the weakening of the role of the family. Besides, in both societies, there exist many frustrations for a human being. Many of his needs cannot be realized. A Soviet man as a rule has no spiritual needs, but his material needs cannot be realized. In America if a man has no spiritual needs, if he is just a consumer, he has the means to at least satisfy those needs. But in the Soviet Union all efforts toward even material self-affirmation meet with barriers. What can an average man achieve there even economically? Well, he can perhaps buy a second suit. It's not enough to sublimate other exigencies. And the alcohol is a quick way to relieve frustration. It is a kind of escapism.

Q. As a psychiatrist, do you believe that it is possible for a human being to live without any spiritual needs? Here in America, for example, you see that many live strictly by materialistic or consumer-society interests. Can such a person live without developing frustrations and neuroses?

Frustrations exist in any society. A society is impossible without frustrations. The very attempt to unite with anyone, even if it's just two people, man and wife, is already frustrating in some sense, resulting from mutual concessions and expectations. Therefore, any society is necessarily frustrating. But the question is, what is the character of such frustrations and in what measure is it possible to sublimate them? There are needs for emotional contact, there are biological, aggressive, sexual needs, there is need for self-expression, a need to seek an ideal. Even the most primitive man seeks for himself a sense of life. The question is, does a given society allow you to compensate for the needs which cannot be realized? Take American society for example. Of course, in some ways a person's needs are frustrated by the society, in some ways by himself. American society doesn't provide for the satisfaction of the spiritual needs—a person must provide for it himself. Suppose he is not equipped to do that? What will he fill the void with? The question is universal. Previously a person could fill the void with religious faith, or by some ideals or beliefs. Now with the general fall of moral and ethical values there is a vacuum.

Q. In your opinion, in which society is it more possible for a man to fill this vacuum, no matter with what, in the Soviet or in the West?

In Soviet society Marxist ideas of changing social relations lost their appeal for the people, but in Western society the classical ideas of "bourgeois" democracy are also becoming unpopular. In this sense we can agree with those who are speaking about the de-ideologization or even of the death of ideologies. Nevertheless, since society in America has less control over the individual he has more possibilities here. There is another question: how successful would the person be at realizing them? Still, there are more ways to utilize one's energy, more canals to channel it. Soviet society, being more rigid, offers fewer possibilities. For example, personal wealth is unattainable or rather it is attainable only by illegal means; one must break the law. In America where society is certainly not ideal and does not provide for spiritual needs, there are many more equivalents available. But it all is a surrogate for spiritual needs.

Q. If we accept the Dostoevsky concept that man does not love freedom, that man prefers that someone should think for him, doesn't it follow that it is easier to live in the Soviet Union?

It is true that an average person, a simpler person, feels himself more comfortable under conditions of nonfreedom, under controlled conditions, so that even though the Government is keeping its power by certain mechanisms—repressions, fear, the KGB—that power is not only maintained by those negative factors. It is also maintained by the positive factors, by the positive attitudes of the people toward governmental power. It may be an unconscious factor, but it's there. This positiveness is created by the totalitarian system. That is, the image of the leaders of the Government is that of a father, omniscient, omnipotent, one who could punish or reward. This is the ideal variation, the variation as Stalin or the Nazis thought of it. The person has a feeling of passivity and of horror before the all-powerful State. But that path is behind. With the degeneration of totalitarianism and as the fear and repression weakened, so too did the forces that supported the system. The process of pluralization and liberalization weakens the stability of society. It depends partly upon psychological factors. A person in a prison camp has no inner conflicts because he is in an extreme situation. Under the conditions of Stalin's regime such conflicts were fewer. For a simple man it was better; everything that could be done and what was forbidden was clear. To the degree that the central power weakens, various antagonistic tendencies appear, alcoholism, crime, and so on.

Q. Do you personally consider that criminals might be sick?

It's the same as with sexual illnesses or alcoholism. There are biological, social, psychological factors. There is such a thing as the genetic criminal. There are people who since early childhood show sadistic inclinations. Such a child is a potential criminal. It gives them pleasure to torture or destroy. There is a great contingent of social criminals. They became criminals because of social conditions. The same with homosexuality.

Q. Do Soviet psychiatrists study homosexuality?

Sexual problems in general are hushed up in the Soviet Union. About eight years ago, after a long and arduous campaign, a sexology laboratory was created in Moscow.

Q. Do they read the Kinsey Report there?

One man who could read English did read Kinsey. They study the same things as they do here only without a sufficient theoretical base.

Q. But if they study and are not able to apply it, what's the sense?

In order to practice it there has to be some organizational system and that doesn't exist. And no one would give any funds for it. A book on sexology was suggested for publication. The publisher accepted it, but the Central Party Committee made a resolution against it. It was not acceptable. A book on sex and marriage was translated from German, but it was more about anatomy and physiology. People bought it up, but there was no second edition. The reason they don't publish such books is not because there is no one to write them, rather they simply don't consider it necessary to allow them.

Q. Speaking of marriage, are there marriage counselors?

Very rarely. We tried to organize it. You see, those things depend on someone's enthusiasm. But the enthusiasm is negated by a society that restricts individual initiative. If one went to a doctor with a personal marriage problem, a doctor who has to see dozens of patients a day and doesn't have time to listen to such things, he'll give him a tranquilizer at most.

Q. Are there tranquilizers manufactured in Russia?

No, they are imported from Hungary.

Q. Can they be gotten without prescription?

Legally, no, but generally one can get them. And they are also prescribed a lot because something has to be prescribed.

Q. I've been to the Soviet Union five times and this last time I noticed a lot of homosexuals in Leningrad and Moscow, and it wasn't so before.

Yes, there is an increase. Because for the greater part pederasty is a social phenomenon. There are genetic homosexuals, of course, but mainly it's a social occurrence. Those who have tendencies could or could not realize those tendencies. It depends on the concrete environment in which they are brought up. If they find themselves in an environment where it is forbidden, they will not be homosexuals. The judgment of a puritan society holds back the tendencies. The same with alcoholism. There are very few drunkards in China. They have alcoholics, genetic ones, but not social ones. And a huge number of others who could have been do not become so because of severe condemnation by their society. The homosexuals who are simply potentials will not realize their tendencies in a severely puritanical society. This social condemnation becomes their own superego. They judge themselves as well.

Q. What is the official point of view in the Soviet Union regarding homosexuals?

From a judicial point of view all homosexuals are looked on as criminals. Until 1924 it was considered by the Soviet penal code a biological abnormality. After 1924 it has been regarded as a crime. However, they are punished unwillingly as are all crimes against the individual.

Q. How do you explain it?

Very simply. In the Soviet Union every crime against the State, like theft of Government property or political crimes, is punished harshly. There are fewer legal articles to cover crimes against the individual. A man who has committed murder can find his guilt mitigated by circumstances, whereas a man who had committed theft of social property will receive a greater punishment. So things like rape or homosexual assault, since it is a personal crime, is punished only when there is a demand for punishment from a victim.

Q. Are there certain problems that are considered typically feminine or typically masculine?

Absolutely not. There is no "sexual psychiatry"—it's not allowed. Such analysis might lead to social conclusions.

Q. Do they admit female problems?

Purely physiologically. I, as a psychiatrist know that psychiatric problems that are purely feminine exist. And the Russian woman is in especially difficult circumstances, though officially it is not admitted. They admit the physiological problems involved with the menopause, but not the psychological ones.

Q. What about the problems of old age?

There are institutes of gerontology, and there are clinics in the mental hospitals. But to get into one of them is very difficult.

Q. But do they admit the existence of psychological problems of old age?

The works that exist are formally descriptive. They describe, for example, the old age psychosis. They are described in terms of syndromes—loss of consciousness, manias—but no one analyzes such things as the feeling of not being needed, of being disoriented. You know, all efforts to understand an individual come up against political repercussions. Why, for example, is it forbidden to study alcoholism? Because at some point one will have to analyze Soviet society and draw some conclusions. One might have to conclude that Soviet society doesn't give an individual a chance to realize himself. If you begin to analyze homosexuality you'll have to admit that in the Soviet Union there are homosexuals. If you talk about old age problems you'll have to say that an old man, as in any other society, is not needed. How can such things be said? Then one might say, "What? The Soviet society is no different from the capitalist one where those problems exist?" This is an anti-Soviet conclusion. Therefore, every investigation of this sort has to be sociological. For example, the study of crime. It was always declared that a criminal is a social phenomenon, that crime is the result of class struggle, that in a harmonious society it will not exist. We were told that crime and alcoholism would gradually disappear, because they were the leftovers from capitalism. And in actuality they grow and grow every year. When sociologists were given an assignment to work out a graph of crime in the Soviet Union and they came up with the conclusions that crime is not only increasing, but will continue to increase, then one of the Politburo members announced that "the sociologists in the Soviet Union haven't matured enough; they aren't yet ready for such work." Because any honest, logical study of causes will necessarily have social implications. Even if you take the problem of being left-handed. In the Soviet Union there are few left-handers because since early childhood they are constantly being shamed: "Look, everyone writes with the right hand and you write with the left." So they switch under this pressure. This helps the conformist mentality. But try to draw this conclusion. It will be considered anti-Soviet. If you analyze anything thoroughly you will come up with the conclusion that the Soviet society had something to do with it. Therefore, people prefer not to study these problems. They prefer description to analysis. A huge number of dissertations that I personally directed were of this sort: "The Changes in the Blood after Such-and-Such Drug Therapy" and so on. And the things that you and I discussed here are considered nonscientific, speculative, not serious. If a young psychiatrist begins such a study, then not only his political boss but his old teacher-psychiatrist will say to him, "What's the matter, why do you occupy yourself with nonsense?" For example, we had one single, only one single dissertation written on homosexuality. The dissertation was failed. And by the way, no one had any Party directive to fail it—the psychiatrists themselves decided that it was some sort of pornography. "Is that a scholarly work?" "This isn't a scholarly work. A scholarly work describes hallucinations." I was the opponent of the others. And the director shouted that it was some kind of nonsense, that it was nastiness.

Q. And what came out of it all finally?

Finally it was defended, but with great difficulties.

Q. Does a concept or practice of group therapy exist in the Soviet Union?

Very seldom. For instance, in Leningrad one doctor tried to organize it for alcoholics. We also tried group therapy in Moscow, but that is all limited to Moscow and Leningrad. There is also one in Kharkov. In short, if a foreigner comes to visit there is something to show him.

Q. Do you mean to say this is done for the purpose of a show?

No, I mean that it is done because some individual is interested in that problem, or is doing a dissertation on group therapy. But if the need arises and some foreigner asks to see a group-therapy session, he'd be brought there. You see, the very system of medicine there is totally soulless. As in every government, the attitude toward a human being is strictly formal. There is no personal interest in a patient. Therefore, psychotherapy wouldn't work there. It demands personal interest. In psychoanalysis, a doctor has to talk to a patient for an hour or two. Who can afford it there? One has to be either a great enthusiast and love this work, or else one has to be interested financially. But a doctor who is simply a government bureaucrat will not spend time on that even if he had it. And he doesn't have it. I'm sure that if American psychiatrists were forbidden to practice privately they would stop practicing psychoanalysis.

Q. Have you heard of transactional therapy?

I read about it in a magazine. You must realize that in the Soviet Union if a book is not translated, it is impossible to get it. Here it's simple. You go to a bookstore and get it. Or to a library. There, unless you read English you can't read it, and besides it's very hard to get a book to read. It's almost impossible to get a book. People in sciences have access to foreign books and are well informed. But people who are close to the humanities, to history, to philosophy, psychology, are under greater control and are deprived of information. A Russian physicist and an American physicist are on the same level. The closer one is to ideological subjects the less informed one is. What does an average psychiatrist there know about Freud? That he wrote something about sex. Now it's not so strict; one wouldn't be arrested for being a Freudian. But if one writes a dissertation with Freudian theories, he will be failed.

Q. How does a psychiatrist to whom a perfectly normal man like Leonid Plyushch or General Grigorenko is brought, how does he within himself resolve the problem of having to keep such a man in an insane asylum and of having to give him medications that are harmful? And does he reconcile this with his oath of Hippocrates?

The oath of Hippocrates has only been introduced recently. The problem of the forced hospitalization of the dissidents is not so simple as it may seem at first glance. To begin with, I want to emphasize that in any society psychiatry is providing not only medical but "defensive" functions, guarding it from antisocial acts. From the point of view of Soviet authorities, in particular psychiatric bosses, their direct duty is to isolate in the insane asylums those people who have anomalies and are engaged in anti-State activities. The statement that in the U.S.S.R. the insane asylums are full of political dissidents is not correct (as Tarsis wrote it). It's an exaggeration. They receive the same drugs as other patients who have been diagnosed as insane. The crime is not in giving them drugs but in declaring them insane if they are not. The regime in these prison-hospitals is very difficult. The state of a patient after those drugs is very burdensome, and all who are given these drugs always ask, if they are able to speak, not to be given them any more. But at the same time it is naïve to affirm that the forced hospitalization of dissidents does not exist, as some Western psychiatrists, like Lopez Ibor, do say. The truth is that as the liberalization of the Soviet regime occurred and the mass bloody terror stopped, the authorities were faced with the problem of what to do with the opposition. The KGB tried to avoid too many political trials that would have a negative resonance in the West, and so it began to ask the psychiatrists about the psychological state of the dissidents. It was more advantageous for the Government if one or another dissident could be found insane. The Government didn't order the psychiatrists to declare someone insane, but to express their opinion. It is quite possible that some psychiatrists, especially the ones connected with the forensic-psychiatric hospital named after

Serbsky, which is closely connected with the KGB and with the police, did give consciously erroneous diagnoses. But most of the psychiatrists were acting sincerely. There is also this: many psychiatrists think that every seventh person is a latent schizophrenic. So when they see a person with some originality or eccentricity they say that he is a schizophrenic, or paranoiac. From the point of view of an average, narrow man, the dissident activities are useless and therefore are symptoms of an illness. It is especially so for the Party psychiatrists. A lot of these doctors are not only conformists but not very intelligent, and they occupy important positions. A person like General Grigorenko, who comes out on Red Square with a protest poster is to them insane. What normal man, thinks such a psychiatrist, would go out on Red Square, knowing full well that he will be arrested and that nothing will come of his protest? To them a normal man couldn't act like that. And they are right, because the designation "normal" means conformist. Such a man adapts himself to society; he doesn't fight it. Take those pre-Revolutionary revolutionaries like Perovskaya who threw bombs and were terrorists, they were also abnormal in that sense.

Q. According to this sense Lenin too was crazy. He didn't adapt to his society?

Of course.

Q. But if they take this theory seriously, don't they themselves have to come to the conclusion that Lenin was not normal?

If a man of Lenin's mentality and behavior would appear on Red Square today protesting the invasion of Czechoslovakia, of course they would say that he was insane. Besides, among the dissidents there are people with deviant behavior, with various psychiatric anomalies, and even with mental illnesses. It is irrelevant that there is no need whatsoever to put them in the psychiatric hospitals. Otherwise Kafka and Dostoevsky and Gogol should have been locked up too. If these people did not occupy themselves with dissident activities, no one would have paid any attention to them. We should also keep in mind that in the Soviet Union not only political dissidents are placed in punitive insane asylums, but anyone with psychiatric deviations or "antisocial conduct." People often are in conflict with some organization, or with some bureaucrats, and they begin to fight them and in this way begin to engage in "anti-Soviet activities." In the U.S.S.R., as in any country, many people are displeased with something aside from politics. They begin to fight for their rights, they write complaints, they demand justice. But in a bureaucratic society this sort of activity brings a person to a confrontation with the Government, the role of which is great. A person who is obstructing the work of a governmental institution or organization could very quickly be sent to a psychiatrist for a diagnosis, and if the psychiatrist finds some deviation in this person's behavior, he finds himself in a hospital. Usually the psychiatrists diagnose "pathological development of personality" or "paranoiac development of personality" or schizophrenia or psychosis. In this way the practice of forcible psychiatric therapy for dissidents is a natural continuation of this tradition. This practice is made easier because Soviet psychiatry in general has a very passive attitude toward human rights. To grab a man and declare him insane is nothing. They don't require a commission or lawyers or anything. It is not a problem and it has never been a problem. It is not a Western society, it is a Russian society, and it was always this way in Russia.

Q. What is your view of the future of this problem in the U.S.S.R.?

Like Americans, I am an optimist. I hope that the gradual, even though unfortunately slow, evolution and democratization of Soviet society will bring it to a more strict observance of human rights, and in this way this shameful practice will be stopped. For this we must hope for progress in psychiatric studies in the Soviet Union. This again is tied up with the question of liberalization and with the increase of scientific contacts with the West.

GALINA TELNIKOVA

Odessa opens up to the sea, and the infinite horizon gives it a sense of limitless possibility. The people of Odessa are known for their direct and bold manner, for their straightforward and colorful speech, for their spirit of independence. When someone characterizes a person as an "Odessan," it might mean cunning, swindler, crafty, but it might also mean talented, aware, candid. Odessa gave the country its best musicians and some of its bravest fighters.

One of the first things that becomes apparent about Galina Telnikova is that spirit of independence. Without makeup, with long, straight, dark hair and slim figure, she looks more like an American teen-ager than a 29-year-old married geographer. She answers questions with the self-confidence of a person who has considered various issues and has come to some definite conclusions based on experience and deliberation. But she also seems impatient, even annoyed, at questions regarding Women's Liberation, as though the inquiry in itself were a mockery of the Soviet woman's situation in her society.

Galina was born in Odessa and educated in an English school there. At the University she majored in economic geography. With that degree and her excellent English she could have had a rather easy life in the Soviet Union. But comfortable existence did not interest Galina. Always a rebel, she was one of the few Soviet children who refused to join any organizations such as the October, Pioneers, or the Komsomol. It was inevitable that her insistence on being left alone would result in difficulties.

Galina at first emigrated to Israel. There she married Vladimir Telnikov, a translator who at present works for the BBC in London, where they live. Also a rebel, Vladimir had been arrested as a student back in the middle 1950s and had spent six years in the labor camps of Mordvinia.

Q. You are a geographer?

Yes. We have a joke in the Soviet Union: "Soviet geographers are also women." I was always interested in history and geography, even while I was in an English school in Odessa. And then in the University, by chance, there was a group of professors who taught geography in English.

Q. How was it that there was an English school in Odessa?

It was a local school, but all the subjects except for math, physics, and chemistry were taught in English. It was for children who had an aptitude for learning foreign languages.

Q. Did you have any difficulties getting into a university in Odessa?

Yes. There was a very strong competition and preference was given to those who had production experience—that is, people who had worked in industry between high school and university. It was Khrushchev's idea and it lasted for about 10 years. Those people with production experience were accepted with very low grades. Otherwise, the competition was very tough. And then there was the fifth column.

Q. What is that?

Designation by one's nationality. I was the only Jewish woman applying to this particular department. And since I went to the English school the entrance exams were not in Russian, but in Ukrainian. One of the committee members, a lecturer, was a Ukrainian, and he simply did not notice my nationality and passed me. Later, when I was accepted on all levels, he had to sign the final papers before sending them to Kiev, and this is when he saw my nationality. He asked, "What's that?" and it was pointed out to him that "you are the one who passed this woman in the first place." After that he had heart trouble for two weeks.

Q. You studied in the University for six years? What degree did that give you?

In the Soviet Union you don't get a degree after the University, you get a diploma. Then I was recommended for graduate work, but since that would have involved being an "ideological worker," I wouldn't have gotten a character reference for an exit visa to Israel. So I dropped the whole thing.

Q. How would you characterize life in Odessa as opposed to life in Moscow or Leningrad?

Odessa is a provincial city. It's different from all other provincial cities in its bright, southern character; it has its own face. But unfortunately Odessa is under the double burden of both Moscow and Kiev.

Q. Why Kiev?

Because Kiev is the capital of the Ukraine and Odessa, in the administrative sense, is subordinated to the Ukraine. Odessa was always a multinational city because it's a port. Traditionally, it is a cheerful city—but that is now dying out.

Q. Do you consider yourself an Odessan?

Of course. I was born there. But I often left it. Recently it has become very difficult to live in Odessa in the sense that the life of the Intelligentsia is concentrated in Moscow and so most interesting people are leaving for Moscow or Novosibirsk. It is still the music center, but not the way it used to be.

Q. When did you first become interested in geography?

I was always interested in economic geography, which is my specialty. If I were in the Soviet Union I wouldn't have had too much trouble professionally because there aren't many people there who are both geographers and know English well. I would have taught in a university, in English, and would have defended my dissertation and received a degree.

Q. So you didn't leave because your life was difficult?

No, I always wanted to leave.

Q. Since when?

Since I was born, as they say. As long as I can remember myself. It's complicated, but again, Odessa is the kind of a city that gives a sense of what freedom is without giving freedom itself. When you walk toward the sea, by the sea, you feel freedom. But when you return to the city itself you have a very clear perception that there is no freedom and never will be. Besides, when I was a child all the organized forms of life were already repulsive to me. Especially since these forms are compulsory. Maybe that is where it all began. Besides, at the age of 13 I already spoke English and met some foreigners.

Q. Was that allowed?

It was officially allowed because they very often needed translators. We needed practice and the representatives found this profitable because they didn't have to pay us. They used to invite the foreigners to our school as a model school. It was a school where everything was taught in English from the beginning. So I often got to talk to the foreigners. This was for about five years, during Khrushchev. Then in 1956 there was the Twentieth Congress, at which Stalin's crimes were denounced, and so, even if I would have been willing, they didn't have time to make out of me a person devoted to the Communist Party, especially since at the age of 13 or 14 one reads the documents of that very Party.

Q. But weren't you in the Pioneers, Komsomol, and all those things?

No, never. I don't like organized forms of life.

Q. Was it possible not to be?

It was very difficult, but it was possible. There exists a very good excuse: "I'm not worthy of this; I'm not mature enough."

Q. And that is accepted?

Yes. Or you could say, "I'm an individualist, I have a bad character." Besides, since our high school was special we did have extra study hours. We studied two additional days a week, and instead of the usual six hours a day, we had eight hours a day of study. So they were more lenient with us.

Q. When you were in the Soviet Union did you hear of the Women's Liberation Movement?

Women's liberation in the Soviet Union means hard labor. If you go along the streets you can see that a lot of the construction workers and road builders are women. But when they come home at night they still have to do the same things as women in the West have to do who do not work outside of their homes. A woman who works in a heavy industry, who works in the streets during winter, who then has to work additionally at housework, is old at 30. When I worked with foreign women as a translator, with American, British, French women, my first impression of them was that I could never tell how old they were. I remember once I had to guide around a group of American women who were 80 and I thought they were about 40. I was amazed at the way they dressed, décolleté and all.

Q. Is it difficult for a Soviet woman to move into a city if she lives elsewhere?

First of all there is a matter of *propiska.* If she is from a village, it's very difficult for a woman to get a permit because women don't have passports, and in order to get one they have to be hired first and submit themselves to very difficult jobs. And if a woman leaves the job, she has to leave the city too. Or else she has to pay a lot of money. But first she must know where and to whom she has to pay money; she has to have access to the "key"—to a person who will take the money and give her permission to stay in a city. But even if she gains this permission, it is hard for an uneducated woman to find a job. Light industry is also full of women. I used to work in a factory where 90 percent of the workers were women. I don't know where they got the machinery, but it was built before the Second World War. In fact, I don't know a single woman who isn't working in the Soviet Union.

Q. Well, but isn't everyone supposed to work by the Soviet Constitution?

Yes, but by the same Constitution a woman who is a housewife is not persecuted if she stays at home. If an unmarried girl does not work, she is persecuted. If a married woman doesn't work it means her husband can afford to support the two of them. But this is very rare, of course, whether a woman has children or not. In most cases she is obliged to work in order to help support the family. But at home the Soviet woman does everything by hand. There may be washing machines in some families, but I never saw a dishwasher.

Q. Does the man help?

It's really very rare for the husband to help. There is also the problem that there isn't enough room. Two families live in one flat; mother, father, daughter, her husband, and their children sometimes live in one room. And they have neighbors in the same corridor.

Q. I noticed from talking to the newly arrived émigrés that it is much easier for a man to adjust to the West than for a woman.

I don't know whom you've been talking to, but from my own experience and observation I would say the opposite. When a woman comes to the West she gets a flat and is not obliged to do a lot of dirty work as she did in Russia. In Israel, for example, it's much easier to bring up a child; they have kindergartens and nurseries and there are no queues. An average Russian woman spends one-third of her life standing in queues. I know in Odessa my mother used to stand in queues as long as five hours.

Q. In comparison with the past, what is the woman's role in Russia now? Have there been any changes in the last 10 years?

Some of the more interesting jobs are still forbidden to women. For example, a woman cannot be a sailor, but she can build a road. I find this interesting. Why can't a woman who can build roads be a sailor or a pilot?

Q. Well, what about Valentian Tereshkova, the astronaut?

She is an exception. I'm talking in general. There are probably 10 women pilots altogether. In agriculture, for example, men do everything connected with machinery, but women do everything with their hands. In the food industry where I worked, all workers were women and the administration was composed of men. A woman meets a lot of obstacles if she wants to go higher. In the construction industry men are engineers and women are builders.

Q. What are considered the prestigious positions for women? I know there are many women doctors, but to what would a woman aspire if she could?

An intelligent woman?

Q. Yes.

Well, in the universities most professors are men. Women work as assistants. But there are many women musicians, art critics—these are respectable jobs. The easiest for a woman is to be a teacher; there are no obstacles at all.

Q. It's the same in the West.

But, I don't think women are singled out for heavy jobs in the West. I don't know. I don't know about the States, but in Israel a woman can be anything. I think that one of the reasons for crime in the Soviet Union is that the children are left alone so much. The woman is busy 20 hours a day between her job, queues and housework—that's the liberation of women.

Q. Well, our women do not mean that when they speak of liberation, when they speak of the raising of consciousness. Do Soviet women know about it?

You shouldn't forget that you *can* get into the Soviet Union, but it is very difficult for a Soviet woman to understand the Women's Lib Movement in the West. The Soviet woman lives under certain conditions that make it very difficult to understand other conditions. Besides, many men in the Soviet Union drink and drink horribly and it's a real problem. It's visible. The Soviet Union will never publish these statistics, but it's a horrible figure. So the Soviet woman has this problem of a drunk husband first of all.

Q. Is it possible that women will organize in the future?

They could, because there is such concentration of women in certain industries such as cotton and wool. There are some cities where these factories are almost exclusively women's cities. So they could organize, but I don't think they will. They don't have time to think.

Q. As far as a child is concerned, does the mother or the father have more importance?

From the legal point of view the courts are usually on the side of the women. In the case of divorce, the child is usually given to the woman. When a man leaves his family he is obliged to pay alimony. Laws there are not so bad—but no one follows them.

Q. By the same token, are women in prisons treated more gently?

Oh no, there is nothing worse than a women's camp. There were very few things that I was afraid of in Russia. And I was involved in some things that could have landed me in prison. But I did not do certain things because I was afraid of women's camps. I don't know how to explain it to you—why the women are treated 100 times worse in prisons than men. Usually everyone associates crime with men, so that if a woman commits a crime she has to be treated more harshly.

Q. Well, if they get more indignant when a woman commits a crime, political or otherwise, doesn't it mean that they have a romanticized idea of a woman? That they don't expect a woman to be a criminal?

No, not at all. It's not that they have a romantic conception of a woman, but simply that women must be a kind of silent cattle. A woman must work and silently accept all kinds of sufferings.

Q. What do you think is the attitude of the Soviet women toward jobs and home? Would they prefer, if they had a choice, not to work, to stay home and raise children?

There is a great difference between the Intelligentsia and the working class and peasants. The Revolution was supposed to have liquidated all those classes, but they still exist. The woman from an Intelligentsia family has a much easier life whether she works or not, while the working-class woman works so hard that she would probably prefer not to. But the problem is that millions of them don't even think about preferences because they don't know that other kinds of life-styles exist. They are brainwashed from birth as to how lucky they are to have been born in the best country in the world and so they believe it; they have no access to information about life in other countries. They can observe that the life of an educated woman is so much easier, but as I've told you before, they are so silent. And when a child is born and it's a boy, the parents are so happy; if it's a girl, they are very unhappy.

Q. It is the same in the West.

Perhaps, although I've seen people happy with a birth of a daughter here. But if so, it's for different reasons, because a family there knows that if they'll have a boy he will have a much easier life than a girl.

Q. Did you know that in the West women claim brainwashing exists against them in that in the mass media men are heroes and women are presented in subservient positions?

We shouldn't forget the limits to comparisons. When I say here in England, "There is no freedom in the Soviet Union," they say, "We don't have it either." If there are instances when freedom is abused in England it is considered a mistake, an injustice to be corrected and to be protested against. In the Soviet Union the lack of freedom is the way of life. So we should keep these things in mind. If what you say is right, the women should definitely complain. But if we are speaking about Russian women and consider those complaints as you've just stated them, well . . . to me these seem to be very funny problems.

Q. I understand your point, but I'm interested in knowing if such things exist in the Soviet Union. In the mass media is the man always in the foreground?

Who can even ask themselves whether that is so on television or not? Who can possibly take television seriously anyway? It's a joke. The problem there, the worst things about life in the Soviet Union, is that you are forced to lie from the minute you wake up in the morning until you go back to sleep. These are the problems we have to think about.

Q. So you would say that the women there accept their position?

Well, they have no choice.

Q. If one has no choice, one can at least rebel—if not verbally, then in one's attitude.

Forget about rebellion in the Soviet Union. I was a fairly independent woman there, but these questions never even occurred to me. I had time to read. I wasn't encumbered with a family.

Q. You weren't married there?

No, I didn't want to. I wasn't crazy to marry there and live with my mother. I was married abroad.

Q. As far as a Soviet Jewish woman is concerned, does her religion suggest something different to her about her role as a woman?

Yes, there are advantages and disadvantages to that. She is responsible for everything in the home and she makes decisions about home and children. But then in an Orthodox Jewish family there is no problem of husbands drinking and wife-beating. Wife-beating is a serious problem there. A Jewish woman is the queen of her home. A man has to earn money, a woman has to raise children, but it doesn't follow that therefore she should not be intelligent or pursue intellectual goals. A woman must give her intelligence to the child. If she is home, she has a chance to read and develop herself. I don't care who wants to be a member of the Women's Liberation Movement, I only mind it when they want to force it on others. If a Jewish woman is satisfied with her life, why must she be "liberated" if she doesn't want it?

Q. Do you mean to say that the lot of a Jewish woman is easier in the Soviet Union than a Russian woman's?

Yes, definitely.

Q. Now, here in the West, do you see any difference in mentality between women?

The difference between the intelligent or intellectual woman in the Soviet Union and in the West is not that great. It is great at the working-class level. Among the intelligent women in both places the interests must be the same; they probably read the same kinds of books, see the same kinds of films, like the same kind of art. But there if you walk down the street and see all those cars driving by you won't see but two or three women behind the wheel. The car owner—if there is a car in the family—is always a man. In the West, I noticed, if you come to visit, both the woman and the man rush to the kitchen; perhaps the man will bring out drinks and the woman some food. In the Soviet homes, the man will always stay in the living room with the guests and the woman will do everything alone in the kitchen. I'm talking about an Intelligentsia home now.

Q. When did you become aware of the difficulties in the Soviet Union?

Well, to tell the truth I never liked it there. I didn't like Soviet society at all, and being Jewish was a second strike against me.

Q. Was that the main reason for leaving?

If any Jew tells you that he left the Soviet Union *only* because he is a Jew, he is either not intelligent or a bastard. No one can live in such a society and be indifferent. You have to commit crimes every day there; you have to betray a friend, you have to remain silent, you have to accept lies. If you aren't willing to do all that, you can't live in the Soviet Union. Otherwise you'll be arrested or put in a mental institution. There is no such word as "rebel" in the Soviet Union. From the beginning you are constantly taught that you must accept this way of life as the best, that you can't rebel against anything. You are taught, and you realize it, that all your efforts to change anything are useless. You are taught that if you are not like others you are crazy. If you don't want to be a member of the Komsomol you are strange. So I think all comparisons between the West and the Soviet Union are fruitless if we forget about Soviet society itself. These are the main problems there and they are applicable to both men and women. I didn't leave the Soviet Union only because I was Jewish. If Israel had the same kind of society I would have run away from it. Thank God it isn't like that.

Q. Was it difficult for you not to join in or did you derive some kind of satisfaction from being different?

I never wanted to be accepted. I refused all these things from the beginning, but it was very difficult to defend myself. I am very disappointed in the West in one respect; the people here can't realize that they have a lot of advantages, that they are left alone in their personal life. The norm in the Soviet Union is that everyone interferes in your life, in your personal life. You have to attend meetings, you have to do certain things, you can't be independent. Everything in the Soviet Union is created for the majority, both in the judicial sense and otherwise. While in the West, though the laws and norms are also created for the majority, they still provide the defense of the minority. This is the greatest difference between the two societies. I wanted only to be left alone. I was a very gifted child, but I spent my life in defending my independence, my right to be a human being. I had two desires: to be a human being and to leave the Soviet Union, and I spent 27 years of my life for this.

Q. Are you 27?

No, 29. It must sound funny to you. It's nothing for you to buy a ticket from the United States to Casablanca. For me to buy a ticket from Moscow to Vienna it took most of my time.

Q. Do you think you were born with that sense of independence or was there some influence in your life.

A combination of both probably.

Q. Was your mother or father of the same spirit?

I don't have a father. My mother is one of the best products of the Soviet society. She always keeps silent. She doesn't think of whether she is satisfied or not. For my mother it was impossible to adjust to the West.

Q. Is she here?

She is in Israel. She doesn't know what to do with her time. She was taught to fight for her bread, to admire the Soviet Union, and now she has nothing to do. She doesn't need the independence she now has. She is very disappointed because she can't understand that she spent 35 years working for nothing. In Israel she doesn't work because women of her age do not work in Israel. She gets money and she doesn't know what to do with her time. She isn't interested in reading or theater. She doesn't know what to do with her time.

Q. Was there anyone in your childhood who encouraged your independent spirit?

I was always very much alone. I didn't like company. I was born into a very poor family, lived in very difficult conditions, rare even for the Soviet Union. Later, when I got everything, more or less, that a person can get in the Soviet Union, I didn't want it. I wasn't a rebel, I just wanted to be a normal human being. I enjoy my life in the West. I see both the good and the bad sides of this society, but I'm satisfied to be left alone here. I dislike some things, I dislike it that the most desirable occupation for women in England is to be a secretary. Now that you mention the fact that women are presented as subservient to men in films and books I don't like it. I would like to change that. But not the way the young generation here thinks of changing things. I have a friend here from Czechoslovakia who left in 1968, and he said once to me that we are one generation ahead of the youth here because we already had to tackle the kind of society they are now striving for.

Q. Do you think that if you were born in the West you wouldn't have this spirit of defiance?

As I told you, unfortunately my life was spent just in defending my right to be independent and to leave the Soviet Union. Having had this experience I do accept now what Churchill said, "Democracy is probably a bad thing, but there is nothing else I can offer you." There is nothing else better that a human being could create. I accept this on the basis of my experience and on the changes that moving here brought me. Had I been born here, I don't know whether I would make the same mistake as do those people here who want the same system as the Soviet Union and China. Perhaps I would be clever enough to understand this without the experience. I hope so.

Q. What was your first impression of the West?

On our arrival at the airport in Austria I was immediately left alone. That was fantastic for me. I loved it. I couldn't get over it for months. In general I was prepared for the West, for the good and the bad of it.

Q. What bothers you most in the West?

The attitude toward money. In the Soviet Union people seldom have money. No one gets on a bus and buys a ticket for himself alone if you are with friends. If we go to the theater there is no question as to who will pay for the tickets: whoever has money will pay.

Q. For everybody?

It depends who has what. If one has more he gives more. Everyone gives what he can and the tickets are paid for. Here everybody pays for himself or else if someone invites you or a few friends he has to pay. If you invite friends it means you have to pay. In Russia if friends go to a pub no one thinks who will pay, no one counts ahead of time like people do in the West. Probably money has more value in the West and people are more careful about it here. I can understand this attitude and even justify it, but for me personally this seems bad.

RAISA PALATNIK

Among the dissidents Raisa Palatnik is known for her courageous and bold conduct during her interrogation and imprisonment. Among the interrogators and the guards she had a reputation for being stubborn, difficult, and defiant. Arrested for typing Samizdat material—not a crime, according to the Soviet law—Raisa was sentenced to two years for "disseminating false ideas defaming the Soviet Union." When she was told by the investigator that she was undermining the foundations of her country, she replied that the foundations had been undermined by people like Stalin, Beria, and those who placed her on trial. She refused to answer a single question unless a legal article was shown to her under which she was obliged to comply. She did not name a single person who supplied her with underground material.

Before Raisa Palatnik's arrest, her 20-year-old sister, Katya, was very much against her activities and did not share Raisa's desire to emigrate to Israel. The KGB, therefore, counted on the sister's cooperation. But when Raisa was arrested, Katya became an activist herself, and devoted her entire time and energy to fighting for her release. After Katya was ordered to leave Russia, she traveled through Europe and America seeking help for her sister. As a result, there were demonstrations on Raisa's behalf, especially in England.

Raisa is tall and her regal manner must be intimidating to anyone who expects obedience and submission; her beauty is totally natural. Unconscious of her appearance, she is conscious of her right to dignity and respect. She listens carefully, patiently, but when she speaks she expects the same attention. What she says is always direct, without frills, and to the point. So in awe of her manner was one investigator that he requested to be transferred to another case.

One of the prison officials told her just before she was released, "When you come out, Raisa, don't tell any lies about the Soviet Union."

"It won't be necessary," she replied. "It'll be quite enough just to tell the truth."

At present Raisa Palatnik lives in Jerusalem and works as a librarian in the Hebrew University.

Q. What were your first impressions of the West?

My first impressions of the West never materialized because I came to the West too soon after my release from the prison camp and was still in a state of shock, of nonperception of any different reality. Looking back, I understand that it was an acute change, but then I could not psychologically grasp anything.

Q. Was there any simple visual impression?

Visually, the West looked totally unreal to me. Even later, when I was in Paris, I could not believe that I was seeing real French people, that I was in Paris, that I was not in the Soviet Union. The newness of everything was painful to the eye. There were things that were pleasant and there were unpleasant things, but, you know, truth is born in an argument, and I had no one to argue with.

Q. You landed in Vienna?

Yes, I was there only one day. I was taken on a tour of the city. The first impression I had was that of incredible silence. It was December and it was very quiet. So this tranquillity and the number of automobiles on the roads and the absence of crowds in the streets was what was striking. In Israel what impressed me on arrival was the bright sun, the warmth and the colors. People seemed so colorfully dressed. It was noticeable especially for me because my eyes were still used to the brown-white uniforms of the prison camp.

Q. What sort of uniforms were those?

The women wore brown uniforms with white stripes and a chest sign: name and patronymic, last name, the number of the division and the brigade to which one was assigned.

Q. Were you born in Odessa?

No, about 150 kilometers from Odessa. I lived there until 1960, at which time I moved to Odessa.

Q. How old were you then? Did you come to study in Odessa?

Twenty-five. I finished high school in my hometown and began working in a library there. That was in 1953, the year of Stalin's death. It was the time of ideological vacillations. They didn't know what to do with all that literature about Stalin. Gradually, about a year later, they began to remove all those books.

Q. Did they tell you to get rid of them?

No, at first we had to collect them and bring them to the cultural division and there they were burned. They didn't trust us to burn the books.

Q. Who made the decision to burn the books?

We received lists of titles from the censorship bureau. But this was at the beginning, when there weren't too many books marked for destruction. Then, in 1956, after the Twentieth Congress, when it became necessary to remove a huge quantity of books, not only by Stalin but about him, or any book that advocated his ideas, they told us that we had to remove anything connected with Stalin. Then we could burn the books ourselves. In more advanced cities, like Odessa, they had factories for recycling used paper, but in our small town there was nothing else to do but to destroy them.

Q. How did you personally feel while burning those books?

By then I had already begun to listen to some foreign radio stations, and after what I heard during the Twentieth Congress about Stalin, I understood that it wasn't such an unpleasant task. There was a different question: the old was being destroyed, but there was nothing to put in its place. Thus a vacuum had occurred and each person tried to fill it within his own capabilities and possibilities.

Q. When Stalin died, did you personally feel a vacuum?

Not at the time he died. I was only 17 and I was trying to understand what the people around me were saying. And the people were mostly afraid. Afraid of the changes because in the Soviet Union they are always expecting the worst. No matter what happens they always say, "I hope it won't be for the worse."

Q. Was there any moment in your life to which you could point as the decisive one in terms of the change in your own attitudes?

I couldn't pinpoint a single moment, no. It was an accumulation of everything since childhood. In school, for example, all the children in our class were Jewish except for one Russian girl. But not one of us could hope to get a gold medal—we all knew it would go to the Russian girl. When I entered the tenth grade I had a chance of getting the gold medal, both because of my marks and my ability. The counselor came to see my parents and told them that I was not studying to my full potential, that if I would just put forth more effort I could get the medal. I told her, "Why should I put forth more effort? We are living without enough food, without enough sleep, without the necessary clothes (it was just after the war), why should I spend all my energies in studying and be disappointed in the end?" I was studying and I was getting knowledge, this they could not take away from me; as for the medal . . .

Q. What was your parents' reaction to her visit?

They were in agreement with me. Indeed, I was very weak from hunger, and they told the counselor they didn't see any reason to force me to do any extra studying, that they thought I was doing well as it was. So I already knew in school that for a Jew life is different, that a Jew must know more, must work more, must try more. They say the Jews know how to get around; perhaps it is because the direct way is not available to them.

Q. Is there any other incident in your early years that you remember as in some way revealing to you?

Yes, the Doctors' Case. The Kremlin Jewish doctors who were accused of attempting to poison Stalin. I remember it very well. I was in the ninth grade. It was scary to leave the classroom and go into the hallway because from all sides you heard, "You yids, you poisoned Gorky, you wanted to poison Stalin, you poisoned all our great leaders," and the atmosphere was very tense. Even the teachers allowed themselves such remarks.

Q. When did you enter the Institute of Library Sciences?

The first time was in 1953, directly after Stalin died, and I didn't succeed because they hadn't had time to "rehabilitate" the Jews yet. A year later, in 1954, I was accepted into the Moscow Library Institute. Then there was another incident that I remember well. That was somewhere in 1965 or 1966. I was working in Odessa. By then I read Samizdat. I read a lot, listened to radio stations, in short was more or less "educated" in that sense. Odessa was preparing for the celebration of the one hundred seventy-fifth anniversary of the founding of the city. Among other preparations there was the compilation of a historical bibliography. For that, one had to look through all the old newspapers in order to find materials connected with the history of the city, such as the date of the founding of a certain square, and so on. Since the work was very time-consuming, every librarian in Odessa had to work on it. Every librarian was obliged to work one week in the Central [Gorky] Library where all such materials were kept. When I went to work there, the earlier newspapers and magazines had already been checked and I got the 1937–1938 papers. Instead of working I read them the entire week. I sat and read about all those trials.

Q. Did they write about those trials in the press?

They had the usual Soviet workers' denunciations, accusations, as now with Sakharov and Solzhenitsyn, the usual Soviet nonsensical chatter, except people were losing their lives because of that chatter. And one could read between the lines. Then I read the 1948–1949 papers and there I read the echoes of these same trials, the trials of "rootless cosmopolites." They began in the capital and then started moving toward the provinces. I read the articles about all those who lost jobs in Odessa for being "cosmopolites"—meaning for being Jewish. The funny thing is that we had supervisors whose job it was to see that we didn't waste time, but seeing the materials I was reading, none of them dared ask me why I wasn't working. You understand that until that time I hadn't had a chance to read those papers because they were from the closed special archives. So I had no access to so many facts before. And it was there that I read a paper by Dmyterko [a Ukrainian writer who delivered this paper at the Convention of Soviet Writers in 1948] denouncing all Jewish writers such as Kaverin, Babel, Bagritsky, calling them dirty names, calling them "passportless garbage" and things like that. And what astounded me was that among all those dogs there was one man who dared to defend these writers. He was a Ukrainian poet, Mikola Bazhan. So he got it as much as the Jews. They decided to check his biography to find out if he wasn't Jewish somehow. Dmyterko's books now come out in hundreds of thousands of editions and are offered to the Soviet readers as the best examples of Socialist Realism.

Q. What was the first forbidden book by a contemporary author that you read?

It was Yevtushenko's *Autobiography*.

Q. Was it forbidden?

Of course. He was denounced for that book; they wanted to expel him from the Writers' Union.

Q. What was dangerous in the *Autobiography?*

Nothing at all. He praises himself to the thirtieth sky and tells of his creative journey. It's in the same style as he himself is, a braggart and a chatterer. The important part was when he talked about repressed poets and writers and how their destiny impressed him. Then the songs of Okudzhava became popular. We sang them, we taped them, and then a small collection of his songs came out, *The Cheerful Drummer*. Of course, even though I had connections in the publishing world, I couldn't get a copy, so a few of us put our money together and got a typist to type them out for us. Then came the trial of Joseph Brodsky. And I was given a stenogram of that trial, as well as his poems. That was in Samizdat, of course.

Q. Don't such documents go into the closed archives of the libraries?

Of course not. Such literature is not in any closed archives except in the libraries of the KGB. Anyway, I got interested in that trial, and began to ask friends for his poems. This was the beginning of my own library of such "publications." Then came Korzhavin, Galich, essays of Lidiya Chukovskaya, then stories by Daniel, then the materials of the Sinyavsky and Daniel trial, the Ginzburg-Galanskov trial.

Q. Was the Sinyavsky-Daniel trial as disturbing in Odessa as it was in Moscow?

In Moscow a lot of people knew them personally. And Odessa is in the provinces. Nevertheless, among ourselves we understood that it was the reemergence of Stalinism. We understood that if we had been able to read Bulgakov and Babel and Platonov since the liberalization, now the picture was acutely different. Such things are especially noticeable in a library.

Q. What kinds of books are most popular in the Soviet Union now?

There is a genuine book hunger in the Soviet Union. There are the people who read Dmyterko and the like, who are only interested in detective themes, or, as we used to say, in "defective themes." They all come with the request, "Give us books about spies"—spy-mania. For a person who is at a crossroads and who needs some sort of spiritual nourishment, it is very difficult. None of the official books or journals could satisfy this hunger. As a result there is a heightened interest in popular scientific books. Books about nature, books by Gerald Durrell, the English zoologist who collected animals all over the world, are very popular, as are books about the human organism, or about the working of the brain. Topics that are very common in the West are only now beginning to be written about in the Soviet Union. For example, there are just a few books about dolphins; they are very popular because those books at least contain some interesting information. Travel books are very popular since the average Soviet man is deprived of this and can only travel vicariously. And of course people ask for foreign travel books, because Soviet travel books are the usual *agitka*. I just looked today at the publication list for next year. It's a nightmare; hardly any foreign authors at all.

Q. Thanks to the copyright agreement?

Precisely because of it, since they have to pay now.

Q. So how did your friends pass those forbidden books around?

Not too openly because everyone knew what it could mean. But we had no opportunities, unlike the Muscovites, to discuss them with people like Sinyavsky and others. We could only exchange our own impressions among ourselves. We had no serious source of information. When the poems of Pasternak came out with the preface by Sinyavsky we were all wondering whether they would tell us in the library to cut it out. They didn't. Then I received Daniel's *Poems from Unfreedom*. I had Yakubovich's article about Stalin, and so on.

Q. Did you keep such literature for a specific purpose?

I considered it part of my private library, especially because in the Soviet Union no one knows what will be regarded as permissible tomorrow, and what was considered forbidden yesterday is allowed today. As for the documents I had about Israel, such as Golda Meir's interview with a *New York Times* correspondent, they were my particular interest. I wanted to go to Israel and wanted to know about it. The article that impressed me most of all was one by a Czech writer, Mlacko, who wrote about his two trips to Israel, before and after the Six-Day War, in Samizdat. He was thrown out of the Union of Czech Writers and the Communist Party.

Q. Did you think of going to Israel before there was any possibility or only after it became plausible?

Before there was a possibility.

Q. Did you ever think of escape?

To escape one has to work out a plan. And since I knew how vigilantly the Soviet borders are being guarded I didn't feel myself properly qualified to make an escape. One needs a long preparation, a long investigation, all kinds of information to which I couldn't possibly have had any access.

Q. Did you expect arrest?

After the search in my apartment I knew that an arrest would follow. However, they let me go free for two months.

Q. What happened in the search?

They came to my place of work and took me home. They showed me an order for a search in which it was written that a nearby school had been robbed, that the robber took a typewriter, money, and some documents, and they had information that those things might be found in my home.

Q. Had there in fact been a robbery?

No. I went to that school the next morning and said to the secretary, "I heard your school was robbed," and she said, "Nothing of the sort. Where did you get such information?" But it was very obvious by the manner of the search that they knew what they were looking for. I didn't hide anything; all those papers were together with my books. As soon as they found that file they didn't look any further. They took my own typewriter, though.

Q. According to the Soviet law was your trial legal?

The article by which I was tried presumes dissemination of false ideas—it means you know that they are false and nevertheless you disseminate them—defaming the Soviet Government. Article 190. First of all no one proved to me that what was in all those articles and poems was false, let alone the fact that I was aware that it was false.

Q. Did you try to defend yourself on these grounds?

I didn't have to defend myself; according to the Soviet law they had to prove my guilt. They didn't even attempt to. They didn't need to. If the KGB decrees that one is guilty, what is there for them to discuss? No proof of my innocence would have made any difference.

Q. Did they at least make a pretense?

Sure they did, but so what? All of it was scattered to the winds during the trial.

Q. Did you have a defense attorney?

I had an attorney who accused me instead of defending me.

Q. Could you not get a good one like Kaminskaya [the famous woman lawyer who defended Bukovsky, Marchenko, and other dissidents]?

She wanted to defend me, but they didn't allow her. Three Moscow attorneys wanted to defend me, but not one of them was allowed. They told them, "Odessa has its own lawyers, there is no reason for you to go there."

Q. Did the court need witnesses?

Yes, they managed to find two witnesses. One of them escaped altogether because she knew what it meant (she left the city) and the other one gave such a testimony that if it hadn't been a fabricated KGB case she and not I would have ended up on the bench for the accused, because it was clear that it was a lie from beginning to end. And since there were no other witnesses they had to use her testimony. So for the verdict in my case there is only the testimony of a single witness. And even if I had given anything to her it wouldn't have been enough for a guilty verdict because according to the Soviet law "dissemination" means giving material to at least three people.

Q. How long was your sentence for?

Two years. The investigation took eight months.

Q. Where were you during the investigation?

I was in prison for ten months, and the rest of the time in the labor camp.

Q. What is the difference between being in prison and being in camp?

How should I put it? In prison one is scared because one is in a cell. It is small and stifling; there is no place to turn around.

Q. How many cell mates were there?

Four usually. There are two bunk beds [wooden benches without mattresses] and if the prison is full they can put in a fifth person. Then the famous *parasha*, which is emptied twice a day. The cell is dark, damp, and very cold.

Q. Did you make friends with the other women in your cell?

What friendship could there be? One was in for theft, the other for prostitution, the third for murder, and I was there for nothing.

Q. Is there still animosity between the criminal and the political prisoners?

No. Not in prison. Every woman, no matter how limited or stupid she is, understands very well what Soviet reality is all about. Even the lowest dregs of society know that. So they knew that I was a political prisoner and they had some kind of respect for me. But after all, they are to be bought. They can earn an easier sentence by doing certain things that the administration instructs them to do. So the administration used them to mock and harass me. This was the most frightening thing of all. In camp these women wanted to beat me. They called me names; they called me a traitor. In camp they wanted to make me work more than the eight-hour shift; they wanted me to work 10 hours a day and 12 hours a day and also during the one day off a week we had. I refused resolutely to work on my day off and they threatened me.

Q. Were there any women prisoners who were also administrators?

Yes, they all were except for the top one. I mean among those who were in charge of labor.

Q. Do you think that the women's prisons are worse than the men's?

I think that in some ways they are easier. All the prisons and camps where I was were "general regime" ones; they weren't the strict regime ones. And also, it is more difficult to handle women, you know. If it is possible to prove anything to a man, women are very disorganized creatures. More is demanded from a man. I had a chance to observe life in a men's camp, since there are a few of them next to the Odessa prison. Also there were a few guards there who used to work in the men's camps and they told us that is easier for them to work in a men's camp because the men are punished much more quickly than the women.

Q. What do you think is behind that attitude?

Among the women there are many who speculated in money or didn't present the right account in a store, or were dentists who practiced privately and made gold plates (which is a crime) for someone's teeth. That is, the crimes which from a simply human point of view aren't even crimes. From talking to the women whose husbands were imprisoned I knew that our regime was a kind of kindergarten in comparison. At least I was allowed to read and to write letters. This is very important—to get letters, although three-quarters of my mail was always confiscated. But that was because it was me; it wasn't a general rule.

Q. Why you?

As a punishment for bad behavior.

Q. Did you behave badly?

Not that I intended to, but I did not react to any kind of pressure. I did not attend political education seminars, did not attend meetings, did not participate in *samodeyatelnost*, didn't participate in any activities organized by the prison administration. I refused to go to Subbotniki. Saturday was my only free day. So it was their revenge.

Q. They still have Subbotniki?

Of course. I also refused to sign any "Socialist obligations" and told them that "your socialism doesn't concern me."

Q. What are "Socialist obligations?"

What a naïve question! Before every "great" holiday in the Soviet Union, all Soviet workers take it upon themselves to exceed their norm of work. By signing "Socialist obligations," they promise to increase their political awareness, their ideological level, and they promise to carry out the decisions of the Communist Party and the Government.

Q. That goes on all over the country?

Yes, only outside prison people do it collectively; each department signs collectively. For example, when I worked in the library we had to take upon ourselves a collective obligation to see that a certain number of books on and by Lenin will be read by our readers, to make sure that 20 percent of the books loaned out would be ideological, to organize political seminars in our reading room for the readers. In the prison camp it was the same thing. The "Socialist obligations" meant signing a promise to achieve a 105 percent norm of work, to elevate the "quality" of work. They all sign, of course, but then they don't carry it out. I didn't sign anything.

Q. What was their reaction to your refusal?

They collected all those "misbehaviors" and put me in a *kartser*.

Q. Is that frightening?

I think it is frightening to lie on a cement floor without any covers in a freezing cell, to have only water and a piece of bread three times a day, and not be able to walk for a week.

Q. What else did you refuse to do?

I didn't wear the chest sign. I told them I wasn't a dog. But what angered them most of all was that I managed to have uncensored letters smuggled out all the time. They could not isolate me and despite their vigilance everything went out beyond the camp walls, overseas. That is why there was publicity in the West. This infuriated them, but at the same time it held them back; they knew no matter what they did to me I'd manage to get information about it to the West.

Q. I can't imagine how one could manage that in those circumstances.

That is why today, a year after I served my sentence, I still can't regain my health or my equilibrium. My nervous system has been shattered in the process. I'm lucky it was only two years.

Q. What did they tell you when you were leaving?

They said they would have a big celebration. The authorities said they'd give a banquet.

Q. Wasn't there anyone who was moved by your spirit of rebellion?

You see, to this day I have a dual attitude toward these people. As human beings, the prison and camp administrators were often sympathetic toward me. Many were quite open about it, and didn't even attempt to hide it in simple human terms. But as members of the Communist Party and as Chekists, they did what was demanded of them. If they were pressured, they pressured me. If they were left alone they gave me a respite. In the camp they had to give a daily report on my behavior, and apparently the instructions they received were based on what they'd reported.

Q. They must have gotten reprimands for not being able to control you. Did they not appeal to you to help them?

They knew that I wouldn't have any pity for them. But they did tell me about the reprimands they'd received on my account.

Q. Did the other women inmates make any protests?

The young women, most of them were under 25, opposed the regime by resisting the "remodeling program." They broke the clothes regulations, they didn't do their work properly, they beat one another and made scandals, they resisted by lesbian love. Very often there were "family scandals" and jealousy scenes, once even a suicide.

Q. How did the administration handle that?

There were various methods: recruiting secret agents and informers, penalizing by depriving them of the right to use the food shop, placing them in the penalty dungeon.

Q. Was there any category of women who were particularly obedient?

Yes, mothers who had children at home. They obeyed everything in hopes of earning an earlier release.

Q. What gave you strength?

Knowing that my friends and my sister were constantly working toward my release, constantly thinking of me.

Q. Why did they let you go to Israel so quickly?

One could say I was thrown out. My release from camp was inappropriately close to an official holiday—the fiftieth anniversary of the birth of the Soviet Union (December 30) in 1972. They were expecting all kinds of official guests from all over the world. They knew very well that I would be in Moscow on that day and that they would have to think of something to do with me. Or they'd have to hide me, or I would meet certain foreigners. I'd applied on December eleventh (six days after my release) and on the morning of December twelfth the director of OVIR came to my house, handed me the visa, and told me that I had five days to leave the country. I left on the fourth day.

Q. And your sister?

She was told to leave much earlier. She left and then she traveled all through the various European capitals and in America trying to get help for my release. She almost made it to Nixon.

Q. I don't think it would have helped you any.

In any case, she placed high hopes on that. He was about to go to the Soviet Union. But she did get to speak to Gerald Ford. And also with Mayor Lindsay.

Q. Did you leave the airport without any trouble?

They made us wait for a long time, and when our turn came they told us to select one suitcase since they didn't have time to check the others. And then I had an "escort," a KGB woman who traveled with me to Vienna.

Q. Why?

I don't know why. Perhaps to see what sort of reception I'd have in Austria.

Q. How did you feel in the plane?

Totally exhausted and numb. Emptied.

Q. How do you picture your future now?

In the usual way—to work and live.

Q. In Israel?

I had enough living in a foreign country for 35 years—I want to live at home now.

DMITRI SIMES

Dmitri Simes was born in Moscow in 1947. Both his mother and father are lawyers and have a reputation for unfailing integrity among the Russian Intelligentsia. After being expelled from Moscow University for organizing a protest against Soviet involvement in the war in Vietnam, Dmitri graduated by correspondence from the Department of History at Moscow University in 1969. At the age of 20 he began working as a research assistant at the Institute of World Economy and International Relations. He later became a research fellow at that Institute, and in 1971 won a prize for the best research project. His function was to prepare reports and forecasts on the United States, specifically on American-Soviet relations. Several of his articles have been published in Soviet journals and newspapers, but mainly in a classified information bulletin for top officials. In the fall of 1971 Dmitri Simes finished his dissertation on the New Left Movement in the United States; it was approved for defense, but he chose to forgo the doctorate degree for fear that it would make his emigration more difficult. Having applied for an exit visa in August, 1972, Simes became active in the movement for free emigration from the Soviet Union. In November he was imprisoned briefly, but upon his release he was soon given permission to leave the country. At the present time Dmitri Simes is working as a senior research fellow at the Center for Strategic and International Studies at Georgetown University, Washington, D.C.

Tall and powerfully built, Dmitri Simes is quite astonishing in many respects. Unlike most Russians, he is totally uninterested in any abstract speculation or sentiments and is conservative in a rather British sort of way. He doesn't think out his answers—he has them ready, formulated, and precise. Always self-possessed and vigilant, Dmitri remained unruffled when he was questioned by William Buckley on the televised program "Firing Line," and again when he appeared on the program "The Advocates." Of the emigrants Dmitri says, "People who emigrate to the United States should have the goal of becoming Americans. Otherwise, there is no sense in it." He characterizes himself as "a Republican to the right of Goldwater." But then this remark is intended to catch one unawares, leaving the listener to figure out if he is being sarcastic, ironic, or earnest.

Q. How did you leave the Soviet Union? On a Jewish visa?

Formally, yes, though everyone knew where I was going, including the authorities. The KGB told me directly, "We know where you are going."

Q. But it's not their business, is it?

It is their business, but also it's the rule of the game. They know where you are going and you still ask for an Israeli visa in order not to create difficulties for yourself and for them. If everybody asked for a visa to the U.S.A. it would be difficult for both sides.

Q. So they understand where people are going when they ask for an Israeli visa?

No, not in everyone's case. There are people who do not know themselves where they are going when they ask for an exit visa. But about some they do know.

Q. And they knew about you?

They knew where I was working and what I was doing and I never concealed from the Jewish movement that I wasn't going to go to Israel. Most of these people have very strong Jewish feelings, and they were only interested in going to Israel and prefer not to have any relationship with those who do not wish to go to Israel. It would have been dishonest to pretend to them that I was going to Israel.

Q. And why did you choose America?

I only wanted to go to America.

Q. When did you first want to go to America?

When I was about 13.

Q. So early? Was it some particular experience or a book you read?

I don't know. There was a big contrast between what I read in the books about the Soviet Union and what I saw in reality. Though no one explained to me why this contrast exists.

Q. At that young age you saw the contrast?

From some inner opposition toward this contrast and toward those negative aspects which are discussed in the press.

Q. And is America the way you had pictured it?

Yes. Perhaps I overestimated a little the degree of organization in the American society.

Q. You think our society is disorganized?

Disorganization has great advantages. I am talking about it not as a defect, but as an advantage and a defect at one and the same time.

Q. In what sense is it advantageous?

Disorganization is an advantage in that in a certain sense it is related to freedom, and one feels himself more independent. And if you quarrel with one organization, you are not afraid that it will reflect on your relationship with another one. But the defects are probably more acutely felt when one is in the process of looking than for people who have already in some way asserted themselves. It's a great advantage. But when one has to still affirm oneself, this disorganization must be an obstacle.

Q. Did you major in American studies?

I was majoring in the contemporary history of the U.S.A.

Q. What was it like to study American history there?

In the University? Well, there was some propaganda there and some objective truth. That is, it was impossible not to tell that there was a war between the North and the South in America. However, it's possible to give a Marxist analysis and to say that the first plan of devastation of the South was worked out by Marx and that what was done afterward was done under the influence of Marx. One could say such twaddle. Nevertheless, we did read in English and we read the American historical sources, even though "Marx was the victor of the American South."

Q. How did you begin to study these subjects?

I began with archeology and ethnography. This was at night. And during the day I was studying in the Department of Biology. But then I was thrown out with the charge of supporting the American war in Vietnam and when they reinstated me I was then allowed to take correspondence courses in the Department of History. And this led me to study not the abstract subjects, not what went on two thousand years ago, but what is happening today.

Q. In what way did you support the war in Vietnam?

There was a meeting in the House of Friendship of Peoples. The students presented their views and then offered a resolution to stop the Soviet military assistance to the North Vietnamese.

Q. You mean it's permitted for students to make such resolutions?

As you see, it isn't.

Q. And you really think that Americans were right?

Well, I don't know on what sources the opponents of the war relied. I worked at that time in the Institute of World Economy and International Relations, and I was in touch with certain circles and knew that North Vietnam was for a long time actively infiltrating the South. I knew that starting from the end of the 1950s North Vietnam began to create a revolt. This I knew not from the American sources, but from my own work experience. One can call it any name; one can call it brotherly help for the people of South Vietnam, but I am in a habit of calling it aggression. Perhaps because I have a Soviet upbringing and Soviet formulations. But if one country first creates a political organization in another country, and then begins a revolt, and then uses that revolt in order to send troops into the other country, this is called aggression.

Q. So after this meeting you were thrown out of the University?

I was not allowed to study biology in the daytime, nor history in the evening.

Q. Did they explain why?

What's there to explain? They said with such views you had better work on a farm.

Q. Was such an act less dangerous than if you had expressed your opposition to the Czech invasion?

Of course. In the first place it was 1966 and not 1968 and everything was much less tense. Besides the participants of the meeting in no way wished to create any kind of publicity for themselves in the West.

Q. What did you do then?

After a few months I tried for reinstatement in the history department, by correspondence, and I began to work. I did my graduate work also by correspondence. I worked from 1967 to 1972.

Q. How do you see the appearance of the new Intelligentsia in the Soviet Union, in the nineteenth-century sense of the term?

In this case I do not believe too much in the new Intelligentsia. That is, I know people who come from very uneducated families and who became brilliant intellectuals. I don't want to say that this is impossible; it is possible, but it demands more ability than from a man who did not come from an Intelligentsia environment. And since the majority of people do not possess outstanding talents, but mediocre ones, I don't believe in much of the new Intelligentsia. Lenin's formulation of Intelligentsia is that it was *raznochinnaya.* This type of Intelligentsia doesn't appeal to me. I call myself a member of the Intelligentsia with pride, as do my friends, but it is because I went the road of the middle of the twentieth century.

Q. All right, if an American would ask you to define this word, how would you define it?

I would say a person was of the "Intelligentsia" if his inner, spiritual life plays a big role or is prevalent over everything else. From this point of view, those for whom the restructure of the external world and their external battle are everything do not belong to the Intelligentsia.

Q. We have a lot of wonderful people in America whose inner world prevails or is very important. Nevertheless, when they see injustice around themselves they don't act.

This doesn't mean that they aren't of the Intelligentsia. Being a member of the Intelligentsia is not a privilege but a virtue. There are active and passive members of the Intelligentsia.

Q. Do you consider yourself a passive one?

I consider myself an active one by the force of my temperament and by the fact that I am occupied with political science. I consider myself an active, antirevolutionary member of the Intelligentsia, in any country and in regard to any revolution, white, black, brown, red, or yellow—Communist or anti-Communist.

Q. You mean you are against revolution per se?

Yes, against revolution per se.

Q. Do you believe in reforms instead?

I think that any half-way reforms and any slow reforms are better than any of the greatest revolutions. Because a revolutionary's task is the happiness of the future generations built on the blood of those who live today. A revolutionary conceives of people as building material for his own model of the "beautiful future." I don't believe that such people can bring any happiness to the future generations.

Q. These ideas were formulated in your mind on what experience?

Well, naturally, I had no such experience. They are formulated on the basis of Russian history and on the basis of my interest in the Russian Revolution, in nineteenth- and twentieth-century events, and in the opposition movement.

Q. How do you differentiate between opposition and dissent?

Dissidents are opposition, but I don't want to call it the Democratic Movement because among the people who now oppose the existing conditions there are many reactionaries.

Q. In what sense, reactionaries?

In many different senses, beginning with the liberal Marxist-Leninists. When I hear "liberal Marxist-Leninist," I don't know what to grab first: a handkerchief to stifle laughter or a holster for a pistol.

Q. You mean the neo-Communists?

Yes. The very combination of "liberal Marxist-Leninist" is inconceivable to me.

Q. Do you consider it to be a contradiction in terms?

Well, because I can't understand what to be a liberal Marxist-Leninist means. Is this a man who only kills SRs [Socialist-Revolutionaries] and doesn't kill his own secretaries of the Raikoms? Is that what is meant by liberal?

Q. Do you consider that "liberal" and "Marxist" can be joined?

Liberalism and Marxism, yes. But when they add Leninism . . . Lenin was a man who did everything that was brilliant in our Revolution. I consider Lenin a genius. Right now I don't have his works, but as soon as I have some money I will buy them. I love to read Lenin, I respect him endlessly as a political tactician. He worked out brilliantly a theory of intolerance, a theory of destruction of enemies. He explained ingeniously whom and when to beat, how to grab power and how to hold it. But the views of this man and liberalism in any usual understanding of the word are so incompatible that the term liberal-Leninist is an abracadabra.

Q. And Marx?

Well, Marx had never given so much attention to the political theory of the Revolution. He was interested more in political economy and in the social organization of society. But Lenin was much more interested precisely in the concrete practice and tactics.

Q. You respect Lenin in what way? In the way one respects Napoleon, or do you agree with him in any way?

No, God forbid. In the Napoleonic sense.

Q. But many think that Stalin corrupted the pure ideals of Lenin.

I don't think that, of course. I think that Lenin from the beginning did what Stalin did later, with individual differences. Lenin would have killed about 10 million fewer people.

Q. I thought Stalin killed 7 million people?

You have in mind only the labor camps. Take the collectivization, take the purges of the 1930s. This statistic is, as everything in the Soviet Union, relative, but the numbers are great enough.

Q. How about China? There is a lot of admiration for China in this country.

This is wonderful. Perhaps things in China are much worse than in the Soviet Union, but I would be happy if the relationship between China and the United States would be warm.

Q. You know that I mean whether Marxist ideals would work in China or not, as some people think here that they are working.

Well, this is simply humorous to me. I would very gladly send those people to China without the right to leave China for five years.

Q. Do you imagine an ideal system in Russia?

If I did and if I could imagine a system of changes in Russia realistically, I wouldn't be sitting here now.

Q. I'm not speaking realistically, but idealistically. Or what about democracy, are they ready for it?

I consider that a Russian man by his biological nature can accept democracy, but the contemporary generation of Russians are not ready for democracy.

Q. What future prospects do you see for dissidents?

They want to change the system, not just the rulers. I mean not just the Politburo of the Party, but the entire layer of the ruling class. The dissidents knew that that power would defend itself, more cruelly than it has so far. The question is not in what the regime will do, but how the opposition will reply. Now they estimate that they have many sympathizers, perhaps several thousand. Let's even say 100 thousand, even though for Russia that's a drop in the bucket. But there is another question: why are the very active people only in the hundreds? Two or three hundred? The dissidents will probably say because they are the courageous people, that the others are afraid to risk their families, their jobs, and their well-being. But cowardice is not in the character of a Russian, so why in such an historic period should only those few hundred people be so brave or so irrational?

Q. Isn't it difficult to remain normal in that society?

I had the privilege to meet Andrei Sinyavsky who, as you know, served seven years in a labor camp. He is a man of amazing spiritual health. And if he would have spent 20 years in that camp, he would still remain the same. Daniel is the same kind of a man. I don't consider them dissidents. I don't consider Solzhenitsyn a dissident. These people are concerned with creating new spiritual values and they have all my admiration and esteem. But people who spend all their energies on redividing the existing things, and not on creating something new, I think these people are repeating the errors of the past.

Q. Then you think that people like Sinyavsky and Daniel do more than . . .

I think that Pasternak, Sinyavsky, Solzhenitsyn, Daniel accomplished more for Russia in the last 15 years than anyone. Much more than any demonstrations on Red Square, though I admire the courage of those who participate in them.

Q. In what way?

It seems to me that the opposition in Russia is not really dangerous. Because while protesting against the regime, while fighting it, the opposition has not been capable of working out new moral values. These four people have done it. They were able not to fight the regime, but to live in a way as though that regime doesn't exist. And this, from my point of view, is the most threatening fact for the regime.

Q. Speaking of that, remember when Osip Mandelstam tells his wife in her book, *Hope against Hope:* "Why are you complaining? You live in the only country in the world that kills its poets." In our country, indeed, a poet is not at all dangerous to anyone. Why is he dangerous in Russia?

I think this is very understandable. Poetry means those very values that are very dangerous for the regime. In the United States society is at least partly built on those values already, so they can't be dangerous. Quite a few of the Soviet political opposition members fight the political system with its own kind of values. And poetry carries a different system of values.

Q. When Joseph Brodsky came to this country many Russian émigrés were outraged that he did not express himself politically: why didn't he do anything? I always thought he had already done more than a lot of them put together.

Exactly, I would add Brodsky to the previous four we talked about. I don't know him personally, but I know his poetry and his role in Russia. Perhaps his significance is less than the other four, but it is still very important.

Q. What hope is there then?

Hope for what? Hope that there will be a really liberal government? I don't see any serious basis for such a hope. But there are reasons to believe that Russia will be a more open country and that it won't return to Stalinism. There now exists a huge new class, a powerful bureaucracy which today is really the ruling class of the country, and which will not share its power with Brezhnev or anyone else. Brezhnev could be its boss so long as he guarantees its security and this is his hold on it. And this ruling class knows very well that when there is a mass purge in the country it's impossible to save oneself.

Q. Because they remember Stalin. But what about the younger ones who will come to power and who will not remember because they didn't have the experience of Stalinism?

This new generation lives by different values altogether. In comparison with the old people, I mean. Of course, they won't make the regime liberal in the Western sense of the word, but in order to employ terror one must grow up in a given social experience. People who live by the category of terror grew up on the idealism of the 1920s and the 1930s, when the goal justified the means, when all was allowed, when the masses were obedient. These people are different. They understand that not everything is permitted now. Before all was permitted. Not now. I know quite a number of people who potentially could be Russian leaders in 10 or 15 years. They aren't capable of terror. They grew up in a different environment with different values. They are more cynical than their predecessors, they are more pragmatic, they are capable of a cruel regime, but not of terror, in order to preserve their positions.

Q. What do you think of our Watergate hearings?

I like it very much. You see, I don't like it that all this has happened. I don't like it that almost half of the President's personal staff is involved in it. One can be mistaken in a person, but one cannot be mistaken in half of one's closest associates.

Q. He wasn't mistaken, he is the same way.

Possibly. I prefer a more cautious formulation, but it seems to me even though I'm cautious my idea is the same as yours. But this event strengthens my optimism regarding the United States. I don't like a lot of things in the United States, not only Watergate. But Watergate, as nothing else, shows that this country is open for changes and that the possibilities exist for the removal of evil. You know Watergate is very unpleasant, so is Harlem. But what is happening with Watergate is convincing to me. And it seems to me that this is the way a lot of Americans think of it.

Q. Do you think there will finally be normal relations between the Soviet Union and the United States?

First of all I don't want to say "between the Soviet Union and the United States." I want to say "between the Politburo and the current [Nixon] administration of the United States." I prefer this expression. The fact that I am a supporter of the good relations between the two, I probably don't have to prove to you. And when wheat is sold to the Soviet Union I am not prepared to yell "How awful that you are supporting Brezhnev" because I always remember that 50 million hungry people are now supplied. I do understand and agree that it is not good for the American taxpayers, but I am not yet so American to be interested in that above all. I understand this argument, but I can't grieve when 50 million people receive bread. Brezhnev wouldn't go without bread.

Q. One of the dissidents told me that a Russian man can take a lot, you can spit in his face and he won't protest, but if you take his bread away he will revolt. Then Nixon, in this sense, is a strikebreaker, is he not?

Beautiful philosophy. What you were told is typical for the Russian revolutionary philosophy, and probably for the revolutionary philosophy in general. The worse the better. We almost burned the house down and you came and put the fire out. Now, on the basis of this you may understand what I mean about the Russian revolutionary philosophy and what I don't like in it. Wonderful example. But on the other hand, I don't think that the Russian-American relations should be based on a long-term American aid, because when one talks in terms of 20 years' credit this is not trade but rather economic assistance. To talk about 20 years when the political situation is unknown is to promise long-term economic help. The basis for a long-term relationship should be on both sides, not on one.

Q. Do you think that a Soviet person, dissident or average Soviet citizen, could really get adjusted to our country, to our system?

It's difficult; very difficult. I think it is connected with one's expectations. I spoke to a very good and bright man in Moscow who thinks seriously that when he arrives in the States, he will go to Senator Fulbright and will tell him the whole truth and Senator Fulbright will instantly change and will run to vote for the right things. Some people thought they'd come here and they'd be met as political activists. This didn't come true. I didn't count on anything. I was never an activist in the Democratic Movement and didn't count on collecting laurels for that. And while I was quite well known in Moscow in the movement for free emigration from the Soviet Union, I understand that a person is known while he is fighting for his right to leave, but when he has already left, he is independent. He should be on his own. I fought, I acted, I got what I wanted. I left. But there are those who think that since they fought for their right to emigrate, they should get a medal for it. When I was leaving the Soviet Union I wanted to go to the United States, to make contact with American universities, to try and do something for those who are still in the Soviet Union through Senator Jackson. I made contact with universities, and I am in contact with Senator Jackson. I am satisfied, even though I don't have a job yet. I am sure that I will get a job in some university. But I understand that no university will give me a job just because I came here.

Q. I don't think you answered my question. Can a man, brought up in the Soviet Union, get adjusted here? I mean, what psychological difficulties is he likely to encounter?

Any answer to such a question would be based on intuition rather than on research. I think the main difficulties will be in that the people there are brought up on values directly opposite to those in the West. Or not directly opposite, but different. Even the representatives of the Soviet opposition often came out with slogans which were the same as the regime's, only from the other side of them. But people like Sinyavsky, Pasternak, Brodsky—and I want to add Amalrik too—they lived and live in Soviet society according to the standards of contemporary civilization. They thought and wrote what they wanted; they understood that the main thing is to reproduce one's own ideas and to create. And they understood that this rather than any political demonstrations or demands is the best contribution to change. So it seems to me that they gave to Soviet society some new standards without which there couldn't have been any Democratic Movement.

Q. You say that the people in the dissident movement haven't worked out new moral values. Could you elaborate?

In general in the conditions of a totalitarian regime it is not easy to work out new moral values. In England the perfection of the system is expressed not only in the perfection of the Government but in the perfection of the opposition. In Russia the imperfection of the Government is expressed in the imperfection of the opposition. The conditions for the function of an opposition are so monstrous that the opposition by its own nature cannot be normal. Then there is the traditional difficulty of any Russian opposition: whether to go underground or be effectively liquidated. Often the logical answer seems to be to go underground, and this is, in my view, the most tragic solution. Because then there is another question: what do you want, to change the ruling group or to really change the situation in the entire society? If you want to change the ruling class then it makes sense to go underground, to construct a conspiracy, and to hope that one day you'll be lucky and will take power. I'm not speaking in terms of reality, but in terms of intentions. But if you want to change society, then you must understand that any kind of work in the underground, anything that has to do with conspiracy, always leads to a definite amorality and the loss of those values which you set out to preserve. So it seems to me that the crisis in which the opposition now finds itself in the Soviet Union is not only the pressure from the authorities but also a moral crisis. An illustration of this crisis, at least for me, is the Yakir case, which I would like to call the Watergate of the Democratic Movement in Russia. You know what struck people about Watergate? Not that a few unknown people broke into the headquarters of the Democratic Party. What struck people was that some people who occupy high positions were trying to hide these circumstances for fear of losing face. Now when I speak of the representatives of the opposition in Russia, I want to emphasize that I'm not speaking about all the people in that movement, and when I speak of the moral crisis naturally I do not include all the people. I speak of tendencies, not of people. So there was a tendency among those people to do everything possible to conceal Yakir's testimony, to gloss over it, to work on the principle of "one doesn't take dirt out of one's hut." This is, by the way, a Soviet principle: if we tell how bad things are in the Soviet Union what would the West say? And so, some element of the dissident movement adopted that same slogan with a minus. If we tell about Yakir how would the Soviets use it.

Q. But no one was present at Yakir's interrogation; no one knows what went on.

As for his testimony, the situation was cleared up in October or November, 1972. Nevertheless, there was an all-out effort to cover it up, starting with pressures on people and ending with some American (émigré) newspapers saying that those people who spoke of Yakir's testimony are under the pressure of the KGB. I personally spoke to people who accused these people. They do not, by the way, stand on those accusations now. They say that it was a decisive moment and the fact that Yakir did testify had to be explained somehow. I spoke to many representatives of the opposition after Yakir had confessed. Yakir was a man who was ultimately convenient for the KGB. Two things astonished me; almost all the people I spoke to said that they had known what Yakir was like for a long time, but since he had a big name they did not turn away from him. In short, the goal justifies the means. One must say, however, that there were people who later took the position of a cover-up, and there were those in the Democratic Movement who wouldn't shake his hand, who wouldn't sit with him at the same table. This is very revealing.

Q. Why didn't they want to sit at the same table with Yakir?

Because of his objective role in the opposition movement. Yakir regularly met with the representatives of the KGB in order to convince them, as he expressed it. Possibly at that particular time he could believe in this, but what he couldn't believe in was that the KGB would let him stay free and allow him to do what he did contrary to their own interests. Yakir told his close friends and even some foreign correspondents that he would be used as a sitting duck. He knew it all. He drank obscenely. In this situation a man must leave a movement. If he doesn't understand that himself, someone should show him the door, whatever his best qualities. They could be friendly with him, be compassionate toward him, but they should have removed him from the movement. And it wasn't done; in my view that makes it unseemly.

Q. Do you think he was given drugs?

I don't see any basis for that. I can name Bukovsky who was and is in prison. Lyubarsky in Rostov, Shikhanovich. Not one of them testified. Krasin began to give testimony only when the testimony of Yakir cornered him. Those who were brought for confrontation with Yakir all had the impression that he was normal, that he wasn't under the influence of any drugs. And also he told the foreign correspondents that "if I'm put under pressure I'll confess." In the West this was understood as physical torture, but he wasn't talking only about physical pressure, beating, he was talking about other pressure.

Q. It must have been a difficult situation.

Let's put it another way. If Yakir was in an American prison there are many more chances that he wouldn't have confessed. And chances are that he would have been acquitted like Berrigan or Angela Davis. I think that one shouldn't try to demonstrate that the Soviet Union is not the United States and it's not necessary to explain what Soviet justice is. But you know, when the authors of *Vekhi* [*Signposts*, a 1909 collection of essays critical of the Russian Intelligentsia, especially the radical Intelligentsia] wrote their book, they were attacked by the revolutionary Intelligentsia, and were told, "You are playing into the hands of Czarism." In reality the question of what Czarism is didn't exist for Berdyaev, Struve, and others. For me the question of what the Soviet Government is doesn't exist. For me there is a question, which I'm trying to solve for myself, concerning who the people are who oppose the Soviet Government, and what can be opposed to the Soviet system. From this point of view, it seems to me, that as Watergate should teach something about the American system, the case of Yakir should teach the Russian Intelligentsia something.

Q. But for the KGB it was very important to kill the faith in Yakir and in the dissidents.

The KGB is a powerful organization, but you can't explain everything by KGB pressure. The fact that people socialized with Yakir knowing about his way of life is not explainable by KGB pressure. You can't explain that people attempted to hide this fact. You can explain the fact that Yakir confessed with the pressure of the KGB, but for me this is the least interesting, the least meaningful fact.

Q. Could the KGB add to his testimony?

No, there isn't any doubt about that. He confronted his own daughter and he said the same thing. Then you probably know about the famous letter Yakir wrote to Sakharov. This letter, in the opinion of Yakir's friends, is written not only in his own handwriting, but in his own style and formulation. There isn't any doubt. It's a fact that Yakir took the road of active cooperation with the investigators. And I want to draw your attention to one more thing: there was no precedent for it. But look what is happening now—Yakir and Krasin are central figures in that movement. Many Democrats say, and probably justly, that in the last months these two were removed from some aspects of the movement. But they were allowed to remain central figures in it. So for the outside world they are still central and the dissidents can't blame anyone except themselves. Now Titov, who also was a famous figure in that movement, wants to return to the Soviet Union, and all this happens at one and the same time. Well, if you imagine that all this is in the power of the KGB, then I must say that I have a much lower opinion of the KGB than you.

Q. What did Yakir write to Sakharov?

Yakir wrote that they were both used by the enemies of the Soviet Union, by the NTS [an émigré group] and Radio Liberty (which translated into Russian terms means by the CIA) and thus that it was time to end this service to American imperialism. It is true that he did add that he was and is an anti-Stalinist. This is especially piquant in a letter of that sort.

Q. So there is no possibility, as you see it, that he was forced?

There is no doubt that he was forced. But, you see, the word *forced* has always been incomprehensible to me. I admire the letter of Andrei Amalrik to Anatoly Kuzetsov. When Kuzetsov made a statement in the West that he wrote the way he did because he was forced to, Amalrik wrote, "What do you mean forced? I don't understand it." I don't understand either. Did they put electric currents through Yakir, tear out his nails? Perhaps for Americans, for those who place a very high value on an individual, who believe that even those POWs who must cooperate with the enemy and give testimony should be understood and forgiven. But in each country there are different rules of the game, and Yakir played by the Soviet rules of the game—and what he did has no justification. Yakir understood what the stakes were. That there was a threat of prison was clear from the beginning, unless he considered that being an objective worker for the KGB would save him. Nothing happened to Yakir that he couldn't expect. Even in Stalin's time they couldn't make everyone talk. They couldn't force Solzhenitsyn. They told Sinyavsky to write a solicitation for forgiveness and he didn't. How Daniel behaved in the labor camp, you probably know. Isn't it strange that some can be forced and some cannot be forced into anything.

Q. In November, 1972, you were falsely accused of participation in a hunger strike. How was that?

It was a hunger strike at the Moscow telegraph by the people who were demanding the right to leave the Soviet Union and freedom for those people who were imprisoned for wanting to leave the country. I did not participate in this strike, since I never approved such types of actions, but because my friends were there I went several times to see how they were doing. Besides, I was taking cassette interviews with them in order to pass them on to the American correspondents who were afraid to talk to the strikers because of the presence of the KGB and the police. But that isn't a crime, and I didn't participate in the hunger strike and was there only half an hour. I was detained when I was walking from a restaurant. The strikers were not in an office building; they were in a public building. They didn't break any order. But there is an article in the Soviet law pertaining to the "disobedience of the lawful demands by the police or citizen's volunteers." This is the article on the basis of which we were detained. But in order to imprison a person on the basis of this article two things are required. That there should be lawful demands given that must be obeyed. In my case such demands couldn't have been made because I was there only a half hour and therefore no one could have made such a request. The people who were there since 7 A.M. were told to leave, but that couldn't be true in my case so it was just laughable. The others did not obey. But in this law there is an additional demand. The people who were sitting there and writing telegrams to Brezhnev explaining why they were on a hunger strike were doing what one is supposed to do in a place like that: write and send telegrams. There were so few of them that they occupied only one table. There was plenty of space at other tables so that the strikers didn't prevent anyone from writing other telegrams. Therefore the demands of the police were unlawful. And if the court wasn't interested whether or not I was at the telegraph, it also wasn't interested whether these demands were lawful or not. The presumption was always this: if the police and the KGB said it, then it is unlawful.

Q. And you got two weeks for that?

Yes, even though every person began his testimony by saying that I did not participate. But already then in the bus the formulation was ingenious. "You see," said the KGB worker, "they all know you, so what do you want?"

Q. And how do you think the Russian middle class thinks about the situation in the country?

I think that the majority of the Soviet people basically support the existing system. I am not saying that the Soviet people are happy about the status of the country. Here, you understand, it depends on how one approaches the situation. If one wishes, it could be discovered that the majority of people are not satisfied. And this will be true. But this majority is dissatisfied with different aspects of life, and as a rule it blames the Jews, international imperialism, international Zionism and those Jews of the Intelligentsia who made it to the first row. Of course, there are those who blame the Secretary of the Communist Party, Leonid Brezhnev, personally. But nevertheless, the great majority do not reach the point of not accepting the system. Tell me, under what other system does an average man, intellectually average first of all, have such opportunities as in the Soviet Union? Where knowledge, talent, initiative will play such an insignificant role in a career as in the Soviet Union? Where else is there such an ample scope for an average man? I knew a few Soviet officials on the Central Committee of the Communist Party apparatus and, indeed, they were totally obligated to the system. In no other society would most of them have any chances for advancement. Imagine an average worker, an uneducated person, who can join the Party, who can become a secretary of a Party organization, who feels that the horizon of the Secretary General of the Communist Party is not any larger than his own. Isn't it encouraging?

Q. Nevertheless, when I was in the Soviet Union on previous occasions—1959, 1962, 1964, 1966—I noticed some kind of faith among the people. They always said, "We'll have this, we'll have that, and we'll get ahead of America." But this last time I didn't hear anything like that.

No, there isn't much enthusiasm there. Only a minority believes in ideology now and even fewer people talk seriously about communism. The only statements colored in some ideological tone that you'd meet would be, "If Lenin were alive now he wouldn't have allowed it." But you understand, I am not interested in who will be at the top, Brezhnev or Shelepin, or whether it will be called the Politburo of the Central Committee of the Communist Party of the Soviet Union or The High Council of the White Tribunal. I am giving that as an example. I'm not interested in that; I am not interested in communism from the point of view of its ideological goals, which are disgusting and hamper one's life and in the end aren't so important. I am interested in it from the view of its being the power structure of the Russian totalitarian regime. I don't want to say that the Russian people are now for communism, but unfortunately the Russian people are not against totalitarianism either. You can, under certain circumstances, get rid of communism. Today that isn't realistic in the Soviet Union, but I can imagine it in a few years. But that isn't important. What's important is whether or not there will be totalitarianism in Russia or not. Today, the greatest majority of the people still think in terms of the political terminology of the totalitarian system.

Q. How do you explain it?

In my opinion this is explainable by history, by tradition, and by the contemporary political situation. I'll give you an example. I used to give a lot of lectures and I was confronted with the following paradox: the majority of the people are decidedly against the Czechs and at the same time the majority of people are sympathetic to the Polish people, why? They say, "We spilled blood for the Czechs, what do they want?" This is a strange statement. Imagine a young woman in the street being attacked by two bandits. A man defends her, gets his hand cut, she is grateful, and asks him to walk her home, and he rapes her. This is called brotherly assistance; he spilled blood for her. And if we speak seriously, blood was spilled for both the Czechs and the Poles. But for some reason the only blood that is remembered is that spilled for the Czechs. What the Czechs wanted is incomprehensible to the average Soviet person. Did they want lower prices, higher wages? What did they want? Freedom? What kind of freedom—they lived well enough. Probably the Imperialists promised them something, otherwise what they did want is incomprehensible.

Q. Was there no sentiment of "did they want to live better than us?"

Yes, and this is also insulting to an average Russian. Amalrik wrote about it; the Soviet sense of justice being that others shouldn't live better than we do. In the case of the Poles it was clear what they wanted. The people said, "See how smart the Poles are. We are cattle, they can do what they want with us, but the Poles are clever." Understandable: the Poles wanted to lower prices; they wanted higher wages. Material values. This is very close to the heart of an average Soviet man. At that time especially there was talk in the Soviet Union about higher prices. After the Polish events that talk stopped. I don't know if that was a coincidence, but in any case, among the people it was thought that the two were connected. So you can see what values are important to the people and what values have no meaning whatsoever. An average Soviet man cannot understand that five people went out on Red Square to protest against the invasion of Czechoslovakia. "What are they, schizophrenics? Probably the West paid them a lot. They wanted glory." But the fact that these people simply could not refrain from expressing themselves, this idea, for an average Soviet man, is a crazy idea. He can't believe in it, and to speak of democracy in such a psychological climate is useless. That is why I think that if we are to speak of changes in the Soviet Union we must choose a less effective but more realistic road: gradually teaching the people to get accustomed to these concepts. To accomplish this in Soviet circumstances is extremely difficult and will be an extremely slow process. And if one hopes to see the results in five years, it's best not to start. In any case I'd like to recall Churchill's words here, that democracy is a disgusting thing but it is better than all other alternatives. So the road I spoke about is not appealing to me at all, but I don't know of any better one.

Q. Is there frustration among the Soviet people that past promises have not been fulfilled?

A typical Soviet person is cynical and suspicious; he doesn't believe in anything or anyone any more.

Q. So this lack of former enthusiasm that I noticed . . . ?

Of course. We are just talking about two different things. You talk about the attitude of the Soviet people toward the ruling class and I'm talking about their attitude toward democratic values. These two things are connected, but not identical.

Q. Yes, but I wanted to know the reasons for the disappearance of the enthusiasm and the aggressive spirit of competition with the U.S.A.

Enthusiasm can be warmed up for a few years. A country cannot function in a continuous state of enthusiasm when the promises are never kept, when plans stay on paper, when each new leadership brands the previous one, when there is an endless race with America, and when the two domains in which the Soviet Union was ahead are today doubtful—because Americans were the first on the moon and even in the field of ballet Russian supremacy is questionable. The French ballet and Balanchine's ballet were admired in Moscow. So it's clear that there is no superiority in space or in ballet. The Soviet Union has always lived with an external enemy. This is very important for the Soviet psychology, and now the United States is no longer a major external enemy. Now they are being accustomed to the idea that China is an enemy. Do you remember in Orwell's *1984* when an orator changes the name of the country with which they are at war? That is a grotesque and marvelous page. The Soviet people now believe that the Americans are friends and the Chinese are enemies. Tomorrow it can reverse once again.

Q. Do they really?

Yes, without a doubt. But then there is a little psychological twist; they regard each consecutive enemy with less enthusiasm.

Q. How can the Soviet Government fill the void created by the disappearance of enthusiasm?

By the military campaign which is now going on under the sign of "China is our enemy."

Q. Is China really dangerous for the Soviet Union?

I don't think so. The Soviet Union is dangerous for China. I know concretely that plans were discussed to attack China with a surgical nuclear strike. That was at the beginning of the 1970s, and the discussions were serious and pragmatic. However, I don't think that is a likely possibility now. Now the Soviet Union is really trying to do something about a higher standard of living. I don't think as some among the émigrés do that it is a monstrous plan of the Kremlin, that it is a monstrous lie. It's another matter that nothing will come out of it because the Soviet economy is not, even with the help of Mr. Nixon, in a condition to simultaneously race America in rockets and missiles, feed the country with wheat, create miracles in space, and spend more and more on the ballet. Something will have to be sacrificed, and it will be the well being of the people. The ballet, space, and arms will get their share.

Q. You mentioned that the return to Stalinism is impossible. Are there any judicial guarantees against it?

You know when a state is not based on any lawful principles. No judicial safeguards, even if they exist, can be reliable. In theory Stalin's constitution wasn't bad. I don't much like it, but if one compares it with what there was before, in the first two decades of the Revolution, the constitution didn't allow what was previously allowed. Even Article 58 of the criminal code, which existed during Stalin, had nothing to do with millions of imprisoned people. They were imprisoned on totally false charges. So no matter what a good judicial system there is or would be in the Soviet Union it changes nothing. So far the jury system doesn't exist in the Soviet Union.

Q. Are there any kind of guarantees?

I see mainly the social guarantee in the new, powerful bureaucratic class interested in the present stability. Such a class cannot allow an individual dictator to be totally independent of his bureaucratic constituency or to destroy his opponents in the ruling class.

Q. What do you yourself think about the personal freedom of an individual in a country such as ours?

For me the freedom of an individual is the greatest value; that is why I am in the United States. I don't know of any greater value.

Q. How would you limit the principle from being abused?

I think that mankind has possibilities to limit it by lawful means. I consider that the American society is open enough for changes, to have guarantees that this principle would not be misused. Otherwise there would be monstrous things, like what is going on now when two criminals who have committed exactly the same acts find themselves in different positions. One telephones his senators and gives them information and advice and the other is on the bench as an accused. Even though in their way, both were idealists. One is Ellisberg; the other, Hunt. Each had his own criteria. One considered that the war in Vietnam was monstrous and anticonstitutional, the other that the Democratic Party is composed of left conspirators and is destroying America. And each of them acted according to his own reason. And each considered that by breaking the law and privacy he is saving the country. Now see the results. I am not sure that if it wasn't for Ellsberg there would have been Hunt. And I'm not sure that Hunt wouldn't have given birth to other Ellsbergs. From my point of view they are moral and political twins.

Q. How do you account for the fact that previously the students always were active in various dissident movements in Russia, while now it's the people over 30?

Because they are "students" themselves.

Q. I see your point. Nevertheless, where are the real students?

I read in Brzezinski about American students. What he said about the students here, I can say about Soviet dissidents. These people are in general without any definite position in society. They are outsiders. From the point of view of the masses, they are outsiders, therefore, in some sense, students. And in contrast to American students the students in the Soviet Union have a definite future; they get *raspredeleniye*. And they try to get as good raspredeleniye as they possibly can. Thus they are much more connected with the system than the outsiders.

Q. Have you noted the spirit of intolerance, a moral intolerance among those members of the Intelligentsia with whom you met?

When I was a student, I did meet with those people. Then there was 1966, the trial of Sinyavsky and Daniel, and for a short time I was rather infatuated with that movement. And the reason I got away from it was not because I was afraid, and not because I realized all the hopelessness, but because I understood the nature of the choices I had. The choice was between two similar things. Only through one could I get interesting work, comfort, a fair salary, and various pleasures of life, pleasures which are valuable to me. The second choice was the renunciation of all those things, and it wasn't clear to me in the name of what this renunciation was to be made. And the other side, the Intelligentsia, from the moral point of view is extremely intolerant. Intolerant of others' opinions, of the views of others. What I like in America is this: I am not in agreement here with a lot of people—in some respects with the leftists, in other respects with the rightists. When we talk about foreign policy, as a rule I disagree with the leftists here, but not always. I support improved relations with China, while the American conservatives are against it. I don't think that the United States should do something in relation to the Soviet Union, to sacrifice national interests in order to change the system over there. I came to the United States in order to be an American, and not to urge the United States to make revolution in the Soviet Union, even if I could. And I think that if the United States is able to help people in Russia from a humanitarian consideration, that's wonderful. But the American national interests are first in my consideration. Perhaps this is so for me because I was involved so much in American studies, and am in the habit of identifying American interests with all that is opposite to the Soviet Union.

Q. Is that why you are for Vietnam war?

You did not understand me. I didn't say I was for the Vietnam war but against the Soviet policy in it. These are two different things. Besides, I am, with some qualifications, for what this [Nixon] administration is doing now and not for the stupidities that were done before, and not for the careless steps that Kennedy took. Today I don't see any other way out. But that doesn't mean that it was necessary for America to get involved in Vietnam, and especially a few years back when it was done.

Q. You want to work in an American university, but do you realize that these views may close all the doors to you in an academic community?

You know, I'm accustomed to this. To express one's opinion is a luxury, but I am not prepared to sacrifice it even in order to open additional opportunities for myself. After all, I had career opportunities in the Soviet Union also. But let's get back to your question. I told you how I felt about foreign policy. On questions of domestic policies I am more on the side of the reformers. That is, as a liberal, I recognize that no society is perfect and I believe in reforms. I have argued with a lot of people, but that didn't spoil any relations for me. I didn't change my attitude toward anyone here and, hopefully, no one here changed his attitude toward me. In the Soviet Union people make friends with those who think like themselves. It seems to me uninteresting. There, to say that you are against the dissidents means you acquire the reputation of being a police agent. They wouldn't be interested why you said it and what arguments you have to offer. If you say that, you are a police agent. This is, in a sense, a deification of a definite political movement which already existed at the beginning of the twentieth century. And we all know where that led. And what is most frightening, why I do not like some part of the Russian opposition movement is that it didn't learn anything and it still repeats the same intolerance.

Q. Do you think that by 1984 the life of the Intelligentsia in the United States will be the same as the life of the Intelligentsia in the Soviet Union?

Why this particular date?

Q. I'm just making an allusion to Orwell's novel, in which he shows that the West is moving in the same direction, toward where the Soviet Union already is.

You know, that question is below the belt, addressed to a person who arrived in America six weeks ago. My arrival here is my answer to you. And my experience here, which could change my theories about the United States is inadequate. Still, my prognosis is optimistic.

MIKHAIL AKSENOV

Mikhail Aksenov belongs to the "lucky generation," the generation whose most impressionable years coincided with Khrushchev's liberalization. It was the time when the ZEKs were coming back from years of imprisonment, when the air was charged with the promise of freedom, when criticism of Stalin was allowed.

The new liberty was intoxicating and it affected people in different ways. For Mikhail it was the beginning of reckless years. As a teen-ager he immersed himself in a bohemian life, or, as he puts it, "in degradation." When he came out of it and after some self-searching, he decided that he wanted not only to be converted to Christianity, but to become a priest. The prospect of having a Christian priest in their family caused much anxiety for his parents. Relieved that the terror was in the past, they had envisioned a secure life for their son; now, instead, he was setting out on the road that could only be difficult and hazardous. But there was no one and nothing that would convince Mikhail to change his mind. At present he is studying at the Saint Vladimir Seminary in Crestwood, New York.

When we met in Paris in March of 1973, Aksenov had been in France but a few weeks. It was one of those Parisian rainy evenings when people, hidden under umbrellas and raincoats, all look alike. I was waiting for him on a street corner wondering how we could recognize each other. But he emerged from the Metro and took my arm, saying that before anything else we must go and see his friend in a hospital. It was a long train ride to the mental hospital in the suburbs, yet it seemed perfectly natural to be with a stranger on the way to visit another stranger who was ill. I felt helpless and depressed by the ward of six people in which a young Moscow girl had no means to communicate her anxieties to doctors or nurses, but Mikhail, sitting on her bed, holding her hand, smiled and laughed and told her the latest news of their mutual friends, as though we had dropped in and would proceed shortly all together to a dinner or a party. I was relieved when we finally left the forbidding stone building, and it was then that Mikhail was silent and looked in need of comfort himself.

Q. I am interested in your reaction to the statement by Mihajlov in which he says that the Socialist intellectual who expresses himself freely before the West begins to feel like a traitor. That this sense of treachery is inhibiting and is much stronger than the fear of reprisals. Do you feel that this sense of betrayal does exist?

It certainly does, though I do not share it. I'll give you an example: there is a young man here in Paris who at the age of 17 suddenly felt that he no longer could live in the Soviet Union. He became a Zionist, learned Hebrew, joined the synagogue, and became one of the most active Zionists in the country. Finally he left for Israel. And since he was one of the most active Zionists, he was surrounded on arrival by reporters who wanted to interview him. And his answer was, "You scoundrels, do you want me to betray my Motherland?" They asked him, "Are there repressions in the Soviet Union against the Jews?" He answered, "No." And in this fashion he answered all their questions. Now he is 20, he lives here, and he goes around to wherever he can meet any Soviets and he terrorizes them. He asks them, "Well, how do you live in that country of yours without any freedom and without any rights?" Do you understand that dualism?

Q. Yes, very well. It's very Russian, very Dostoevskian. But Mihajlov says this sense of betrayal is in regard to both one's country and to those who fight for freedom in the capitalist societies.

Mihajlov is right, but I think it is more complex than that. He tries to explain it on the ideological level and it exists on the subconscious level.

Q. What do you think is the source of this dualism, the system, the upbringing, the psychology of a Russian?

At the source of this is the concept of Russia as a phenomenon which is a spiritual sovereignty. Russia is not just a country, it is also an Orthodoxy.

Q. And what does socialism have to do with it?

But what is socialism in the Russian variety? At its beginning Russia was the Third Rome, the only Christian domain in the world in which there was no Christianity. Greece fell. This consciousness has such strong roots that I find it everywhere in the Russian people. This is the country that for centuries thought of itself as the only truly Christian country. Before 1905 Christian and Russian were synonymous. And in the psychology and consciousness of a Russian this is so fused that for a person to renounce his country is a betrayal. Remember, when during the reign of Boris Godunov 17 students went abroad to study for the first time in Russian history and never returned, the Russian Embassy demanding their return asked one of them, "But how is it possible to renounce one's nature?" In other words, the nature of a person is not his personality, but his nation. This is very typical. Nation not as a natural category, but as a spiritual category, a religious category. That's where it all comes from. And these are the people who haven't thought of Christianity for 55 years. Why did the Russians win the war? Certainly not because they loved Stalin or were better equipped than the Germans. It was again an absolutely religious thing. As Pasternak has said in *Doctor Zhivago,* it was a purification. When culture and values were stamped out, all of a sudden the people were united by the defense of the Motherland. And it wasn't by accident that at that time the church was revived and the Metropolitan Sergius, who sinned much against the church, spoke with such a pathos on the radio, for the first and only time in his life. He spoke first and then Stalin.

Q. Who allowed him to speak before Stalin?

Well, when the Germans attacked, it was so unexpected, the Government was totally lost. They thought themselves an absolute power in their own country, and here is this invasion from the West. They were grabbing at anything. And suddenly the hierarch of the church speaks up. True, the church was demolished, the priests imprisoned, but still, someone was able to address the entire nation.

Q. And why wasn't he in prison?

There were three at that time, Sergius, Archbishop Alexius, and Metropolitan Nikolai. They managed to remain free as a result of a very clever and at times unjustified policy. But that speech was very courageous. He said that we must forgive everything, we must leave all our ideological differences, all that divides us, and he took the line that the Russian church is the mother of the country. Now, he has said, we have a chance, because in the history of our country, at its most difficult moments, the church always is resurrected. It was the first time that he used such a sentence. Not by accident did Stalin change his policy toward the church.

Q. But how did Stalin react to this speech?

Just think who could before the war speak about the Motherland as a religious entity? That isn't a revolutionary category. The revolutionary category is that it's International, World Proletariat, solidarity of the oppressed. Here all the national slogans were revived. And the church began to talk of itself as a force whose spiritual mission was to guide, resurrect the country.

Q. Were you interested in religion in childhood?

No. I am absolutely a Soviet man. I was brought up in an absolutely Soviet family. When I was six, I remember this very well, I had a dream that Stalin would one day come to our house. Because at that time there were rumors that Stalin had been dropping in on average citizens. And so I had this dream of childhood, how Stalin will come and see what a wonderful cook my mother is, how marvelous this will be to see Stalin in person. He was truly a religious figure. You know, a year before I left, I had a very interesting conversation with a close friend of mine, a Jewish woman. She belongs to the Intelligentsia, a woman who had suffered a lot, who understands everything, and who back in 1950 already opposed the system. And so we were talking about the possibility of leaving Russia, and she said, "How could we possibly leave?" And then she said, "How difficult it is to live now. I watch my daughter who is 15, she doesn't believe in anything any more. She is skeptical of everything; she understands that the system has decayed, that all the ideals are worthless. I too understand it. But when Stalin was alive, how we believed and how easy it was for us to live then. I remember being in tenth grade, how all of my friends believed in communism and in Stalin; now our friendship is still intact because we have shared all this." You see, even though they have changed there is this nostalgia for the religious unity of souls.

Q. What about yourself? When did you first become aware?

I was an average Soviet schoolboy. At the usual age I became a Pioneer, and so on. But at the age of about 15 I got acquainted with a group of people older than I, those who at the age of 19 or 20 began to be disillusioned with Communist ideology and came to search independently. They read such innocent things as Romain Rolland and they gathered to talk about life, art, culture, on a very primitive level. They were all imprisoned in 1949 for talking. And among these people was a very impetuous boy, Boris, 16 years old, very passionate, very individualistic, and, you know, in our society, especially at that time, it was unthinkable. He used to speak up in class, used to criticize the Government. And then he was approached by a provocateur, who said to him, "You know what, Boris, let's stop just talking, let's do something, let's organize." So they organized, five more agents provocateurs and two or three others. Naturally they couldn't do anything, they just continued to talk. But they were accused of planning to assassinate Stalin, and everyone, except the provocateurs, was shot. Boris, because he was under age, was given 25 years in prison.

Q. Did they really plan the assassination?

My God, who could even think about such a thing? Don't you remember how in 1937 they used to shoot people for intended assassination? This was 1950, the year of new purges. Boris was imprisoned, but was let out in 1956 because of Khrushchev's amnesty. I met these people in 1958, their lives were broken, they hated everything. They had a great influence on me. So by the time I was 16 I was a passionate anti-Soviet. There was especially one person there who influenced me. He is in prison now; he was one of the leaders of the Democratic Movement.

Q. And this is how you began to be interested in religion?

No; I still wasn't interested then. What happened was that this becoming anti-Soviet threw me out of the normal routine of a Soviet student: grades, studies, school amusements.

Q. What then pushed you toward a religious quest? A person, an idea, an event?

All three, but mainly my own way of life. My own degradation. I joined a circle of bohemians and this was for me not even a protest against the social system, but a way of life. Then, at 17, I got acquainted with our Intelligentsia—Bukovsky, Vladimir Osipov, Yuri Galanskov, Yuri Titov. We used to meet by the Mayakovsky monument and read poetry. Amalrik called it aptly a "cultural opposition." Then the first exhibit of abstract art began. I participated in it as an administrator.

Q. Public exhibits?

Oh no, it was in private homes. Anyway, I was an unformed person, got into this bohemian circle, *not* the Intelligentsia, but those others I mentioned, with people who had lost their life's source. And when a man falls out of the social system, opposes everything without yet knowing what he can affirm, when not knowing what he wants—he only knows what he doesn't want—then he falls only one way—down. That is, a man opposes his inner anarchism to the structure that is orderly even though it is totalitarian and unacceptable; he desocializes. But since he must express himself somehow, he falls into drunkenness, into drug addiction, into the lowest depths. My friends who fell all the way can no longer rise by themselves, without the forces of Grace.

Q. And how did you come out of it?

Mine is an extreme nature that takes everything to its limits. Do you know how we used to spend our days—I was then at the University—we used to meet early in the morning, collect the money that our parents had given us (one ruble each) and spend all our days at the movies or playing cards. We forgot everything, our former interests, literature, art, philosophy. It was a totally meaningless existence. We played as many as 300, 400 games of cards a day. And in this state of nonexistence the problem of my own life suddenly arose.

Q. Suddenly?

Perhaps not so suddenly. You know how a young person always has an illusory picture of life and of his own place in it. He thinks he defines life and suddenly this definition disintegrates before his eyes. In such moments of self-consciousness I began to question myself. Perhaps it was a lucky coincidence. I was in a hospital, ill; it gave me a chance to read, to think. In my childhood I read a lot. By the time I was 13 I had read all of Russian literature. Then between 14 and 20 I read absolutely nothing. And there, in the hospital, I reread the classics, Dostoevsky and Tolstoy, writers in whose works the problem of identity and its moral meaning is the predominant one. And this is what had shaken me up.

Q. At the moment, and for a long time, there is no self-affirmation in Western literature. While in Russia it does exist. The literature of human values comes from the Soviet Union now, as in Aleksandr Solzhenitsyn's novels. Why is that?

Yes, I thought a lot about it. I even wrote an article about it for Samizdat. There is a profound basis to it. I think that the self is not just given us, but posed before us as well, and we must actualize it, realize it, struggle for it. And it seems to me that in the West, the period of creation or a struggle for one's personality is over. I mean the period of great revolutions—Cromwell's in England, the French Revolution, the Protestant Revolution in America—when a man was in the process of conquering his right to be himself in a social environment that was hostile to him. And now youth is the heir to this victory, and they receive the possibility of the self, the possibility of being, without struggle. They don't have the opportunity to battle for their place in life. And though it was a wolf's world, in which their grandparents and parents had to fight for their place tooth and nail, they created a situation for their heirs in which it is difficult to affirm one's self. For a religious consciousness, suffering is, in some sense, a gift. We can't enter God's Kingdom without it. But it doesn't mean that people must put each other in prison camps to help each other enter the Kingdom.

Q. Perhaps your country and mine are moving toward similar goals by different ways.

I know very little about America. I've been in France for about three months now and have never been to America. But it seems to me that what is happening in America, all those movements, must be different from the European ones because of the differences in culture and traditions and age. It seems to me that in the American culture there are more constructive beginnings, that the society is more creative, or rather is still in the process of creation. Perhaps I idealize it. The United States society is freer from traditions, strictly empirical ones. While the traditions of Europe are measured by centuries of Christian culture that is already degenerating.

Q. What about the Soviet society?

Before 1968 the social structure was still largely the highest category for the self—if one was a Communist—and after 1968, even after the Khrushchev period, disappointed in its social structure per se, the Soviet Intelligentsia began to search for the affirmation of the self as it exists. That is, at the moment, the Soviet man faces the same problem as in other times the European and the American men had faced: how to gather, preserve, and affirm his own self-forces in the face of such a social structure. So the Soviet man is now in the position of explorer-conqueror. He is not an heir to anything, he is standing on the ruins. He is not on the ruins of society, though the society is ruined and another one has been constructed. He is on far more frightening ruins. A young European, or an American leftist, is on the ruins of some kind of social idea. But the man of the Soviet Intelligentsia stands on the ruins of his personality.

Q. His own individual one?

His own and in general. On the ruins of the idea of the self, and on the ruins of the self in its empirical existence, his own. How can he put himself together? What can he oppose to the ideal of a Communist society? He needs to say, "I am," in order to say to the society, "You are not right." Otherwise, from what premises will he judge this society? It is, after all, a society that wants to construct the world of absolute values on earth. Even if it is not successful, nevertheless it presumes to want to construct the world of absolute earthly values. So to judge it, one can do it from the position of the self, which is not presupposed in the world of absolute values. Ideally, the Soviet society is an abstract world society in which the self is nothing. It is a perfect social structure in its conception objectively, in which there isn't any subject, isn't any "I." So one must discover this "I" in himself; one must put together his own "I." And a spiritual man in the Soviet Union must find a basis on which he could build his "I." He begins to look inward. Inevitably he must come to some metaphysical reality in which his personal beginning has its roots. That is why among the Russian Intelligentsia today, as nowhere else, there is such a movement toward Christianity and why Russia, it seems to me, is potentially the Christian nation, while France, a Catholic country with a strong priesthood and a powerful religious tradition, I don't see as a potential Christian country.

Q. So you do not see the religious movement in the Soviet Union as a protest against the official atheism, a sort of forbidden fruit?

Any protest is a push, and by itself it cannot be constructive. As for the forbidden fruit one can only say, "You don't allow me to eat this apple, so I'll eat it." But one cannot reach God out of sheer protest.

Q. What if religion was allowed and encouraged, would it be the same?

We can make suppositions and experiments in physics, but we can't talk about it in other spheres. If Russia had a free religion it wouldn't have been Russia. We must talk about what we have at hand.

Q. So what you are saying is that the Russian Intelligentsia is searching for its personal self, and the self cannot realize itself on the social or political levels?

These supports are also necessary. A person is a social animal; he can't live alone. But at times these social foundations close to us various metaphysical roots of our being. In the Soviet Union these roots are naked, because in the regime of totalitarian social structures man is deprived of his socio-political foundations. Unless, of course, he belongs to it, as any bureaucrat or civil servant does, then he can live by it. Even if he doesn't share all its ideological aspects, he still lives by belonging to his society, and he represses all his doubts, so that he may belong to it, and I mean not only materially but existentially. I tried to talk to some of my friends, who are thinking people supposedly, who already have their Ph.D.s, who are my age, and I saw in them a reluctance to speak on the subject of existence. I saw the expression of fear in their faces; they were afraid of those questions; they didn't want to know. They say, "We live here, in this society. Why do you disturb us? Why do you call us to other things? We don't need religion; we don't need to ask any such questions. Even if we are scoundrels, if we have sold out, so what? We have built our own, secure world. We live in it."

Q. Why do you think Christianity would help them? Why not some other religion?

Every religion is true, but Christianity is the most human religion. What does the Soviet man need most? He needs humanness. It's not God that has been stamped out in him, but man. So he must find that human being in himself and he can only do that through God-Man (*Bogochelovek*), through Christ. Because Christ is the Human Being who is indestructible. Christ has absolute humanity because in Him this God-Manness is indestructible, because it destroys Itself on the Cross and resurrects Itself. And that is why one can find in Christianity this humanness and say, "My humanity is indestructible; even if I'll be destroyed by this society, by this system, by this force, I will be resurrected in my own humanity."

Q. Do you believe that there is such a thing as universal intellectual communion? Or do you, like most Russian émigrés, feel condemned to aloneness in the West?

I think there is a mixture of conceptions here. Let's take a primitive example. Let's say that science is a building that is being built by all mankind. Einstein's theories or some Soviet scientist's discoveries belong to the entire world, to the intellectual community of the world. That always existed. Now it is more clear that it transcends all ideological systems, and even the leaders of the Soviet Union must take that into consideration. But that is an intellectual union. There are other unions: a psychological union, the union of experience, the union of understanding. For example, people who went through the Siberian prisons together, or through the tortures of the KGB or the German camps, they—despite all their intellectual closeness to American or French scientists, say—have absolutely nothing in common psychologically with them. Because the more important reality, the existential experience, is different. In this I see the main difficulty of any émigré—when a man finds himself in a society of people of different experience.

Q. Do you feel that here in the West you are torn, that your strength is weakened?

After my conversion God gave me strength, so I can't say that I am deprived of strength. But I am deprived here of people whom I understand and who understand me without words, with whom I made the same journey, the same search. There are people whom I loved all my life, with whom I lived all my life, whose souls are ingrown into my soul, and this ingrowing of the souls I lost here. But that is natural and it's a psychological difficulty.

Q. Do you think that in time you will find such people here, or with whom at least you can feel a spiritual alignment?

I am convinced I will.

Q. Do you see any parallels between the Western youth and the Soviet youth? Right now there are student riots going on in Paris, how do you view all that?

Let's take first your last question. Why is the 50-year-old, the 40-year-old, or 30-year-old not protesting here? Is it because at 30 you know less about the negative aspects of the system? On the contrary you see more. Because the 18-year-olds have no adequate relation between the responsibility and that against which they are protesting. It's a named protest. In essence, though, the psychological motivation behind protests here and in the Soviet Union is the same. Among youth, that is. In a sense it is a self-consciousness, the need to place oneself, to create an individual world-sense, to grasp the world around. In this sense my particular generation was more fortunate than any other; in another sense it was least fortunate. My generation is one of "in-between time." We grew up during the time of relative liberalization, Khrushchev time. Once when we were talking about that, a friend of mine, a physicist, said, "How sad. In a few years they'll talk about our time as the time of relative freedom." We who are conscious of the fact that we are living in a state of slavery, lawlessness, we turned out to be the generation that was lucky enough to breathe for a moment. This must sound comical to a Western person, and it is a comedy, but until the age of 14, a crucial age, we lived in a totalitarian situation. My parents, for example, never told me until I was 17 that my relatives were in prison.

Q. Why didn't they?

What do you mean, why? They were afraid. My uncle was in prison for 20 years. And I didn't know that my father's brother, the son of my grandmother with whom I lived in the same room, was in a Kolyma prison. They were afraid even to think about telling me.

Q. When did you first find out?

In 1958, when he returned and bought me a pocketknife. Then gradually I began to find out about his prison life. The same with General Yakir, who was also a close relative and who was arrested in our house in Moscow, and also his brother, not a small figure himself. Pyotr Yakir is my third cousin. But these subjects were taboo, the memories were forbidden, my parents were scared to death. And if I don't have the sense of fear that the old generation has, it's not to my credit. There were six searches in my house, my parents and grandparents absorbed the fear, and they, who witnessed so much, did not believe that it would ever change. They think that even if there is some kind of easing up now, it'll be worse in the future. Fear becomes a part of one's texture of existence.

Q. You mean it becomes a normal state?

Yes, normal. And they think that it's best to live like everybody; find some kind of a safe niche, some specialty, that will always be of value. This is the consciousness of my parents who gave all their energy to put me on that road. They wanted to push me into some scientific sphere, or technical one, to protect me. After I was converted to Christianity, many years later, I tried to explain to my parents why I wanted to be a priest. They were, of course, radically against it. They are atheists, but in my case it wasn't their atheism that was the motivating force, but that which was nourished in them by the social structure.

Q. They were upset that you were Orthodox Christian?

Sure, they were. My conversion took place without them, naturally. Intellectually, I was already independent from them at the age of 15. But what scared them wasn't so much that I was a Christian, but that I was a dissident. This frightened them; by being different they thought I was putting them under the axe. This is the main danger when you fall out from a unified, social structure—you are doomed. For years they have asked me, "How will you live?" "What will you do?" And it's not an idle question, how to live outside the social structure, if the structure happens to be absolute, when a man is programmed into it like a detail of a mechanism. It's not an ironic image at all. In 1950 Stalin himself said that, "You are little screws, all the Soviet people are little screws of this great mechanism which is the Soviet System." And, besides, it was a great joy for the Soviet people to be functioning screws. We can sit here and be ironic about it, but it isn't ironic there; the Soviet Government is a powerful apparatus and each person has his or her own function in that apparatus.

Q. How old were you when Stalin died and how did you react?

I was seven or eight. I was in the hospital then and I only heard that there was a huge crowd and that hundreds were killed in the stampede at the funeral. This was a religious event. Everyone wept. The government members wept even though they knew who he was, because it wasn't just a political system he created, but a system of being, and then the main source of it, the one who personified it, suddenly wasn't alive. There is his corpse, they'll take him away now, how will we live tomorrow? This was everyone's question. This is why I think although my generation was fortunate it was also split. Because it wasn't formed in totalitarianism. People who were 10 years older and were mature by Stalin's death had a kind of wholeness, the wholeness of the people of Stalin's epoch. They could change later, but they had it. The faithful ones. The generation which is 10 years younger had it. The generation which is 10 years younger than I didn't know Stalin at all, and grew up in a cleared-up atmosphere. And my generation was in between. Because what does it mean to be 13 or 14? This is the time of explosion, an inner explosion of a human being, and suddenly this explosive time coincides with the period of liberalization, when people are returning from prisons, from labor camps, do you understand this? And they begin to talk, for the first time, about the cult of personality. And suddenly some strange books are being published . . . The feeling was that we are on the brink of freedom. Here is freedom, in the air, you can smell it already. So you live your crucial years in this exalted atmosphere, returning to the time of Lenin.

Q. Did you think that Stalin had corrupted Lenin's ideals and you were on the way back to those ideals?

Your question is either naïve or you are taking me for a naïve person. I had in mind the people who were returning from prisons. They were on the level of neo-Communistic consciousness, romantic neo-Communists. Because who was put in prison in the 1930s? Not the enemies of the Soviet Union or the Soviet Government, those were wiped out in the 1920s. Average people, faithful people.

Q. Are there any people now among the Intelligentsia who believe in Lenin's ideals?

It seems to me that during Khrushchev's time, among the Intelligentsia that was coming back from the camps, there was the belief that everything after 1935 was abnormality. This Intelligentsia, after all, was born from the system, bred on Communist ideology, and regarded Stalin's repressions as abnormal. And I think that this was still so until 1968. Then it began to die, and now, among the Intelligentsia, it is completely dead. Lenin's communism totally lived itself out in Khrushchev's politics. This is when people understood that there'll be no liberalization.

Q. Do you consider yourself an active dissident?

Yes, I signed letters and so on.

Q. Do you, like some other dissidents, consider that *Doctor Zhivago* was the first impetus for the dissident movement?

I was young then, but I think it's true. It's a comical fact, but the Soviet Government is really afraid of writers. An ideocracy based on the word is afraid of the word. Pasternak was a Soviet writer, in some ways he accepted the system.

Q. In Nadezhda Mandelstam's book *Hope against Hope* she says that he even had a kind of a cult of Stalin.

Yes, even historically he had some idealization of Stalin's system. And his novel, it isn't so much an autobiographical thing, perhaps some sort of self-reflection of a member of the Intelligentsia of that era who, having accepted the system, then finally has to perceive it. And his perception of it is aesthetic, not as a thinker, not as an intellectual, but as an artist. And it is his artistry, his creativity that is protesting. Zhivago is a very symbolic figure. It's a sort of a substance of humanity. All the humanitarianism of the nineteenth century is focused in Doctor Zhivago, even his professional responsibility as a physician. He represents an indivdiual in that world. Not ideologically, for he doesn't belong to any system, he is by himself, but he cannot accept that system which came with the Revolution. Not because he will not try, he even wants to accept it, but he cannot live in that atmosphere which is stifling. He is dying. He isn't put in prison, he has a chance to work as a doctor, and he leaves that social structure because he cannot exist in it, he becomes a *yurodivy* (saintly fool). And here Pasternak goes back to the deepest roots, traditional roots not only of Russian literature, but of the Russian concept of human nature and religion. *Yurodstvo* is a protest against the meaninglessness of the world. And in this particular case this revolutionary reality appears as a total objectification of this meaninglessness that kills human beings. So that in the very fate of Yuri Zhivago this dying is personified. It kills him not with an axe, not by the walls of KGB, not with prison, it kills him with itself. He has nothing to do but die.

It is interesting that the novel is divided into two parts. In the first it's life, life of society, Russian Intelligentsia, bourgeois world, noblemen's world. That life is strange too, polarized, antithetical, disputable, torn by strife and controversy and conflicts, but still in it a man lives. He exists like a human being. The first part of the novel is the narration of life. The second part of the novel is the fixation, the constancy of dying. The dying of Zhivago. In it time disappears. Remember, there is an episode in which two friends of Zhivago are sitting together, after the war, and reading his poems. Look at the life of these two—one is Gordon and the other Dudurov. Actually, these are good people who suffered much. Both were in prison; both were in the war. They didn't sell out; they didn't sin against their social conscience. On the contrary, they are victims of the system, but they are shallow and they know it. Why? Because in the depths of their being, in the very heart of their "I" they did accept this inhumanness of the system; they began to live in that atmosphere. They didn't die, they lived. They said to themselves, we must survive. And they did. And in this is their sin. So that in this novel what occurs is the reexamination, reperception of all values. In it the world evaluation of the average man is turned upside down. Zhivago comes out the victor even though he is dead. He is weak, he gradually dies, in poverty, in pitifulness, but he in his death turns out to be stronger than death, because he triumphs over this pseudo-life which others live. And now, at the end of their lives these two people read his poems. It's symbolic that these poems are about Christ, about the dying and resurrecting of life. And the name of Zhivago is symbolic; when Jesus asks Peter, "For whom do you take me?" and he replies, "For Christ, the son of God-*Zhivago*"—*zhivago* means *alive*. That is, you are alive, you possess life no matter what will happen to you here. And thus Yuri Zhivago is the most alive of all the characters in the novel though he dies. He accomplished the replacing of all values. And with the writing and publishing abroad of this novel something did happen to the spirit of the Russian Intelligentsia. It may also be symbolic that Pasternak died after the book was published, as though with this book he expiated all his life, all his compromises before the existing reality. This book is his atonement, his redemption.

There is something in common between him and Osip Mandelstam. Pasternak himself said that Zhivago wasn't him; it seems to me that Zhivago is much closer to Mandelstam as an image of life. In the 1930s' poetry of Mandelstam there is a leitmotiv of sacrifice. Mandelstam was asked many times why he didn't emigrate. And he used to say, "I can't. For me emigration is not a question of changing a place of residence; for me emigration is the question of escaping from my fate." He sensed his predestination to be sacrificed. Mandelstam's poetry is a song before the sacrifice; it is the very music to the rhythm of which he is walking toward his Golgotha.

Q. Do you see any similarities at all in the fate of Solzhenitsyn?

They are people of two different epochs. Pasternak and Mandelstam are the spiritual symptoms of the sunset of old Russia. And Solzhenitsyn is the foreteller of the new Russia. He isn't responsible for the past. In this is his strength. He is young, younger than the young. He went through prisons and an almost fatal cancer and yet he is young. Perhaps he is outside of time. Solzhenitsyn is a quality of the new. Therefore we cannot compare them even though in some sense he may be continuing the life of Pasternak and Mandelstam.

Q. If the novel *Doctor Zhivago* was the first impetus for the Democratic Movement, what was the second in your opinion?

In my opinion the Democratic Movement was born in 1968 with the arrest of Ginzburg and Galanskov. Though Sinyavsky and Daniel did open the door to something. But practically speaking it was the Ginzburg trial.

Q. And Czechoslovakia?

Yes, that was a turning point where everyone lost faith.

Q. In order to find another faith?

Those who could found another faith. But I'm talking from the socio-political point of view. With the Czech Spring there was a great hope that the liberalization had begun, that democratization was in progress, that gradually it would come to the Soviet Union too, that we too would be democratized. Then we understood that without ourselves alone starting something, assuming full responsibility, nothing would happen, that liberalization was an episode and not an orderly progression, that it is only a possibility for which we must fight. But also, the Czech invasion undermined the faith of many in the possibility of such a struggle. And that is why people are leaving Russia now; there is a sense of doom.

Q. Are some of them leaving to save their skins?

Of course there is this element, but it is more complex. It's just unbelief. What did Czechoslovakia demonstrate? That the Soviet Union is not a Socialist country, but an empire. You look through history you'll find the same thing; it's an empire, some kind of

Fatum, the Bronze Horseman. And the people, the Russian man, is deaf. You are shouting to him and he is deaf.

Q. What about the Jewish exodus?

That is another subject. The Jews in Russian history and in Russian politics are an episode which is measured by centuries. They entered active political life in 1880. At the beginning of the twentieth century there was a split. One part assimilated and went into the Revolutionary movement; the other, into national Zionism. The Jews who were left in Russia accepted the Communist norms of life in one degree or another, and in the same sense they became Russianized and non-Russianized. Because it was both a Russian affair and also an international, Socialist affair. The Russian-Jewish Intelligentsia today, who took part in the Democratic Movement, after all the events of 1968, consciously or unconsciously began to sense that in Russian society there are separations. Not on the principle of democracy or religion, but on the principle of nationalism. Despite the fact that there is a lot in common between the Russian and the Jews, there is this watershed. And in Russia the note of nationalism begins to sound louder and louder. And so the Jews began to feel alienated. But when we think of a man of the Russian Intelligentsia we must know that this is a lost man. Pomerants called him a man of air, a rootless man, and this applies to any Russian regardless of his nationality. So in a part of the Russian Intelligentsia there is this search for roots. Solzhenitsyn expresses that very phenomenon. In that search for roots the Intelligentsia finds them in the national tradition, and for a Jew this is very difficult.

Q. You mean it is difficult for a Jew to be a Slavophile?

Yes, it's unnatural. While for a Russian it's natural even though it might not always be good.

Q. And why did the Government begin to let them leave?

Because the Jews turned out to be stronger than the Government in some sense.

Q. Not because they want to get rid of the dissidents? So the West can eat them up?

Do you mean why they are letting out the members of the Democratic Movement?

Q. Yes.

Oh, yes, they are letting them out exactly for that reason. Because it's better to have the enemy outside the walls of the fortress than within it. Because in the West a Democrat may die of the plague and in Russia he may make mischief. All those who come to the West are no longer dangerous for the regime.

Q. Why did it take 50 years to come to this conclusion?

They didn't arrive at this conclusion by reflection. This came about by the force of events. All that happens there doesn't happen on the level of thought, but on the level of the instinct for power.

Q. Does it occur to them that those who leave could get together in the West and do some harm?

No, because it's impossible. Their instinct tells them that the people who leave are not émigrés like before, they are just running away from that swamp. I left Russia without any hope of returning, and so it is with the others. It's much more tragic. It's not like the emigration of the nineteenth century when people left for the sake of the country, for the sake of Russia. Now people leave the country. The time for that other one hasn't come yet, but it will come.

Q. It will?

Well, naturally. History repeats itself. At least in the Russian history it's very apparent; it's very cyclical.

Q. Why was the Democratic Movement conceived among the scientists instead of the humanitarians? Usually it's the other way around.

But that is very understandable. The people in humanities are helpless in our system because they are more tied up with the system. A person who year after year fulfills some kind of ideological function cannot, at the same time, retain his freedom of consciousness. But a physicist, a mathematician, he is still free spiritually, he is occupied with his formulas and no one invades his soul. He's not a philosopher or a historian who is obliged to produce so many pages every six months in order to have his bread. So that the scientists are coming to Christianity now with greater intensity and in greater numbers than those who are in the humanities. Generally, a person in the humanities is already a degenerate by the time he is 30. He's a person who already for 10 years, right from his student days, 10 years in a row must step by step say what he doesn't think and then begin to think what he says. And that's it.

Q. And how do you regard such occurrences as General Grigorenko?

This is a miracle. It happens that God's spark suddenly strikes a man and explodes in him. He is not an ideologue, not anyone but a warrior, a general, a military man who is of flesh and bones, a peasant. And suddenly his conscience did not allow him something and he made a protest. And then he confronted the system and was enlightened to all its lies and so he began, in his own way, a general's way, to try and break the wall. And now that wall is literally trying to crush him. He is simply being murdered in that insane asylum. He has been in it for several years and I don't know what is left of him.

Q. And do you think that there is hope that this resurrection of spirit that occurred will continue?

There is always hope as long as a man is alive.

Q. But in the last 40 years, they succeeded in suppressing this spirit. During Stalin, I mean.

Nothing can be built without a spirit; even to destroy one needs spirit. When Stalin was alive, there was a great spirit. To bring so many sacrifices one must have a great strength. Spirit is needed for evil deeds too. And they are at present powerless in this sense.

Q. So that Brezhnev and Kosygin . . .

Who are they? Just functionaries of the system. The system itself lived itself out.

Q. And the fact that the active members of the Democratic Movement are leaving or are being imprisoned will not stop that spirit?

No, I don't think so. First of all, not all active people are leaving. And in the same way that the spirit of liberty was born in those people, so it will be born in others in the future.

Q. Could you tell me about your first day in the West, your first impressions?

My first day was just a kind of adjustment to the new exterior. Then it began to astound me purely emotionally, that is, by psychological pressure—the advertising, for example. Because in the Soviet Union we live in a world in which there is little external emotional pressure. And perhaps our inner sense is sharper.

Q. Doesn't the propaganda affect emotions?

Propaganda is a different matter. I don't think it affects us emotionally or intellectually. It's a different channel to which a person adjusts quickly. But here what I mean is this brightness, the intensity of colors. It's not the grayness, the scarcity of our life. It's like a person who steps out of the room with closed shutters into the bright light. And naturally it hurts. It burns. And this is the impression I had from the bright streets in the center of Paris or Vienna. But maybe it is my own personal perception.

Q. Do the ads irritate you?

They do and don't. Because that loud, colorful sight of a Western city in contrast to our grayness is an irritation in itself. And at first it was very difficult for me; it is still difficult. That is why I avoid these bright streets of the city's center and always try to go by the side streets.

Q. Are you used to the idea that your future lies in the West? Does it scare you?

It scares me, of course. But I would use another word. What scares me is not fear, but a different perspective of existence. Before, I lived with different postulates of existence. And coming here I suddenly am confronted by the fact that my postulates of existence are . . . that in this world, not that they are not needed, but that they will lose value. Every man to remain being a man must build these postulates of being in order to oppose the social system over there. I built mine. It was a kind of spiritual skeleton, or a world which I have been constructing for a long time in order to live, in order to preserve myself. And of course it was very valuable to me. So I came here with my own structure, my own home. And I saw that my world is not of value here. I had such suppositions while still in the Soviet Union, but when I had to confront the fact itself it terrified me.

Q. That world is not of value to others?

Yes, but . . . No. That world doesn't have the same value for me that it had there. And thus I will have to rebuild my attitude toward it. What frightens me is not the external differences in the West, not even the separation from those people whom I left in the Soviet Union, but this dilemma. Not to be unfaithful to myself, which is very easy to do when one changes the environment in this way. And it is also easy to close up. I don't want to do that. This fact of existence is facing me now.

YURI SHTEIN

When Yuri Shtein decided to apply for an exit visa in June, 1971, he had to wait for nine months for an answer. Inquiring at the Soviet visa bureau (OVIR), he was given to understand that his case would not be decided at that office. It might have been so because Yuri Shtein was the first of the most active dissidents to ask for a visa. In a way, he had created a precedent, and when his case was being deliberated in higher spheres than the OVIR, it was probably a decision not only whether to let Yuri Shtein emigrate, but whether to allow the dissidents to leave.

Though Yuri Shtein, a film director in Moscow, was himself not too willing to talk about his role in the Democratic Movement, I have been told that it was considerable. His house was a home for all those who came to Moscow from other parts of the Soviet Union to seek counsel or make contact with the dissidents. Indeed, when people speak of Shtein, they usually speak of the Shtein home or the Shtein family: Yuri's wife Veronika, warm, motherly, hospitable; his 20-year-old daughter Lena, somber and quiet; and his younger daughter Liliya, bright and effervescent. Liliya, who was 12 when they left Moscow, says, "These were the best, the most memorable years of my life. It could never be repeated again. I met so many remarkable, wondrous people. I will live with those memories the rest of my life."

In New York the Shtein family is still a home for many Russian emigrants; their Woodside apartment is always crowded. As in Moscow, people gather for warmth and food and conversation. But it is now more a shelter than a place of action. And although most of their income goes for helping their friends who are still in Moscow, Yuri Shtein looks bereaved in this country. The help they can render is not action, and Yuri is one of those people who cannot be satisfied with just a job, a splended family, and many friends.

Q. Do you think that the majority of people before 1953 thought their system politically illegal and that after Khrushchev's thaw they felt that the system was legitimate?

Until 1953 the system was totally repressive, but there were people who still believed in it. The authorities had support. But the Twentieth Party Congress cut the roots of the system; not just the Khrushchev speech, but the reexamination of the criminal code and the promise of freedom. In general, people accepted the Twentieth Congress not with malevolence but with hope. People who never before thought of joining the Party wanted to join, wanted to be a part of what they thought would be a healthy process. I don't recall that there were any kind of disturbances following the Twentieth Congress (except perhaps in Georgia) even though such horrors were revealed. If before there were only individuals like Raskolnikov who would dare write a letter (he wrote to Stalin) and pay with their lives for it, now people saw that the price was different. So they'd kick you out from your job, or they wouldn't let you defend your dissertation. Even when they took Khaustov from the demonstration on Pushkin Square, they only gave him three years and everyone was outraged, even though three years was child's play. In Stalin's time it would have been considered extremely fortunate to get three years. In this way people began to see their own possibilities.

Q. Does the average Soviet man have any notion of the Democratic Movement?

Those who want to know, do know. But the majority of people are preoccupied with their jobs, everyday concerns, and are very far from it all.

Q. Are there any people in this movement who are not Intelligentsia, the so-called "simple" people.

Yes. Khaustov is a worker. Gershuni is a stonecutter. Professionally they are not Intelligentsia, but in essence they are because they are concerned with the values of freedom and justice. The first protest letters were written primarily by scholars, but the main body of those who fought repressions were professional people.

Q. Who or what pushed you onto that road?

I was friends with General Grigorenko and others, but the decisive moment was the Czech invasion. I had known Pavel Litvinov, Larisa Bogoraz, read their letters, admired them, went to Pushkin Square but didn't participate, even though I did sign some letters in 1966 in defense of Galanskov and Ginzburg. And perhaps if it had not been for the Czech invasion I would have remained inactive. But when it happened I went to Red Square with Pavel Litvinov even though I finally didn't dare to demonstrate with them.

Q. How did the people react in general?

People in general didn't think about it. They accepted the official version. They didn't care. They passed by the headlines on the streets without stopping. Where I worked a meeting was called. Usually, in such cases, meetings are called and a designated person makes a speech and then a resolution is made. But a resolution is never put out for voting. But this time they asked for votes on the resolution. That was unprecedented. And I voted against the resolution all alone.

Q. Did you know what the consequence would be? Or was it emotional?

No, not emotional. I simply didn't have any right to vote for it. Perhaps if I'd known what would happen at that meeting, I wouldn't have gone, but since I found myself in that situation I couldn't approve of it. I understood that it was an intervention. I was already on that level of consciousness when it's impossible to make deals. When they ask you directly, "Who is for, raise your hand." Here I crossed the line of the possible. It is said that there were about 80 people like that in Moscow. It's very little, but also it's a lot. I didn't pay too big a price. I lost my job, but I was revealed and had to become active.

Q. What kind of a childhood did you have, the usual Soviet childhood with Pioneers and Komsomol?

Not exactly in such steps. My father was arrested in front of me in 1937. True, he was freed just before the war and he died in the war. Then my mother got married the second time and her husband was arrested. So I had some kind of preparation in childhood. But I was a Pioneer and then, at the age of 17, I went to war and I was in the army seven years, 1943 to 1950. I was thrown out of Komsomol, but not for any political reasons; it was an incident with a soldier.

Q. Did you serve in the country or overseas?

I was in Romania, in Poland, in Germany.

Q. Did you see anything revealing on those trips abroad?

I didn't see, but I heard. I wasn't in the infantry, so I didn't walk through towns; I was flying in and out the airports.

Q. And when the war was over?

I served until 1950 and then took correspondence courses at the University of Moscow.

Q. Was there a GI Bill of Rights for former military people?

No, the education is free anyway. Even before I finished the courses I already was working at a television studio and there I got interested in films. I edited a television-film magazine, then wrote some screen plays myself, then began to work as a director.

Q. What kind of censorship exists in the films?

I worked in educational films. The censorship is special there. Every inch of the film is checked by a special censor. He must see that no military object gets on the screen and so on. In the regular films they have a general censorship as they have for literature, theater, and radio, but we had a visual censor besides, from the point of view of national defense.

Q. For whom are these educational films made?

Well, for example, for medical schools. They film the human brain, things like that. But when you film factories, mills, here they must check every object.

Q. What kind of censorship did you have in screenwriting?

The editor is a kind of censor. The big screenplays are sent to the Committee of Cinematography and there the censors read them. But the educational screenwriting is censored by an editor.

Q. Generally in America the criterion for making films is whether the film will make money or not; how about in the Soviet Union?

No, the commercial aspect is the least important. The educational films bring no profit at all, and the other films have, first of all, ideological considerations. True, in the second stage, the distribution stage, people are interested in making money, but they are powerless to approve the film before that. Sometimes they can influence the censor if they are sure that the film would bring a lot of profit. After all, they have a certain plan to fulfill, not a personal plan, but a work plan, and they can pressure the censor. This was true with the film *Andrei Rublev;* they managed to get the film on the screen after six years.

Q. What was wrong with that film?

They found it to be anti-Russian, that it distorted Russian history. It was sold in France, but it was forbidden in the Soviet Union. The distributors knew that the film was sensational and that the West would buy it. So they managed to prove that there was no sedition in it. The same thing happened with the film, *We'll Live till Monday*. The distributors knew that this film would be even more popular than *Rublev* because *Rublev* is interesting only to a cultivated audience.

Q. Who gets the profits?

The distributors have a schedule of payments they make to the Government. Films are one of the two main sources of profit for the Government.

Q. What's the second?

Vodka. So the distributors are interested in fulfilling the payment schedule. They get their salaries, but if the schedule isn't fulfilled their career is affected. But the censors are not at all interested in how much was spent and how much profit could be made. Their sphere is ideological. So they shelve the films that aren't ideologically correct.

Q. What happens to the people who make a film that isn't approved?

Nothing, they still get their salaries. But it's unpleasant, and not so good for a career.

Q. In America an unknown director can become famous overnight if he makes a very successful film. But if then he makes bad ones, he can be forgotten overnight too. Is this true there?

It's not at all like that in the Soviet Union. The name of a director is made not only by public success but also by his reception with the authorities—by the Ministry of Culture and Cinematography. If a film is political, a director can be promoted, given a title, and become famous not because the public likes him but because of the propaganda value of the film. Sometimes the two coincide. A director who has become famous can then make weak films, but his title is for life and his position is stable. Even if he makes a very bad film, no one will fire him. We have Chukhrai, who made some good films, then didn't make any and then made some mediocre ones—he is still a Laureate of Lenin's Prize, still a People's Artist. A category cannot be taken away.

Q. What category?

We have four categories: third, second, first, and highest. I was of the second category. Your category may be taken away only for political reasons, but that's rare. That's the advantage of that system. If a director is really very weak, he can be transferred to a documentary studio, but he won't be fired.

Q. You mean because he works for a studio owned by the Government?

Yes. A director is not worried about his livelihood; they are obliged to guarantee him work.

Q. For how long?

A master director makes one film in four or five years. He can make a film and then take four years to write a screenplay. And all the while he gets his pay. If he is a People's Artist, then he is elite. He doesn't have to work creatively at all, in fact. I never worried there whether I'd have work or not.

Q. Is it possible for an unknown director to make a film and become known overnight because the public liked his work?

Yes, it was this way with Tarkovsky. He made *Ivan's Childhood* and became instantly popular. His second film was *Andrei Rublev.*

Q. Well, after he became popular did his opportunities increase? I mean could he do what he couldn't before?

Not quite. Here you have a good example. Even though he became very popular and became a master, his film *Rublev* was not allowed to be shown. Now he has made another film, *Solaris.* In *Rublev* he wanted to show the Russian Christian period, but his concept was not acceptable. The only requirement is to maintain a certain level. Even a master director is not allowed to do what he wants. He has a name, he wears medals, he is bought by the Government and must do what is wanted.

Q. When I was in Moscow in 1966, I met a young director who made a film called *Never.* The film was shown for a week and then Jean-Paul Sartre wrote a very favorable review of it, saying it was the first psychological film and so on. And the film was then taken off the screen.

So? It's natural.

Q. Natural? But why was it allowed in the first place if there was something in it?

You know how this happens. They allow a film to be distributed. Then some very influential person happens to see it and he says, "What did you allow on the screen?" And that's all. It was this way with *Sadko.*

Q. But isn't that a totally harmless fairy tale?

Yes, harmless. But after one high official saw it and found a mockery of the Russian people in it, it was taken off, though later it was reinstated.

Q. A single person can do that?

Depends on what kind of person. If he is from the Central Committee or the Politburo, it takes a single phone call. Nikita Khrushchev liked to watch the popular educational films, especially those in which the collective farmers were glorified. One time he didn't like a film—a film about growing vegetables on stony soil—and there was a scandal. The director and the editor of the film were fired. And no one knows what he didn't like about the film.

Q. Do they still consider Eisenstein the greatest?

Yes, he was a major figure in film history. As for the greatest, everything is relative. The people don't know him too well; he isn't popular. But the directors learn from him.

Q. Are there special schools for film directors?

In Moscow there is an Institute of Cinematography. It trains directors, cameramen, screenwriters, editors, producers, and film critics.

Q. How free is a film critic?

It's the most unfree work. It's a sphere of journalism and of literature and subject to censorship of the press. If the film is already approved, then he can praise it.

Q. Can he criticize it?

No, not too much. And if it's approved by the highest authorities, not at all.

Q. What about such films as Tolstoy's *War and Peace* or Dostoevsky's *The Idiot*, can they be considered ideological?

War and Peace, yes. With *War and Peace* the decision was made by the Ministry of Culture. Since America made one, it was decided to make it better and not to spare any expense whatsoever. It was a "social order."

Q. What is that?

A Government order, from the highest authorities. It's carte blanche for everything. If you need an actor who is in the theater, his director can argue that he is in the middle of a play and can't be spared. But when it's a social order, then there can be no argument.

Q. And it was a social order because America made one first?

That was the original push. Then they were interested in getting foreign currency for it. That is why it was made with the West in mind, and that is why there are all those folk dances and horses and balalaikas. And, indeed, it did earn a very big foreign profit, much bigger than from inside the country. And because it was a social order, the Ministry of Defense participated in it.

Q. The Ministry of Defense?

Well, yes. They needed 30,000 Cossacks and horses, and they were mobilized from the Don region.

Q. Real soldiers?

Yes, a real mobilization. No one asks questions if the Government requests 30,000 troops.

Q. So they didn't think about ideology at that time? They thought about how to best make the film?

It was a question of prestige, for a Soviet film to enter the world screen. Space is also prestige. But here it was dual—to show the West and to make money. And that's politics.

Q. Besides *War and Peace*, what other films were made as a result of social orders?

Many. Under Stalin there was film about a happy life in a collective farm, *Kuban Cossacks*. Then there was a film which was made in order to justify Stalin's repressions—*Party Card*, it was called. This was during the purges and it was about the enemies, spies. Then in 1965–1966 there was a series of films about the Chekists.

Q. But take the film *Dvoye* [Ballad of Love] with Viktoriya Fedorova, there was nothing ideological in that film, it was just a love story.

That film didn't have too much press coverage. But, look, not all films are social orders. A certain percentage of propaganda films must be made, but otherwise one may make films about love, so long as there is nothing forbidden in them. *Dvoye* is harmless. There should be some films like that, but not too many. As in literature, they can have stories about human relations, but not too many. The audience longs for films like that and so all of a sudden the theaters began to have plays (Volodin's, Rozov's) on intimate subjects—but there was a special decree not to exceed 20 percent with such topics.

Q. How long is the director's training?

Five years. That's a standard in the Soviet Union; everything is five years.

Q. What does he study in the Institute?

For the first two years he has to study mainly Marxism, the history of the Soviet Union, the history of the Communist Party. Then gradually, beginning with the third year, he begins to study the films. But it's like this everywhere; the first two years are devoted to general political subjects, then begins the specialization.

Q. Could it happen that after graduation a director can find no work?

Every graduate is supposed to get work. True, he can be sent to Central Asia or Siberia to work.

Q. Does he have a choice?

Not always. If he really excelled, or if he is someone's son, he can even get to stay in Moscow. If 12 films a year were made under Stalin, then 100 to 120 films a year were made between 1955 and 1965. But now, I know, that there are people without work.

Q. And where can he go if has no job? Is there unemployment insurance?

No, he has to find another job. But there isn't a problem in unemployment there. Where one person could do the job, we have five.

Q. Where do actors and actresses study?

They have actors' studios. They don't learn there, but they practice there what they've learned in the film institutes. The film directors go there to cast for films. That's how actors get into pictures.

Q. What do they do in between pictures?

They have to be there and mark time; they get paid for it. Sometimes a theater casts them in a play.

Q. How about famous actors and actresses?

They can do what they want in between films. They don't have to work but once in a while; they get a salary in any case and also have categories like the directors.

Q. Do you have a star system like we do? Can an actress demand any salary she wants?

No, of course not. The top actress makes top salary; 50 rubles a day when she is filming. If a man is a People's Actor he gets this top salary when he makes a film; he can get 40 or 60 rubles a day. The other actors get from 12 rubles a day and up.

Q. Are there no exceptions?

The single exception is for the role of Lenin. This is a command, that anyone playing the role of Lenin, even if he appears in one episode, is to get 75 rubles a day—even if it's an inexperienced child who plays Lenin as a child.

Q. What's required to play Lenin?

Resemblance and luck. This was decreed after Stalin.

Q. And during Stalin who played him?

Only one man could play Stalin on the screen, Gelovani.

Q. Did Gelovani play any other roles?

No, he played only Stalin. This was his specialty. People's Artist Gelovani of the Georgian U.S.S.R. He died right after Stalin.

Q. By natural death?

Yes. He devoted his entire life to this role. He didn't do anything else, and when the one whom he played died, he died too. He wasn't old.

Q. Did he resemble Stalin?

In the way that Stalin wanted to be resembled. Stalin, as you know, was little and pockmarked. Gelovani was tall and impressive, that is, he was the way Stalin ought to have been. He was taken everywhere by car. His salary was of no concern to the directors, and he had his own bank account, which was unprecedented.

Q. Can an actor refuse to play a certain role?

A known actor can. But he can't refuse to play for a certain salary; that is all set.

Q. What if a film makes millions of rubles—does the actor get anything extra?

The group can get little extra money. An actor can win a Lenin or Government prize. That's money.

Q. Is there such a thing as a buildup of a certain actor or actress?

No. There is such a thing as a buildup of a writer, an obliging writer. The press glorifies him. But there is no publicity for films in general; it's not needed.

Q. I heard an expression, "a KGB film." What is that?

Well, the film about the Chekists was a KGB film; it glorified the work of the KGB against the CIA and other enemies.

Q. Can an actor refuse to play in a KGB film?

No, he or she can say that the role is not suitable, but it's impossible to reveal political motives.

Q. And then?

Then they can try and convince an actor. He or she can be called for a discussion. But he can't be forced to play it, especially if he isn't a Party member.

Q. And if he is a Party member?

Then it's simple. They'll say, "the Party asks you," and that's it.

Q. So it's better not to be a member?

Of course. Usually the untalented actors are members. The talented don't need the Party. It's different with production; an engineer for example, no matter how talented, must be a Party member in order to occupy a certain position.

Q. Why does Party membership help?

The film about the Chekists was made by a Party director. It's a deal.

Q. Are there any people who believe in the Communist Party for idealistic reasons?

Not now. It's only deals. A Party card is a bread ticket. Under Stalin, and even during the Twentieth Congress, there were people who really believed. Not now.

Q. Do they ask you if you are a Party member when you look for a job?

They don't have to. The question is in the application you have to fill out. Lately they have a new decree that certain jobs are not available except for Party members. That's to have more control over the population.

Q. What do you think is the future of the Democratic Movement?

The situation is too complex to judge without being there.

Q. Will others start?

Probably, but it'll be a different kind of battle.

Q. I don't understand how a court can override the decision of the medical doctors if it's a psychiatric hospital.

Humanely speaking, it's impossible. But over there everything is possible. This is how these things are done. At first someone in the KGB in Moscow decided to give the command, "Let him out; he'll die soon anyway." So he is pronounced well. But then someone who is higher up decides that he shouldn't be free. Or, "What? You didn't ask me? No, he can't be freed." So the court reverses the decision.

Q. Practically speaking, what harm can a man like Grigorenko do now?

Nothing. It's a machine which doesn't arrest people too easily nowadays, but from which it is far more difficult to free a man.

Q. And what about Amalrik?

From their point of view they have more reasons to think that Amalrik is dangerous because he is still young (35), even though his heart is bad and he was ill with meningitis and almost died. With Grigorenko it was pure mockery.

Q. How do you compare the present Democratic Movement with the nineteenth-century Intelligentsia movement?

It's a different situation altogether. In the nineteenth century there were legal avenues. The people were respected and conducted a normal fight. They had publications as an outlet. All this led to the creation of the Duma, for example. Both the nineteenth-century Intelligentsia and the present one are Westernizers, but the situation is now totally different. In this new movement there was a threat from the beginning, the threat of arrests and repressions, and the only outlet was Samizdat, and such journals as the *Chronicle*, *Syntax*, and others. One of the main merits of the movement is that it showed what was possible for those who were capable of understanding it and wanted to participate in it. Because even after the Twentieth Congress the people continued to live with past fears and didn't know what was allowed, and it turned out that a lot was allowed. It was possible to speak with foreigners, to say what you think, not to attend some meetings, not to vote in the elections. This is what we did; all those things that were unthinkable before. As Amalrik said, "It turned out that a police state was forced to function liberally."

Q. What was your first Western city? And your first impressions?

Rome. I found many surprises. In the Soviet Union mass culture is not on a high level, and for me Rome was always the symbol of culture, of ancient culture. And when I saw that, except for a few films, most of them are on such a low commercial and sexual level, I was shocked. It was insulting. And I understood that the Soviet propaganda that tells us day and night about those things was not lying. With TV it's the same thing. The second thing that was shocking was how little people read. And that they seriously read comics. It's degrading. In the United States there were other disappointments. I thought of America as a strong country, more unified than it is. And the life-style is so different. No one walks, everyone rides. I think it's easier in Europe. Because in Europe a newcomer, a person from a big city who is used to large crowds in the streets, does not feel lonely.

Q. So you think that for a Soviet man America is very difficult?

For a Soviet person, if young and unformed, like my younger daughter, it won't be difficult. But for a formed person, a member who is of the Intelligentsia, it is very difficult, at least in the beginning. There is this isolation in the American life-style. In Italy it was nice to walk in the streets because the Italians always walk around you. Here, in Washington, it's not frightening to walk, it's just sad to walk, because no one walks for the sake of walking. And the human contacts are not the same, all those lunches . . . It's not the same as people coming to your house in Moscow to talk all night.

GRIGORI SVIRSKI

In 1941, when the German tanks were surging into Russia and the airport was burning, Svirski, an aviator in the Northern Fleet, saw a cart full of children passing by. Because the children looked exhausted and hungry he ran after the cart and threw his ration of dry fish and bread to them. Suddenly he heard the voice of his commander, "What, you saw your own?" It took Svirski some minutes to understand what he meant. The children were dark-haired and probably Jewish. Because it was not a German who said it but a soldier in the Red Army, the incident remained with Svirski as the moment when he understood what the word "nationality" meant in his passport. Before that he never thought of himself as other than a Russian. When he returned from the war he became a writer and a journalist and began his fight against anti-Semitism. Today, 30 years later, Svirski is still writing (*The Hostages* is his latest book), and during the Yom Kippur war he served as a free-lance correspondent in Israel where he has lived since 1972.

The interview took place in March of 1973, in Paris, where Svirski was the main witness in an unprecedented trial in which the Soviet Information Service was convicted for publishing an article, "The Obscurantist School," in its September 12, 1972, issue. Svirski produced a 1906 Czarist pogrom document, "The Jewish Question: Of the Impossibility of Granting Rights for Jews," and proved that many excerpts from this document corresponded sentence by sentence to those in the Information Bulletin.

Because of his formidable eyebrows, ruffled hair and the impatience that spills into every movement of his strong body, Svirski can impress one as ferocious. But that ferociousness is fleeting; it can turn instantly into humor or sadness. Although Svirsky has spent his life fighting anti-Semitism, one doesn't have a feeling that he is truly at home in Israel. He is still wandering, seeking for the end to Exodus.

Q. Do you consider yourself basically a writer or a journalist?

Basically a writer. Though I've been a correspondent as well. I belong to the generation of writers that came with the war, and I began to write because I wanted to tell about my comrades who were killed in the war. I was in the Northern Fleet's naval aviation; we battled the Germans who were flying over the American and English convoys going to Murmansk. And while it was possible in other places to parachute, it was impossible here, because underneath us was the Barents Sea, that sea plus three degrees. If a man jumped he would have had a paralysis of the heart within six minutes. And when I came back, I had nine government medals and they told me at Moscow University that they would be unable to accept me in the Department of Russian Literature. I grabbed the dean and shook him, and instead of calling the police he locked the door and said, "Never mind, never mind, it will all work out in the end." In a little while, a friend of mine, a pilot, who wasn't a Muscovite, came to Moscow because he wanted to enter the diplomatic service. He stayed with me. He had 12 war medals. By then I knew how a Jew is sometimes treated, so I told him, "Put on all your medals and I'll put on all mine and we shall go together. And if they won't accept you, we will turn all their tables upside down." And so we came to that diplomatic school, ringing like horses on parade, and ready to create a great scandal if someone would try to lie to us or to cover up. But instead, a rather suave, half-diplomat received us and told us plainly and directly that he will not accept our documents at all because the only people who get accepted in the diplomatic service are people of "the needed nationality." It was in this way that I found out that anti-Semitism exists not only among the uneducated, not only on the kitchen-scandal level, but that it exists on the highest state level. Can you imagine the terror of it? When having come back from such a war, a war for Russia in which you were ready to die gladly for your country, to come back from the Barents Sea and find out that you are not a part of "the needed nationality," that you are an inferior human being? And that is why, no matter what I wrote later, I always addressed myself to the theme of anti-Semitism. Because it was not only my affair, not only my thought, but my pain.

As soon as Stalin died I wrote an article, "Vagon Molchal" ("The Railroad Car Was Silent"). I described how a drunk man shouted in the car, "Hitler didn't get all of you kikes," and everyone in the car was silent. I wasn't interested in that drunk fool. I was interested in the many people who were in that car. Why were they all silent? And when he began to swear, they all screamed, "Don't swear, there are children in this car!" But as soon as he began to shout anti-Semitic slogans, everyone was silent again. For five years I watched that kind of drunkard and each time I would try to bring him to the police, so that for once they would just make a file about an anti-Semite. But not once did I succeed. Once I was so fed up that I took out my Writers' Union membership card and said, "Either you make up a file or else there'll be a scandal," and the lieutenant on duty, at the Kursk subway station in Moscow, asked me to step into another room. "Look," he said, "if I'll write that this man is an anti-Semite, we wouldn't be able to give him even 24 hours. But if I'll write that he was disturbing the peace, we can give him 15 days."

I didn't believe it and went to court to find out if that was true. The judge was very smart; he understood exactly what I wanted and he said, "Tomorrow I have a similar case. Come and you'll understand everything." The next day in court there was some loose female who had apparently insulted a middle-aged watchman, who was a Tatar, and the judge asks, "What did you call him?"

"Tatar's pig ear." The secretary of the court doesn't write it down.

"What else?"

"All Tatars are speculators." The secretary remains in the sphinx position.

"What else?" the judge asks.

"An old fool," she answers, and the secretary of the court writes it out immediately.

And thus I understood all the mechanics of this uncomplicated lie, and it became clear to me why the statistics of nationalistic crimes do not exist in the Soviet Union. In every court, in every police station there is that cipher through which all those cases are sifted out, and that is the reason there are no files. So that the leaders may quite honestly say, "There isn't any anti-Semitism in the Soviet Union."

Q. Did you want to write before you went to war?

Before the war I was only a schoolboy. I went to war directly from high school at 18. Like all children I wrote poems as a child, and the teacher praised my compositions; in short, I was more attracted to literature than to science.

Q. But it was the war that crystallized your desire to become a writer?

Yes, exactly. Because my closest friends perished and I wanted others to know about them. Among those friends many were *shtrafnye*, that means people who were put in prisons during Stalin's repressions, imprisoned for nothing. Those who were aviators among them were freed to fight in the war. They were soldiers, but they were never given any medals, even though they had very important tasks and were very courageous. It was thought that since they were prisoners, they had to wash with their own blood the crimes they had never committed. My desire to tell about these beautiful people made me pick up the pen.

Q. What did you write first?

I wrote a short novel that came out in 1947 and was called *Commandment of Friendship*.

Q. Did you encounter any difficulties in publishing it?

Well, I came to the publisher with a lot of medals. They needed war stories and had nothing about the Northern Fleet. So they accepted it. It wasn't too good. It was a book by an airline mechanic rather than by a writer. Later I rewrote it completely because the subject was very dear to me and I felt its helplessness.

Q. From the artistic point of view?

Yes. Then I wrote a film scenario from it. Much later it was made into a film. I took the entire studio to the airport where I fought during the war. The film was called *Here Places Are Quiet*. It was a powerful film and it would have been significant if the censors hadn't cut one-fourth of it out. They cut it because of those shtrafnye. Because there weren't any shtrafnye, just as there is no anti-Semitism in Russia. We had the best director, Mikhail Romm, who died recently. The film came out, but it was crippled because the main character was one of those shtrafnye and the main hero was cut out.

Q. Did you try to do something about it?

Of course, my God. I had a pass for the Mosfilm [Moscow film] Studios and I threw it in the face of the Mosfilm's manager and left. I knew there was nothing to do about it. Millions of rubles were invested in that film; they couldn't ban it—and I wouldn't have wanted it banned because all those people, actors and workers, who worked devotedly on that film would have lost their salaries.

Q. Did the film bring you recognition?

I don't know. Films do not bring recognition to the screenwriters. What did bring me renown was my book, *Lenin Prospekt,* which is written in a very juicy, peasant language. And even though, again, it was crippled by the censors, it raised one of the most important questions of the Soviet Union—the silence of workers, the theme of "people are speechless." Unfortunately, because of censorship requirements I had to stuff it with superfluous "labor heroism," otherwise it would have never come out. But my main theme is pretty clear. They were afraid of that theme—the silence of the workers—because it's never been done before. After all, the Revolution was accomplished by the workers, the State is considered to be a Workers' State, though the working man has no power, no voice. Still, the novel did come out in 1962.

Q. Well, of course, the post-Stalin thaw.

Oh, under Stalin I would have been arrested the minute I showed up with the manuscript. There were a lot of reviews designed to stamp me out. I was told by my friends who worked in one of the publishing houses how they planned it. But a well-known writer, Stepan Zlobin, ex-prisoner of Hitler's camps, a brave man, took up my defense. He was a madly courageous man, an old Russian nobleman, about 60 years old. He understood what the novel was about and wrote a good review.

Q. You mean he defended you publicly?

Yes. In Russia it's this way: if one newspaper publishes an article or a review it means that the opinions expressed in it are approvable, that they are in accordance with the Party apparatus. So within a month of Zlobin's review, 50 or 60 newspapers and journals published other favorable reviews. In this way the book was recognized and came out in a second edition of 150,000 copies. If I hadn't had that book and that success, I wouldn't have been allowed on a tribune as a public speaker, as nine-tenths of the members of the Soviet Writers' Union are not allowed.

Q. But how did Zlobin manage to write this first review, or have it printed?

By being clever and cunning. The main thing was not to say what the novel was about, but to praise it.

Q. From the point of view of Socialist Realism?

Of course. He emphasized the production of the workers. As for my main theme he . . . not that he was totally silent about it, but he was very careful about what he said. And so for the second edition I shortened all the production stuff and put some other things back that the censors had previously taken out.

Q. How could you do that?

Since the novel had once been approved for publication and this was the second edition, they didn't look carefully—they just told me to prepare the second edition. So I put in two or three chapters. My editor didn't notice; it was a half-liberal time, 1964, and people were not so careful. But it was the end. In 1964 Khrushchev was kicked out and for about six months it wasn't clear where the cart was going to go, to the left or to the right. At that time we all tried to turn it to the left, but it went right. Then I decided to speak out. It was a very risky thing to do because I spoke against censorship, which no one ever spoke about. It was two years before Aleksandr Solzhenitsyn spoke up against it. I called it "osoboye soveshchaniye of literature. Osoboye Soveshchaniye [special board] was a trinity during Stalin; three people could decide to execute people without any trial. Just like that, three people could call someone and pass a verdict of 15 years, 20 years, or a death sentence. Three minutes and the fate of a man was decided. And I said that even though this practice was abolished in the criminal law, because of censorship it was still in effect in literature. Censorship forbids without explanation. There is the censor and yet it is as though he doesn't exist. There is a precise word in Arabic, *mafya,* and it means that which doesn't exist. There are elements of mafya in everything in Russia: anti-Semitism doesn't exist, censorship doesn't exist. And when mafya becomes the face of the State then we can consider that nothing exists.

Q. But what about observing Soviet laws?

They are observed if at a particular moment it's not necessary to break the law. For instance, I once tried to defend some collective farmers in a certain village. The farmers asked me to come. They sent a collective letter from Mordvinian villages, saying that they had been driven to complete beggary there. They asked me to come and see for myself how many crooks there were. I went and saw it and tried to defend them, but my report was taken out of the newspaper, *Sovetskaya Rossiya.* They took it off the galleys. The Secretary of the Central Committee explained to me that since that region gave a lot of bread, it was no use criticizing them. If it had been Sverdlovsk country, he said, that was weak on bread delivery, and then it would have been all right.

Q. All right to denounce them in other ways?

That's right. You see, they have their own inhuman norms. They think that we should not blame the secretary of the Obkom because he did deliver the bread. The fact that his farmers are dying is not important. If they were dying in Sverdlovsk, then it would have been all right to write about it, because they not only die there but they don't deliver enough bread.

Q. These farmers asked you specifically, and they asked you to write it in a newspaper?

Yes. This was a scream for help, a soul cry with 300 signatures. They asked me because they knew me as a person of sharp words. They knew a soft writer would never go there. It's a risky business; it's necessary to argue with the secretary of the Obkom, who is usually a member of the Supreme Soviet. So I went. But to answer your original question: the laws exist, but they are observed only when it is profitable. The attitude is always pragmatic; pragmatism is the philosophy there, a way of life.

Q. Did you ever try to write anything else that was risky?

Well, I told you I wrote "The Railroad Car Was Silent." That was never published. I still have it. I used some of it in my novel. I tried and couldn't publish anything on the Jewish question. But I did manage to publish some short pieces. For example, in 1955 I wrote an article, "How One Is Untaught to Think on Marxist Faculties."

Q. Where was it published? And how did you manage it?

It was published in the Party magazine, *Partinaya Zhizn*. I managed to do it because it was the end of 1955. I didn't yet know what they knew, that in a month there was to be the Twentieth Party Congress and the dethronement of the "cult of personality."

Q. You mean they knew ahead of time that Khrushchev was going to dethrone Stalin? It wasn't a surprise?

No, of course not. What do you think? Every report for such an occasion is in preparation for at least three months. It is prepared by the apparatus. Do you suppose Khrushchev prepared this all by himself? My God, nothing is done that way. Khrushchev was a personality; he gave directions and told them how to work them out. But Brezhnev receives everything ready-made; it's the apparatus that prepares everything now.

Q. But surely for the people it was a bombshell?

Of course, for the people it was. But the people who worked for the *Partinaya Zhizn* journal understood ahead of time what was what. They worked in the same building as Khrushchev, on the Old Square, in the office of the Central Committee of the Party. That's how I was able to publish this particular article. I wanted to research how people are taught to think in the universities. I attended a graduate seminar in philosophy, and heard a graduate student panning some plays. He did not just criticize them, but pretended to be doing it in a scholarly way. I raised my hand humbly and asked, "Which of these plays have you seen or read?" And he answered, "I haven't read them, and I haven't seen them because they were never staged in Odessa." So I said, "Excuse me, but on what basis do you criticize them?" And he replied, "There are reviews, there are articles in the papers." In short, I saw a bright young man, not just some amateur, but a fourth-year student of philosophy who gave a report at a scholarly meeting based not on his own but on someone else's opinion.

Q. Surely that was nothing new for you?

No, but it was an excuse for a serious discussion. His attitude was sincerely that "if the newspapers write about it, it's irreversible. Why study the subject or think about it?" So I used it as the starting point for my article, to analyze the situation. Here was a man who was going to be a philosopher in a year: how was he led in four years to the conviction that it was possible to base his research on newspaper reviews alone?

Q. Was his professor there? Did he say anything?

The professor was there and he was only concerned that everything should go well, smoothly, quietly, so that the professor himself wouldn't be worked over by the Party bureau. So I began to look into this situation. Was the professor a fool? No, he was not. I began to pull different strings and it came out that his chairman of the department of Marxist studies was a bandit who had put hundreds of people in prisons in 1937. If a man would have said something on his own, he would be denounced as a corrupter of Marxism, and so on. These scoundrels created an atmosphere in which people were afraid to think or to say something that wasn't written down officially. That's the way they train their students. And a student doesn't know that his professor lives and works in fear.

Q. A student doesn't know it?

In general a student doesn't clearly understand the underlying relationship in an educational collective. How could he? But he does see that the professor lectures without taking his finger off the prepared lecture, with textbooks and footnotes, how he never deviates. So the student begins to do the same. And when several generations are brought up like this, for 40 years, it's difficult to know that things could be different. This is the difference between the West and the Soviet Union. In the West there are 20 newspapers, and one can fish out the truth from them, and there they have one single newspaper and one must have a tremendously keen mind to arrive at some kind of truth through all the lies. There isn't any comparison.

Q. And when you printed this article was there a reaction?

Yes, a scandal. You see this was the magazine of the Central Committee of the Communist Party, the most official Party journal there is. The editors are all Secretaries of the Central Committee; you couldn't go higher than that.

Q. I still don't understand why they published your article.

Only because they heard that at the Twentieth Party Congress there would be some kind of new moves. Something was in the air, something new. Perhaps they thought it would be timely to publish such an article.

Q. That was before the publication of *One Day in the Life of Ivan Denisovich?*

Oh, sure; six years before. *Ivan Denisovich* came out in 1962, the same year as my novel, *Lenin Prospekt.* It was a bright interlude, but soon after there was the famous meeting between Khrushchev and the Intelligentsia and everything was closed up after that.

Q. What meeting was that?

In March of 1963. Khrushchev called the meeting, and he screamed at Yevtushenko and Voznesensky. He stamped his feet and shouted wildly and accused the artists who were abstractionists of being agents of Imperialism. And after that everything was closed, one couldn't publish anything serious. Solzhenitsyn published a couple of small things and that was that.

Q. It's always been unclear to me, though I've been to the Soviet Union several times, why Khrushchev, who more than anyone else initiated some liberalization, is not liked in the Soviet Union. Can you tell me why?

Because he did not justify the hopes that he called forth. The people thought that since he told everything, how millions were killed in Stalin's time, that there was real hope. And then he began to dance the other way and sat down on the throne himself. In three years he became the czar himself.

Q. So that is the main reason?

It's too complicated. There are many components. Some didn't like him for that. The military hated him because he cut their pensions. The generals' pension was cut in half. The party workers hated him for the cleanup. The peasants hated him because he interfered in agricultural affairs without knowing anything about them. The artists and writers had this ironic attitude toward him because Khrushchev considered himself a great specialist in art and gave everyone directions in aesthetics. He was a talented, self-made man, ignorant to the limits, who thought himself an expert in everything. Therefore, it was impossible to have any kind of relationship with him. At first he brought out an indulgent laughter in people, then not so indulgent, then the heads began to fly. And so the members of the Central Committee, being afraid that he would take them on next, kicked him out.

Q. And could Khrushchev have done all that?

Very simply.

Q. One man?

Of course. He did throw out Molotov, Kaganovich, Malenkov—the old guard. Leaning on the army, on Marshal Zhukov, he threw them in the garbage. He could perform the same operation on the others.

Q. And how is it with such a stubborn and fiery temper as yours you were not put in prison?

It's more difficult to deal with writers than with the others. The writers exist verbally. All my strength was in *glasnost'*, a word that means the opposite of silence. What is said from the speaker's stand doesn't go through the censorship to start with, but there was a possibility of giving one text to the censor and saying something else too.

Q. How is that?

You add to the text you've given them. It doesn't work with the printing press; the censor would catch you. That is why Yevtushenko first read his poems from the podium. So I, too, was obliged to get on the podium and speak from there. Then those ideas exist like a stenogram, in Samizdat, and one's speech is disseminated in 100,000 copies. My speeches about censorship, about anti-Semitism—I saw them in Irkutsk, in Murmansk, in Samarkand.

Q. Weren't you threatened?

Of course I was, all the time.

Q. And were you not afraid?

I got tired of being afraid.

Q. And when Sinyavsky and Daniel were arrested, didn't that scare you? After all, the trial was designed to scare the others.

It didn't make me afraid because my line was different. I went directly, like a bear. I didn't hide. I had support. Thousands of people applauded me demonstratively, to show that they thought the same way. When people are all together they are more courageous. Later, when they are divided and taken away, one by one, it's different. But when they are all together, they feel the power of an elbow. I knew that my strength was in my being open and loud. *Le Monde* devoted a full page to my speeches, about censorship, about Solzhenitsyn, about Stalinism, and so forth. The more they know you in the West, the more difficult it becomes to deal with you in the Soviet Union. Because if they had put me in prison they could have had an international scandal, and they already got burned with the Sinyavsky and Daniel trial. If they weren't afraid of that, they would have taken care of me long ago.

Q. Do you have an impression that there is now a new Russian Intelligentsia, in the sense that it only surfaced eight or ten years ago?

There exists a new Intelligentsia, and it doesn't know the horrors of 1937. That was such a terrifying time, as though the tanks were moving on and squashing the people. It was a time when no one knew what would happen tomorrow, when in the editorial offices it was asked before publishing an article by someone, "What, isn't he in prison yet?" When people were afraid to say a word to their wives under the blanket at night because tomorrow they might land in Lubyanka or get a bullet in the back of the head. Mass terror had no limits. One could have been imprisoned because a neighbor who wanted your apartment wrote a phony report on you. And so the generation that knew this terror and lived it was broken absolutely. There were only a very few people left who remained whole, and they were usually in labor camps, people who went through everything and didn't break. Now this new Intelligentsia at times acts very sensibly against all the injustices, and at times it's just a dance of the boys who jumped out from the edge of a forest and don't know that the field has been mined. They haven't heard that they can be blown up.

Q. Well, they aren't so young. Most of them are over 35, aren't they?

It doesn't matter; they don't know 1937. They don't know what mass terror is. They don't know the consequences of playing hide-and-seek with the Government.

Q. Would you call it bravado?

No, not bravado. It's just ignorance of the dangers. One moves chest forward, thinking, "So what? So I'll spend a year in prison"—not knowing that in a year a man can be crippled completely and in two months he can be killed by being sent to work in uranium mines.

Q. Do you think that they have accomplished anything though?

Yes, they have accomplished a lot.

Q. Do you think they will continue to be effective?

No, absolutely not. Now there is a full squeeze in the Soviet Union. In view of the fact that the economic situation is getting worse all the time, it will be necessary to look for some scapegoats, and they will increase repression. And the main danger—in terms of an internal one, not in terms of external dangers like China—is that the young ones will come who, unlike Brezhnev and Kosygin, do not remember 1937. Brezhnev and Kosygin remember 1937 with their spines. They remember that mass terror is not controllable. They know that when a bloody bacchanalia begins it cannot be stopped, and it'll end up in your own office finally. Kosygin and Brezhnev not only understand it, they know it with their skin because they lived through the terror, and even though they rose through the terror, they know its reaction is circular. The young ones only heard of it; they don't know it with their gut. And that is why they can start mass bloodspilling.

Q. What was your main reason for leaving the Soviet Union? Your son?

Perhaps not the main one, but a basic one. I wanted to spare him the bitter cup of humiliation which I had to drink. But there were also other reasons. I ceased to believe in the possibility of assimilation. Because all Jews in Russia are branded as a fifth column. In the letter I wrote, I said that I am leaving an anti-Semitic State because I don't believe in the assimilation of the Jews. I wrote, "How many times have I been branded? Is it possible for a branded person to be assimilated?" Mimicry is possible, but that isn't for me. No doubt I will be nostalgic; I am a man of the Russian language, of Russian culture, and nevertheless I want to part with it because of that other, base aspect.

Q. You wrote that letter after your departure?

No, before. I placed that letter on the desk of the KGB general.

Q. Was it published in the West while you were still there?

The letter went into Samizdat and then out. It was published in *Survey* in the spring of 1972, and when I came to Israel the editor sent me a copy.

Q. Do you recall your first impressions of the West?

It's difficult for me to say because I've been in the West before. As a member of the Soviet Writers' Union I had the privilege, for my own money, in a group of 20 people, surrounded by all kinds of officials, to walk down the streets of Paris, Sweden, and Norway. So

I've seen the West, visually. Therefore, there wasn't a shock. What is difficult for me now is the competitiveness, and I find the same lack of principle here as there. For a writer there is freedom, of course, a chance to speak up. For myself it opens up gigantic possibilities, all those things that have accumulated in me can now come out.

Q. Do you think it will be expressed now?

Of course. I'll write at least two books and this is just on the material that is on top of my head, so to speak. But the most difficult thing for me is my wife's situation. I am not concerned with this Western competitiveness; I am a Russian writer with my own theme, my own material, my own ideas. I can put my desk anywhere in the world. But my wife is an important scholar. I plucked her out of the collective where she'd been working for 20 years. She is a chemist, a specialist in hybridity, those elements that kill the killers of crops. She has 22 patents that brought millions of profits to the Soviet Union and are still there, of course. When we came to Israel it took her several months to find work. She now works in a different city from the one we live in, and only because she was helped by two American scientists who know her work and took her in their car, drove around half of Israel to help her find a job.

Q. Did she want to leave Russia?

She did because my son and I wanted to leave. But there in the Soviet Union she was a student of the Academician Zelinsky, the most important chemist in the country. She left because I was cornered by my struggle, and because our son was growing up—he is 18 now.

Q. Do you think that you would have been arrested?

There isn't the slightest doubt about it. I was followed all the time.

Q. So from now on your life will be in Israel?

I don't know. Everything depends on my son, how he will get assimilated in Israel. I came to Israel in order that my son wouldn't have a feeling of being an immigrant, so that he would have a Motherland. I want him to have a country. Later, in about five years, he could go anywhere, so long as he has a sense of having a place of his own in the world. Because a man always feels badly without it. But for now it is very difficult. My wife works in one city; I live in another. Division of family on the basis of unity, you might say. And how long can that last? Six months perhaps? And if nothing works out we will be obliged to take off and search again.

MAYA ULANOVSKAYA

In the first decade of the twentieth century, many young Jews in Russia considered that a revolutionary struggle was necessary to liberate their country. They were not as concerned with anti-Semitism as with the destiny of Russia itself. In fact, they usually broke with the Jewish tradition and participated simply as revolutionaries in the nation's radical movement. Such was the family of Maya Ulanovskaya. However, by the time Maya was born in 1932, both her mother and her father were disillusioned, and when she was 15 her mother, and later her father, were arrested. Nevertheless, Maya did not question the political theories of the Revolution. She accepted all the injustices as deviations from Leninism and not as its consequences. At the age of 18 Maya herself was arrested. She was sentenced to 25 years. Thanks to Khrushchev's de-Stalinization, she served only five.

When she returned to Moscow, Maya gradually found herself in a circle of people who were either former political prisoners or their sympathizers. She married a literary critic, Anatoly Yakobson, who is a well-known dissident. Having concluded from her own experience that dissent in the Soviet Union was doomed, Maya was not active in the Democratic Movement, though she remains in sympathy with its goals. Yet despite the fact that many of their friends had been arrested and her husband was under direct threat of arrest, Maya did not want to leave Russia. Their only son, Sanya, however, a brilliant 14-year-old, began to feel a strong affinity with Israel and wanted to go there. They arrived in Israel in September, 1973. In a sense the family has returned to its roots. But the return is only physical; Maya's nostalgia for Russia is not simply homesickness, but also a traumatic sense of the loss of the true source of her being. Maya is dark-haired and frail, but the fragility is only superficial; in moments of stress another quality quickly surfaces—the quality that she must have drawn upon when at the age of 18 she had to spend one year in solitary confinement.

Q. Tell me something about your family and your own background in that family.

Both my parents come from the Ukraine. My mother came from a more Jewish environment; her childhood passed in a typical Jewish commune. Her grandfather was a well-known rabbi, thus she was brought up in a very orthodox family. But already as a very young girl she was infatuated with the Revolution. My father, who came from a much less traditional family, was much better assimilated; his background was proletarian. So their marriage was a misalliance. My father broke with his family in his early youth and became involved with the revolutionary ideas, specifically with anarchism. He was very active in the Revolution and had he been a member of the Communist Party he would have a larger part in official Revolutionary history.

Q. How old was your mother when she married your father?

She was 16. They broke completely with their background—my mother even forgot Yiddish—and dedicated themselves completely to liberating Russia from the czarist regime. They lived totally by ideology.

Q. When were you born?

I was born in 1932. By then my parents were rather disillusioned with the Soviet regime and in 1937 they simply turned away from it in horror. So I wasn't brought up in the orthodox Soviet tradition, but in the democratic one. I believed that the pre-Revolutionary regime was unjust, that we must all fight for justice and that everything that happened in Russia was a gigantic error. I was brought up, then, to believe that the Revolution was tragic, but inevitable.

Q. Nevertheless, you joined the Pioneers and went through the usual steps?

Being a Pioneer is totally automatic in the Soviet Union, but I had not been a Komsomol—first of all because by then my parents had been arrested. But unlike my parents, I wasn't a politically aware child. I was a very ordinary girl who, it is true, was interested in women's equality and thought that a girl should not spend her time being attractive. Perhaps I was myself unattractive and knew that even if I tried with some frills and things I still wouldn't attract anyone, and hence this theory. But I wasn't really socially aware and remained unaware until the day my mother was arrested.

Q. When did that happen?

In February of 1948. I was 15.

Q. Were you aware that people were being arrested before that?

I once saw a photograph of a stranger in our house and asked my mother about him. She told me that he had been arrested and that just before the arrest he asked his son how he would react if someone told him that his father was "an enemy of the people." The son replied that he would kill his father with his own hands. To the end of his life the son was tormented by that reply. And then my mother asked, "And how would you have reacted?" I replied, "I wouldn't have ever believed it." We didn't discuss it any further, but I always thought that imprisonment was a very romantic thing. In any case, my parents were to me an example of honor, courage, and morality.

Q. Were you home when your mother was arrested?

No, I was in the library reading an astronomy book. When I came home my father said that my mother was picked up by a car and taken somewhere and that he didn't think she would be coming back. That night they came to search the house.

Q. What were they looking for?

They always looked for something and they never found anything, even though they turned the house upside down. They couldn't have found anything, anyway, but they did it to make a bigger impression. My little sister was taken to my grandmother in Chernovtsy, as I was for a while; then I came back in order to have a Moscow passport, which is not an unimportant thing to have.

Q. Did your father explain anything to you?

Yes, he did. He told me everything, what he thought about the Revolution and the Soviet Government, and I believed everything he said, even though like every Soviet child I believed that Stalin was a great leader. Even though in our family they didn't discuss Stalin with us, there was an imperceptible atmosphere of skepticism and irony about him. Remember, there was a saying in Russia that a child must love Stalin more than his parents. Once I expressed doubts about it to my mother, but she only sadly shook her head. At that time the parents could not talk to their children about all that, but after my mother was arrested my father spoke to me openly.

Q. Did he try to do anything about it?

He wrote a letter to Stalin—knowing it was useless—reminding him that he and Stalin were exiled together in Turukhansk and that he could vouch for my mother. But, of course, his letter went unanswered and he was ashamed that he had written it. He just said to me, "Don't ever reconcile yourself to any injustice." A year later he too was arrested, in March of 1949.

Q. Do you know why your mother was arrested?

I found out only in 1956. During the war she was working with foreign correspondents in Moscow. She knew English and was a secretary to one of them.

Q. What did you do when your father was arrested?

I was left all alone. My younger sister went to my grandmother's again. It was a very painful period, between the ages of 16 and 18. I longed for the companionship of someone who could understand, but there was no one. I was very lonely, spiritually very lonely. It was also very difficult because the parents of my girlfriends didn't allow them to see me; they were afraid because I was a daughter of "repressed parents."

Q. What did you do after you finished school?

I sold our piano to eat and tried to get into the Institute of Foreign Languages. Of course, I wasn't accepted. Nor was I accepted in the Philological Institute. Finally, I got in the Nutrition Institute and there I met Tamara, a girl whose parents were arrested in 1937, and we became friends. We both noticed Yevgeny Gurevich, a young man in our class who was at the same time taking correspondence courses in philosophy. Yevgeny was slight and very handsome. We both lost our hearts to him and listened for hours to his views about philosophy, though until then we knew nothing about it. He then offered to organize a circle of philosophy studies and we enthusiastically agreed.

Q. Where did you meet?

The first time we met in my place. He brought a friend, Vladik, and we discussed *Ten Days That Shook the World* [by John Reed, the American journalist who is buried next to the Kremlin wall], a book which was then forbidden; Lenin's *Government and Revolution;* and the fourth chapter of the *Short Course* [Stalin's version of the history of the Soviet Communist Party]. We talked a lot about arrests and prisons and the life of the people, and we agreed that Stalin wasn't great, but Lenin was. I asked at the end how we could fight this injustice, and Yevgeny answered that it was possible, that there are young people who are willing and that there is an organization where not everyone is so young. On this mysterious sentence the evening ended.

Q. What was your personal reaction to all that?

I was very excited. It seemed like an end to my loneliness. I found people who thought as I did. Among them was such a remarkable person as Yevgeny. When, the next day, he asked me if I wanted to join the organization which was dedicated to fighting the existing injustices and was for the resurrection of Leninism, I didn't hesitate for a second. Tamara refused. She had a sister who brought her up when their parents were arrested and who was now very ill with Parkinson's disease, and she didn't want to get into anything. So she never again participated. I was joyful that I was involved in a "people's cause."

Q. Were you not afraid of arrest?

No, I wanted to be with my parents. The letters they were allowed to write me were tearing me apart. My mother wrote how lucky she was having broken her arm, because she could then be in the prison hospital. She wrote about the beauty of the Northern Lights.

Q. How long were you involved in this organization?

From the end of October, 1950, to February 7, 1951. We called ourselves the "Union of Struggle for the Revolutionary Cause," and we talked about how socialism in the Soviet Union became state capitalism, how innocent people were being imprisoned, and so on. We had a manifesto that said the same in a more scholarly manner. Yevgeny was arrested on January 18, 1951; so was Vladik and a few other young men whom I didn't know. I was arrested on February seventh at night and Tamara was arrested on April fourteenth.

Q. Since you expected arrest and wished for it, how did you feel when it happened?

The first shock after arrest is the realization that you are treated as an object and that this object is being treated by completely indifferent people. In these first hours some cardinal changes occur inside a human being. He isn't what he used to be several hours before. There is a line in a prison song, "and habitually, handcuffing himself." This habit doesn't come gradually; it is acquired immediately. From this begins a long journey, but those first hours are decisive. Of course, perhaps a person can remain free inside; spiritually he may be able to transcend all the humiliation—but that isn't for an 18-year-old.

Q. What prison were you placed in?

Lefortovo. I was in solitary confinement for over a year. I know that some people prefer the solitary confinement to a crowded cell where one is not able to be alone for a moment. My father thought that way. Perhaps a person with a rich experience and who is used to contemplation doesn't suffer in isolation, but at the age of 18 without inner resources. . . . I wouldn't say it's unbearable, because we stood everything, but it was very, very difficult.

Q. Were you allowed to read?

Yes, we were given three books for two weeks. The prison libraries are very good. But we had no choice and at times we were given the same books again and again. I got Gorky's *Mother* three times. It was most lucky when I could get poetry, for then I could memorize the poems. The biggest event for me was when they gave me Byron's *Prisoner of Chillon*, which I've memorized. But three books for two weeks is not enough.

Q. What did you do the rest of the time?

Walked up and down the cell; it was pretty big, seven steps long. The most difficult thing is the sense of time being wasted. In the labor camps everything is different, every free moment is perceived as a gift. I spent a lot of time sitting on the bunk bed wrapped up in my fur coat. My mother bought the fur coat in America, before I was born, and the salesman told her it would last forever. When my mother was arrested she took the coat with her, but later, when my grandmother went to see her, mother gave it to her for me. Not long before my arrest I tried to sell it but couldn't. When I was arrested I took the coat with me knowing that everything gets confiscated but one's coat. It was with me in prison and in camps and during *etappes*. In prison, looking it over, I found all kinds of little things in it which my mother hid in its seams, a piece of wire, one tooth from a comb with a little hole in it to be used as a needle, a pin.

Q. How did the prison administration treat the prisoners?

In Lefortovo, no one talks to you. You aren't a human being, but a ZEK. Even if you ask what day it is they'll say, "Ask the investigator." All questions are answered with this sentence. In provincial prisons, I heard, they treat you rudely, but at least there isn't this depersonalized indifference. In Lefortovo, the questioning took place during the night and during the day it is forbidden to sleep. It is also forbidden to sit leaning against the wall. If they caught me singing or leaning on the wall or making something out of bread balls, they'd bark at me in a whisper.

Q. Were the prisoners watched that closely?

There is a little opening in the door called *volchok* or *glazok* [eye] through which they look at you from time to time. There were many depressing details; walls were dirty green and the floor was black. We were not allowed to have a piece of paper or a piece of cotton; during the periodical searches they took any shred of a cloth. In short, in that sense it was much more difficult for a woman than for a man.

Q. Were you ever in the punitive cell?

Yes, three times in Lefortovo and one time in Butyrki Prison after the trial. The cell is very small, it is cold and you can't get warm by walking around. In the corner there is a small triangular seat on which one can sit. The food ration is two cups of hot water a day and 300 grams of bread. The cold is so tormenting that you feel hunger only toward the end. They take everything away from you, short of leaving you naked. Once I asked a woman guard for cotton; she slammed the door and I heard how she told about it to the head guard and how he laughed. He told her how in 1949 they had a man in there who was almost naked and how much fun they had. But you can't imagine the state of bliss when you are returned to your prison cell, back to your fur coat, back to the books, to a leftover piece of bread.

Q. How did you get into the punitive cell?

The first time for arguing with the investigator. The second time for scratching my name absentmindedly on the table during questioning. The third time for washing my blouse in a sink and for not stopping after they told me it was forbidden. I was furious to think that my mother too could have been in such a cell. She was placed there, I found out later, for knocking on the wall [this prisoner's communication system among themselves is best described in Yevgeniya Ginzburg's book *Into the Whirlwind*].

Q. How long was the investigation?

Almost a year. They questioned me about once a week. The sound of a door opening didn't bring me a sense of horror as many prisoners say. After being in solitary confinement even the interrogation is a diversion. During the year I had four different investigators. At first I was surprised that the investigator did not write my answers as I phrased them, but when I asked about it he replied that "protocol must be composed in a literate way." His rendition seemed to me illiterate, but it was no use disputing it.

Q. Were those investigators different from one another?

The attitude of a prisoner toward the investigator is a very interesting aspect of prison psychology. When these are the only people you communicate with, it is inevitable that you think a lot about them. One of them, Smelov, seemed to me kindly and even—how monstrous!—resembling the poet Zhukovsky. He was never rude and that was most important to me. He was the first who raised the question of terrorism with me. He asked if we had ever discussed terrorism as the means to our ends. I said that we never did because we were Marxists and terrorism is not a Marxian method. And that, besides, it is immoral. He wrote down my answer as follows, "Even though I consider that all means are good in a struggle, I rejected terrorism as not purposeful." Because he was kindly I was embarrassed to point out his doctoring of my words and signed the protocol.

Q. Why was Tamara arrested when she refused to be involved in your organization?

For failure to report the rest of us.

Q. How many of you were arrested and what were their ages?

Ten women and six men, the oldest was 21, the youngest 16. But some of their parents and friends were arrested too. Yevgeny's parents were arrested and also Vladik's.

Q. Exactly what had your organization achieved before the arrests?

The "theoreticians"—there were three—drew the programs and collected materials in order to create an objective history of our country. One of them, Grisha, tried to produce a hectograph. We assembled, read various books, mainly Marxist classics, and discussed the methods of resistance. At one of those meetings Yevgeny did offer to discuss the possibility of terrorism against

Stalin and Beria, but everyone rejected the proposition. Our "secretary," Alla, kept the notes on our meetings which were confiscated during the search. We collected membership fees. That was all.

Q. When did the trial begin?

In January of 1952. It lasted two weeks. We were very excited because we were all going to see each other. There were 16 chairs in a big room; at a distance there were three people, sitting at a table, the members of the Military Division of the Supreme Court. We were referred to as a "Jewish anti-Soviet Terrorist Youth Organization." We didn't mind the pomposity and the tone of all this since we thought of ourselves as "serious activists." The prosecutor was absent. The man who read the accusatory statement announced, "The accused are being freed from witnesses and defense attorneys." Of the 16 people I knew only three. No one knew all of them. Every one of us spoke with great sincerity. No one interrupted us; they even listened somewhat kindly. After all our testimony we were asked if we had any requests. Most people asked to see their parents. I asked them not to confiscate everything from our house, to leave something as a memory of our home. The stenographer took everything down. Not one request was granted. Then we were asked to say "the last word." I'm sure no one slept the night before; each must have thought what she or he would say. Every one of my comrades said that he or she was repentant, that it was wrong to fight the Soviet authorities, that in prison with time for contemplation they now understood that they were wrong.

Q. And you?

It was very difficult for me to be alone in feeling no repentance. I said I felt none, that I felt alien to our system and our reality. It wasn't an act of courage. What kind of courage could there have been under the circumstances when everything was decided ahead of time? I just said what I had to say.

Q. And the verdict?

Yevgeny, Vladik, and Boris were condemned to be shot. Tamara, Nina, and Galya to 10 years in labor camps, to be followed by five years' exile. The rest of us to 25 years in labor camps to be followed by five years' exile. The verdict was final and without the right to appeal. Still, we thought that our three friends would not be shot. But they were. We didn't find that out until we were freed.

Q. How does the transformation from solitary confinement affect one?

After the trial I spent a month and a half in Butyrki Prison. First of all there is the constant desire to talk. An excessive need to talk. Had they put me in a general cell before the trial together with a stool pigeon, I would have said everything.

Q. Was Butyrki Prison easier than Lefortovo?

It was easier for me because I was no longer alone; it was good to be among people. Only I still had romantic notions about being in prison. I didn't know the rule about not speaking up on behalf of others, so that once when I tried to stand up for my cell mates I was put in a straightjacket. It's a canvas shirt with special shirt-sleeve belts. The prisoner is thrown on the floor and his arms are twisted behind his back. The feet are pulled to the back of his head and he is left in this condition for some time. In my case it was ten minutes. A doctor has to be present to check the pulse, but there was no doctor with me because everything happened too fast. When you are untied it is impossible to move, but they tell you to get up and walk and you do because otherwise they threaten you with another straightjacket. It passes rather quickly with no apparent consequences, as does the beating over the head, shoulders, and face with a bag of sand just before the straightjacket is put on.

Q. What followed after you had to start serving your sentences?

The *etappe*. It comes from an old Russian expression *poetapno*, which means moving in stages under police escort. I was en route more than a month from Moscow to Kuibyshev, then to Novosibirsk, then to Taishet where we stayed for a while, then on to the camp. At that time the inmates were mostly political. Of course, we were not called "political" since there is no such thing as "political prisoners" in the Soviet Union. Political dissent is called "slander of the Soviet Union" and is treated as a criminal offense. There were women of all ages, even women younger than I, mostly Ukrainian. And the mood was completely different than it was in the camp where Yevgeniya Ginzburg was. Mostly they were innocent women, separated from their husbands and children and trapped there.

Q. Was there no solidarity among them?

The solidarity was rather weak. When men and women are imprisoned together there is solidarity as there was in the camps of Karaganda where there were rebellions, put down by tanks and machine guns. I haven't been there myself, but I know a lot of people who were. Some of our 16 were there. It wasn't exactly a rebellion, it was a strike; men and women refused to go to work. It happened in many different camps. But ours was different. And when criminals were brought in, they didn't terrorize us—they were pitiful creatures themselves. To distinguish us from the criminals we had to wear numbers on our backs and our skirts. Unlike them, we were allowed two letters a year.

Q. Could you write that you wanted to?

We couldn't complain. We were told to write that we were well and healthy and that we could request parcels. Unlike the present limitations on parcels in camps, we had none. But then people had different attitudes toward ZEKs and very few received parcels.

Q. Did you feel any difference in atmosphere after Stalin's death?

Yes, about 1954 there was a relaxation of the rules. We were allowed to write without limitations. This is when I wrote my parents, when we finally could correspond. Before, no one paid attention to our morality; now they began to "reeducate" us. Although there always was the Cultural-Educational Department, but it meant access to a bad library—for some reason libraries in camps are always worse than those in the prisons—and also the amateur theater. Even in the most difficult times we had this; I once sang in the choir, with disgust, but I still sang. It was a diversion. In the saddest time we put on *Snow White* with great success.

Q. Were there other changes connected with Stalin's death and the Twentieth Congress?

The parents of those in our group who were not arrested requested that our case should be reexamined. The case was reinvestigated [in February–April, 1956] and as a result we were given amnesty. That is, the sentence was lowered, for example to five years in my case—which I had already served. Tamara was rehabilitated.

Q. And those three who were shot?

Their parents received a notification that the case of their sons was reinvestigated and that their sentence was lowered to ten years' imprisonment.

Q. How do you think those five years affected your psyche?

Of course, it was a great trauma. But any experience is profitable for a person, if it doesn't destroy him; for me it had also a positive effect. Still, I have observed that often people do not deserve their destiny. I've seen people who had suffered much, who went through tragedies, and who still remain nonentities. The experience doesn't enrich them a bit. In a book by Varlam Shalamov [a Soviet author who wrote about prisons and camps] there is a sentence, "I saw what a human being should not see and should not know."

Q. Did you return to Moscow?

Yes. I returned to prison in Moscow for the duration of the reinvestigation of our case. But we didn't travel by etappe but by a regular train, in a convoy. After the new verdict we were set free.

Q. They just let you out on the street?

Yes. A friend and I stepped into the street in our prison-camp clothes.

Q. Did the people stare at you?

The people are busy and in a hurry in Moscow. Besides, we were in a state of shock and we didn't notice how the people were reacting. But when we came out we didn't know which way to go, and a young man, a KGB man, took us to the taxi stand.

Q. Did you go home then?

I had no home. I went to some relatives who kept my younger sister. But there wasn't any place for another person and I lived in different places. Then my parents were freed too. I started working in a library and took correspondence courses in library science.

Q. You were 23 when you came out. What course did your life take then?

When we came back we found ourselves among those who later became "active." It happened that our friends were mostly ex-prisoners or their friends and relatives. And around us the young began to gather; for them our return was the same as my parents' arrest was for me. This is also the story of my husband. When we met, in 1956, he was a rabid Marxist. He used to argue endlessly with my father, by then a thoroughly disillusioned middle-aged man. He would come to see me and instead would argue with my father. And gradually the influence came by itself, the fact that we were imprisoned, that we knew something from experience. Thus my husband became a protester and became a known dissident in Moscow. Then, of course, came the trial of Sinyavsky and Daniel.

Q. Did you know them personally?

We knew Sinyavsky, but Daniel was our close friend. So the trial concerned us personally. Though Daniel was our friend we did not know that he published abroad. It was a big surprise because we knew Daniel as an apolitical man. He lived by his inner life. But here I distinguish between being political and temperamental. I too was apolitical, but I cannot remain indifferent to such things. The people were suffering. Perhaps for an orthodox Soviet it's okay: the sacred struggle of the classes in which some must suffer. But I considered that if people suffer then let all goals go to hell. Perhaps it was a deficiency in my upbringing, which wasn't genuinely Communistic.

Q. You mean your parents were a stronger influence than school and environment?

Yes, their influence was the strongest. I remember during one of my first interrogations the investigator, having found out that the arrest of my parents played a big role in the forming of my own convictions, told me that my parents hated the Soviet Power, and I answered, "If that is true then the Soviet Power deserves it." At this point he sent me to the punitive cell.

Q. And your own son?

My own son did not undergo any transformation, he understood everything much earlier than I did. He always thought as we did.

Q. When did you first think of leaving the Soviet Union?

When I was serving my sentence, it seemed to me that if I had any chance to leave the country I would leave it happily. There were some fanatics in camps who thought it would be better to remain in prison in Siberia than leave. I had a girlfriend who thought that way. But later I didn't consider leaving because it wasn't feasible. As I said, from my freedom to the end we lived at the very center of all democratic, intellectual, and Zionist activities. The Zionists repelled me by their narrowness, but I also understood that our own "largeness" came from the fact that we had no real purpose, that one has to be narrow in order to fight for something. Of course, I always stood apart because my experience had taught me that to fight the Soviet system makes no sense. I did sign some letters of protest because it is difficult not to when everyone around you is signing, but I didn't have any hope that it would do any good. Besides, when we were arrested a lot of people were arrested because of us—parents, brothers, friends—and I felt our guilt before them acutely, so this had its influence on my attitude later as well. After this, after I knew my three friends had been shot, I understood that life is the most significant good and that one must live quietly. But then the events were such that they were in conflict with my innermost convictions. I could not but react when my friends were arrested. And when my friends were demonstrating against the Czech invasion, I knew it was madness, but I could not judge them; I had nothing but compassion for them. And despite all that I did not want to leave the Soviet Union. The question came up in our family very often, should we leave or shouldn't we leave, and I knew that I wouldn't leave.

Q. Did you feel any affinity toward Israel or did you feel yourself Jewish?

When in 1948 Israel was declared a state and I saw how people stood in the streets near the loudspeakers and listened to the news, I was interested in it, but it did not concern me personally. When my uncle said that such and such a writer or artist in the Soviet Union was a Jew, I considered it stupid. In short, I was indifferent to all that, and if it weren't for the anti-Semitism I would have remained totally indifferent to it. Russia's destiny is my destiny, although of course I'm sympathetic to Israel. But despite all my hatred toward the regime, I had a sense of belonging in Russia and a feeling of responsibility for Russia. And I felt I should not leave those friends of mine who can never leave because they are Russian.

Q. So why did you finally leave?

My husband, who has his own history, and who feels Russian no less than I do, felt that we must leave for the good of our son, that the child must be brought up in a free land. The child himself voiced such sentiments, because unlike us he did confront anti-Semitism rather early. Besides, he was aware at a very early age of what was going on in our own circle, who was arrested, who was on trial. He heard all the discussions and knew everything. He knew that on Friday Bukovsky was in our house and that on Saturday he was arrested. He also knew the story of our family, and was very sensitive to it. Gradually, he became infatuated with the Zionist movement and began going to a synagogue (though remaining sober about it), and I felt a very strong desire on his part to leave. Still, I wanted to disregard it. Both my son and my husband tried to talk me into it, but I resisted. Then one day my husband had to face a direct possibility of arrest. That was after Yakir's confession. He was not so much afraid of an arrest, and I felt that if a man took risks he should be prepared for arrest and prison, but he was afraid that he would be put in an insane asylum, like Gershuni or Grigorenko. And that is very frightening. One day a year ago he said to me that he had talked everything over with our son, and he asked him whether or not the boy would be willing to leave without me. The child replied that he was willing, in the hope that I would follow or join them. I took it as a verdict. I knew I couldn't leave my only child. We left September seventh.

Q. Did you land in Vienna? Do you remember your first impression?

Yes, we were accompanied by the gendarmes—this was the time of terrorists' threats—and it brought back memories about the camp convoy for me, only this time they were on my side, they were guarding me.

Q. And Israel?

I loved it at first sight, though I'm still depressed that I left Russia. The visual impression was shocking, I called it in one of my letters "therapeutic shock." Israel heals wounds. We came directly to Jerusalem, where friends met us and took us to the Mount of Olives and showed us the view of the Old City. I was shattered by the magnificence of this place. It is indeed a Holy Land, a motherland of mankind's spirit. When I ride the bus and look out the window, the city's beauty is very impressive. And when I see soldiers I feel tenderness toward them. But all this is on a more universal level. During the 1973 war I felt myself a part of these people, of Israel's destiny. Still, my identity with Russia is so irreversible that the separation from it is very painful.

Q. Are there any circumstances under which you would return to Russia?

I know it's terrible, but I would return to Russia even now. But it is impossible; I can't leave my son, and it would also mean telling lies about Israel, selling your soul; it's not possible for me. I envy Americans who seem to be able to leave their country without any nostalgia.

Q. Is there any feeling of betrayal?

A betrayal of those who are still there. I left very dear people there and this separation cannot be compensated by anything here. I'll have many friends here, but those I left, I can't live without them. I feel also that I cut myself off from the Russian culture. I read Chekhov here and I feel that I left all this behind. It's not that I just emigrated to the West, as people used to do in the 1920s and at the same time still belonged to their culture. Coming to Israel means in a sense renouncing the Russian culture, or rather no longer belonging to it. I have to make a choice; I can't remain at the same time a Russian and be an Israeli. You see, we came here in September [1973], and the war began in October. Knowing the role of the Soviet Union in that war, I was ashamed to feel homesick, to miss my friends—it was even difficult to write letters to them. I felt that I must be *here* more now. I crossed into a different sphere. And this schism is very painful.

VADIM KREIDINKOV

We met in January, 1974, a month after Vadim Kreidinkov left Leningrad with his wife and son. It was in Rome at the Termini Station, an unlikely place to find a person whom one has never seen. But there was no difficulty. I recognized him in a crowd of Italians and tourists and other foreigners. Perhaps because he is very tall and stands erect, observing the scene calmly as though it is a passing show or a circus, that I spotted him immediately. Perhaps because he did not look as if he belonged there, either as a visitor or a native. Vadim Kreidinkov would appear a stranger in any land. It is this estrangement that probably makes him look so tranquil while his eyes are restless and searching.

Vadim was born in Eastern Siberia in 1936. At the age of eight, while his father was at war, Vadim, his brother, and mother moved to Akmolinsk, in Kazakhstan. It is a naked steppe and the town where they lived was surrounded by labor camps. Vadim asked no questions. It never occurred to him to verbalize any of them. And he always distrusted appearances. Once, during a great hunger, his mother was able to get a few grapes and she placed two by his bedside. On awaking, Vadim did not eat them, taking them to be made of glass.

At the age of 18 he boarded a train for a five-day journey to Leningrad, where he wanted to study. He did get his education, not in the University, which he attended for five years, but outside of it. As a student he did not feel a part of the University; the city seemed confining and made him long for the expanses of the steppes. When Kreidinkov applied for an exit visa it was because he felt that he belonged elsewhere. At present Vadim and his family live in New York, hoping to find work outside of the city, somewhere where the fields stretch out to the sky.

Q. In your opinion, what was the source for the reemergence of the Russian Intelligentsia?

The general opinion is that it was due to the Twentieth Congress, but it seems to me that this wasn't the primary cause. The primary cause is more metaphysical. The very psychosphere—psychosphere is my favorite word—became more plastic, mobile, more tranquil and freer. For a short time the burdensome gravity disappeared.

Q. And the Twentieth Congress didn't contribute to that?

Yes, but I don't think that history is made by a decree of some congress. It is made in a more transcendental sphere, if you'll forgive such a philosophical expression.

Q. And in your own personal case?

In my own personal case I sensed this change before the Twentieth Congress, back in 1955.

Q. How old were you?

I was 19. I arrived in Leningrad shortly before that, at the age of 18, from a very backward province in Kazakhstan.

Q. Were you born there?

I was born in Siberia. I lived in Siberia the first eight years of my life. And for the next 10 I lived in Kazakhstan. I was born in 1936 in Nerchinsk, the town which in Russian history is known as the place of the Decembrists. I remember being walked, as a child, in front of the museum of the Decembrists. After 4 years we moved to Chita. My father was in the war from 1941 and I lived with my mother and grandmother and a half brother. My mother's sister and her husband, who was a veterinarian, lived in Kazakhstan. He was imprisoned, accused of being a Japanese spy, and since she was left all alone, my grandmother went there, too.

Q. Were there any Japanese in Kazakhstan?

None. And since it was very difficult for them there, my mother decided to move there too. We came to the city of Akmolinsk, in the center of Kazakhstan. It's a naked steppe, a hungry steppe, and when we arrived there was a *buran*, a steppe wind that carries snow with it, and I remember how we arrived and my mother put down our suitcases to ask some passersby for Engels Street, on which my aunt lived, and the suitcases were instantly covered with snow. The very name Akmolinsk means "white grave." Khrushchev later renamed it into Tselinograd, meaning Virgin-land-town.

Q. So your childhood passed there?

Yes, from eight years on. By the way, a childhood is a childhood and I have many beautiful memories. I often had ecstatic states. But we were surrounded by labor camps.

Q. Were you aware of them?

I had already found out in 1943 what a concentration camp is, in Chita. I was six then.

Q. Did someone explain it to you?

No one had to explain anything to me; it was in our own backyard, in the center of town. I was a very lonely boy. My mother, who was a medical doctor, worked 14 hours a day in a military hospital, and when she would come home she would drink a cup of carrot tea and fall asleep. My grandmother had already left. We lived in a huge house surrounded by a typical Siberian high log fence. There were five apartments, and all the people worked from morning to night. I seldom saw anyone. But I had a cat. That cat was my only friend. And my cat died of hunger. He was probably old and couldn't find food for himself. At that time we only had potato peels to eat ourselves. First we had potatoes, and we could exchange the potato peelings for milk if someone had a cow and needed to feed it. But then came the time when we ate the potato peelings ourselves. There was nothing for the cat. The cat died in my arms. So I took him and went to the far end of our yard to bury him.

But two or three days before that, there appeared some people at that end of the yard, *dokhodyagi*, with green and yellow faces, with sunken cheeks and eyes, hunched and bald, and very quickly they built a guardhouse. On top of that guardhouse appeared a uniformed man with a machine gun, then the territory was surrounded by barbed wire. In short, a small concentration camp had been built. And I watched all that. So I went to that far end of the yard to bury my cat. But since I was too upset I forgot a shovel, so I placed my cat on the ground and ran back for the shovel. When I returned I saw, through the barbed wire, a man's hand. In his hand was a piece of bent wire and he was trying to get my cat. I said to him, "What are you doing?" and he replied—I still remember his words now clearly—"Little boy, give me the cat, I want to eat. I'll give you a skate." Apparently, while making the guardhouse he had found an old, rusted skate in the ground and he wanted to exchange it with me for a dead cat. I grabbed my cat and held it close to me, and he repeated, "I want to eat." I ran to the neighbor's yard where they had some potatoes, pulled two out of the ground and brought them to him. He took them, and without shaking the dirt off, grabbed them with his mouth. He only had two front teeth, and I remember a piece of earth stuck to his teeth. This is how I found out about the concentration camps.

Q. And the cat?

I buried the cat.

Q. Did you ask the man what it was all about?

I asked him nothing; I understood. Simply, there was a perception that people were behind barbed wire, that an armed guard was guarding them. Besides, the guard swore at him and shouted, "Go back to work," but he didn't take the potatoes away from him. In the evening I got punished for stealing them.

Q. Still, did you not ask your mother any questions?

It wouldn't have occurred to me to ask questions. I lived in my own dreamworld, and the very reality by some vibrations made it clear to me what was the heart of the matter. I didn't need to transform these vibrations into concepts or words. I had impressions of events that were bright or gloomy, but I didn't need to know how these impressions were called. Besides a little earlier (I began to read at the age of four) when I was about five-and-a-half years old I used to go to the library to read, and on the road to the library there was a prison and I used to see faces behind the iron bars. But it was a part of life; there were stores on this street and markets and there was a prison. So when we got to Akmolinsk I knew what the camps were.

Q. Is there any other memory of Akmolinsk that you still hold?

Yes, there was a terror in town which came from the Ingush and Chechen [mountain tribes in the Caucasus]. They were angry because Stalin exiled them from the Caucasus and they held the whole Kazakhstan in fear. They were very religious [Moslems], very united, physically very strong and had an animal-like, furious courage. The male population was at war or in camps and so they held everyone in terror even though they made up only 5 percent of the population. By the way, Akmolinsk was a very international town. There was a boy in my class who was Norwegian; heaven knows how he got there. There were two German boys who had it very rough during the war and two Poles. Probably because it was one of the places of exile.

Q. How was your own life in that town?

Well, in the morning I went to school. Although they changed shifts on us all the time and sometimes I had to go to school in the afternoons. I remember that we were obliged to learn the Kazakh language and that was difficult and unpleasant. But I still have beautiful memories of this period. I have a memory of a Kazakhstan steppe in the spring.

Q. A visual memory?

Visual and also emotional. It's something incredible; the sensation of space, of limitless space, the young grass, wild onions and the air is such as you would never encounter anywhere else but in the steppe. Around you is that illusory freedom that seems to stretch into thousands of kilometers. Of course, these were the very kilometers that were saturated by the concentration camps. There was a famous camp, Dolinka, and another one, Karabas. My uncle was in one of them, about 40 kilometers from where we lived.

Q. Did you ever see him?

Yes, I remember it very well. One day a big group of prisoners was being taken through our town, and suddenly one man disengaged himself from the column and began to walk toward the house where my aunt was living. I ran after him. In fact, I ran ahead of him and told my aunt that some man was coming toward her house. He entered. There was this mute scene. Everyone froze in their places. My aunt ran toward him; he stopped her. They hadn't seen each other for about two and a half years. He sat down and for about five minutes he remained seated silently; then without saying a word, without touching his children, got up and left. The prisoners were still going by and he joined the column.

Q. He actually didn't say a word?

No, he probably was paralyzed by the wave of emotions that he had; he could not say anything. It was a mute scene that is still among my lasting impressions.

Q. Do you suppose he was allowed to leave the column or . . .

I suppose that because he was a veterinarian and probably the only one in that whole region, and it was an agricultural region, that it was a kind of favor he was allowed by his superior. He probably told him, "This is my home; let me look in." And the superior probably said, "Run ahead," knowing he couldn't escape anywhere.

Q. How long did you live in Akmolinsk?

In 1949 my mother remarried, because when my father came back he divorced her, having found a new family. We moved to Alma-Ata, the capital of Kazakhstan. There was a magnificent panorama on the Tien Shan Mountains. It was an unbelievably backward place, even though it was the capital. But there were new impressions there; it's the very south of Kazakhstan and it has a lot from Central Asia, which borders it. The population was mostly dekulakized Ukrainians. They are very cheerful, very lively people, people created for material life and there was no possibility of having any spiritual contacts with them. Before my eighteenth birthday I had seen only one student in my life, and he gave me some books to read. He gave me books on psychology. These books were really anachronistic, but nevertheless they awakened an interest in me toward the humanities.

Q. How did you decide to go to Leningrad University?

It was totally sudden, without any prior thinking. In my head there was this word "Leningrad," and I just had to go there.

Q. But you must have heard of it or read about it?

It was totally irrational. I am now an adult, able to think analytically. I would like to know myself concretely where this idea came from. I don't know. It was "Leningrad" and "journalism" that were in my mind, though I didn't know exactly what journalism really meant. I've never seen a journalist in my life.

Q. Was it allowed to go to Leningrad?

Yes. If a student goes there in order to try to get into a university, he gets a temporary *propiska* and if he is accepted, he receives automatically a propiska for the duration of his studies.

Q. How long did it take to get there?

It took six days and six nights by train. I had no difficulties because I was a medalist [one who graduates from high school with a medal—the highest honor]. The medalists were accepted without entrance exams.

Q. And the fact that you were half-Jewish didn't bother them?

You see, in my passport I am designated as a Russian because my father was Russian.

Q. How did the city of Leningrad impress you?

I came in by train. As you know the train station runs into the Nevsky Prospekt, so when I left the train I found myself in the very center of the city. It was the end of June. I was used to running barefoot, swimming in the lake, climbing the mountains, fishing, walking the steppes, and here I found myself in a stone bag. I didn't notice any architectural splendors, everything was unpleasant to me. Still, I had a goal and this was a strong motivation to overcome this impression. Later, of course, I saw the beauty and the mystique of the city, and in my destiny Leningrad occupies a very large place. But initially I sensed the stone bag.

Q. So where did you go from the station?

One of my mother's patients gave me an address of some distant relatives and I slept there at first. Then I received dormitory privileges. This was temporary until the decision was made about my acceptance into the University. I didn't have to pass exams, but I had to have a "talk" with a professor. I found out that I had to go to this talk on July third. I arrived at the designated building; it was a green building—as my friend said, "The only green building among the yellow ones." Yellow house is a synonym for an insane asylum in Russia. And there was a line of medalists. I joined the line but was soon pushed out by some tough guy. Since I was from a province I didn't say anything. When my turn came I was shown into the office of this professor and he told me to sit down and asked me, in his lazy voice, why did I choose the profession of journalism. This moment is the most shameful moment of my life. I don't know where it came from, but I suddenly began to spiel such a Party-line nonsense, such orthodox banalities, ultravirtues, ultra-right nonsense, that to this day I feel ashamed. I didn't think—it was like some devil was guiding my tongue without my will. But I still had a feeling that I didn't make it, because at the same time the critic in me told me what foolishness I was saying. So I was really surprised to see my name on the list of accepted students a few days later. But I still had to live until September, and so I got a job at a construction place out of the city.

Q. Did you have any previous work experience?

Yes, back in Alma-Ata during the summer vacation I worked at a brick factory. I was the only "free" person there, all the rest were the people who just arrived from the concentration camps. It was the year of mass rehabilitation after Stalin's death, so that the atmosphere and the spirit at that factory was actually camp-spirit. They laughed at my naïveté and they exploited me, but at the same time they protected me. They were wonderful people. I worked on the night shift and they always came by to get me because it was dangerous to walk around alone at night. It was my first "university" in a sense.

Q. How was your life at Leningrad University?

The courses began in September and already in a few months I stopped going to classes.

Q. Was there no obligatory attendance?

Not in classes. Rather the classes were so large, 300 students, that no one knew if a student was there. The seminars were obligatory though, and since there were only about 20 students at the seminars, one had to go.

Q. What kind of seminars?

On Marxism-Leninism, rather on the history of the Communist Party, and these could not be missed. So I attended those and didn't attend lectures. Though I was a provincial I understood that the spirit and the atmosphere of the lectures weren't it. So the change occurred in me about four months after entering the University, and although that change was developing in different ways, I found one of the counterpoints. One day, having skipped classes, I went, heaven knows why, to a small art exhibit. It was an exhibit of some small artist, a Socialist Realist, but since childhood I hadn't been indifferent to painting and even the smell of paint excited me. So I was walking around this exhibit and it was all rather boring, but one painting stopped me. It was a landscape and it was one of those moments when scales that block one's vision fell. This moment is fixed in my psyche.

Q. What kind of landscape was it?

It was a wintry landscape, the usual Finnish pines with branches bent to the ground by the weight of the snow. The landscape was very airy, this airiness was felt as wetness, a typical Leningrad gray day but the nature had saturated it.

Q. Did it remind you of anything?

It reminded me of nothing. I just meditatively left reality, dissolved in that painting, my "I" ceased to exist and it was one of those moments . . . And after that, something pulled me toward the Academy of Art. And instead of going to lectures I began to spend hours in the reading room of the Academy of Art, to read and to look at the old journals of the Silver Age, the beginning of the twentieth century when art and poetry flourished in Russia.

Q. Was it easy to get those journals?

At that time it was very easy. Later they became forbidden. It was a discovery, a discovery of the world in those magnificent journals of the world of the arts. *Appolon*, *The Golden Fleece*, *Vekhi.* Year after year I read those journals. Every day for me was filled with discoveries. I've learned about all the artists of the art journal *World of Arts*, and I've approached the Russian abstractionists like Malevich.

Q. And what did you do during summers?

During summers I wandered around the country. I traveled on the roofs of trains and places like that, without tickets. I used these travels to visit various provincial museums. I gave them tales about being an artist or an art historian and I always made my way into museums. This way I got to know all the Russian artists, those who were hidden from the museum-goers, like Kandinsky, Benois, Chagall, and the others. The other important factor in my education was a students' circle. They were all marvelous people, every one of them an autodidact.

Q. But you studied alone in the library of the Academy of Arts?

Yes, but I used to see some of them there. This library was also very pleasing to me because of its interior: walnut-tree bookcases, books magnificently bound, a nineteenth-century atmosphere. There were very few people there. And tranquillity.

Q. But even though you didn't attend classes you had to pass exams?

I managed. I'll give you an example. Once I was taking an exam in the history of twentieth-century Western literature. The program was planned in the way that Louis Aragon and André Barbusse were part of it. I drew the ticket with the novel by Barbusse, *Lights.* [During exams students draw tickets, as in a lottery, with questions on them.] Naturally I've never read it. I asked another student, "What is this novel about?" He replied, "Years of the First World War." I did read two novels that naturally were not in our program, Hemingway's *Farewell to Arms* and Remarque's *All Quiet on the Western Front.* So I wrote that the novel by Barbusse in its general atmosphere and plot reminds one of those two novels, and I began to analyze those novels in detail. The professor was a very lovely woman, delicate and rare. Vanovskaya was her name (she is dead now), and she liked it that I had done extracurricular reading. Hemingway was very popular then, but in Russia very few knew him. Dos Passos was not even mentioned in the University. In short she gave me an A.

Q. What about history of the Communist Party exams?

That was easy. We were allowed to use the syllabus. I took everything off the syllabus and just enlarged it and interpreted it, using synonyms. And anyway we heard those slogans all the time. But the days in the library were indeed discoveries. Each day I found out about things that cultivated people knew a long time ago, but for me it was a revelation.

Q. So your education . . .

. . . was received in the Academy of Arts. And in the University I was there simply on paper. But I must say that there was one absolutely remarkable faculty at the University—it was the hallway. Here we met, smoked, joked, talked, told each other the news, discussed things. Then came the Twentieth Congress.

Q. How did the students react to it?

Very stormily. They began sending us the "classical writers." Aleksei Surkov arrived (a Party-line hack poet) to "explain things" to us. And I remember he was asked all kinds of questions and he was vacillating: "This you can write, this you can't." Then I shouted at him, "Please define what is correct literature." He replied, "All that is for the Soviet Power is correct and is Socialist Realism. All that is against the Soviet Power is not Socialist Realism." We were all elated by such a definition and had a lot of fun during such sessions. Then came Dudintsev (*Not by Bread Alone*), though, by the way, a few people are still in camps for their too frank discussions about the book. So the hallway was the second source. This small circle had some extremely remarkable people. There was a Rid Grachev; he will finish badly; he already began his journey through the insane asylums. A fantastically talented man, a man of very acute, of unique humanitarian sense. He has absolute musical sense, is a talented artist, a wonderful writer and poet. I have his one collection of stories. He had a chance to publish several brilliant essays on French literature. He was the first to translate Saint-Exupéry for Samizdat. He and I used to walk dozens of kilometers back and forth along this hallway discussing things. These talks, at times in the hallway, at times walking in town, at times in someone's room with a bottle of beer, were our school, the school that taught us independent positions in life. So that this generation of the Russian Intelligentsia actually came out from the generation, and over the heads of its immediate generation, of the Silver Age. It's the Godfather and the Godmother of the Intelligentsia. But there is one factor. No one guided me toward those artists or those writers or such philosophers as Berdyaev or Shestov. I'm not putting an emphasis on this in order to underline my own originality of thinking, but to point out that the irrational way in which each of us separately made such discoveries was characteristic for this particular time.

Q. Once you made these discoveries, did you try to tell others about them?

At the beginning, of course, I was certain that I alone discovered all that, and I actively began to share this enthusiasm with my friends. And I think that my enthusiasm was of such high voltage that I probably infected dozens of people with it. Thus a lot of people, like myself, can say that they not only discovered this world of culture but the world within themselves. In this way I came also upon the philosophers of that time, especially Berdyaev and Shestov.

Q. Could you read Berdyaev's *Origins of Communism?*

Of course not. What do you think? Only those books that were published before he emigrated. But you see, also, the library workers were rather ignorant. Once they gave me three brochures by Berdyaev from 1918 in which he criticizes Lenin.

Q. Did you and your friends feel yourselves different from all others?

Yes, we felt that; there were we and there were the gray mass of other students, not because of any contempt or snobbism, but because they were truly unawakened. Our circle began this self-education in the 1950s, but in the early 1960s there was a kind of mass awakening. And I don't know why in the 1960s.

Q. Do you think this is something purely Russian, this occurrence?

I think so. It was as though those people escaped some spiritual imprisonment. This was forbidden and that was forbidden—all the names that created twentieth-century Russian culture were forbidden. The circle that I was talking about, I would say, is a purely Russian occurrence. We felt the fervor of the first pioneers when we could read such forbidden authors as Nietzsche or Schopenhauer or Freud.

Q. And if all these books were available, what would have happened? Would it have been the same?

It would have been different. It would have been healthier. Imagine if you'd have discovered Pasternak you could tell someone else about it. In our situation no one told us about any of those writers. I find some footnote or a mention about Pasternak. Who is Pasternak? I try to find out; I make a discovery.

Q. How, then, did you reconcile what you were taught officially in the University with what you learned yourself?

We regarded the University as the necessary, boring ritual. We didn't take it seriously.

Q. But if you had to write a long term paper?

I'll tell you, once I chose a subject for which I almost was kicked out of the University. I took courses in Polish specifically so that I could read the Polish press. At that time the Polish press was full of anti-Stalin articles, and all the modern writers such as Camus or

Kafka were translated into Polish. So many of us studied Polish. There was a wonderful newspaper, *Przeglad Kulturalny*, and I wrote a paper about anti-Stalinist articles in the Polish press, basing my work on this newspaper. Of course, they failed my paper and there was a meeting where I was given a scolding. After this I couldn't stand the University. Then I was thrown out of the dorm. There was a preelection campaign and an agitator came to the dorm. It was a dorm for foreigners actually, Chinese students and students from the so-called democratic republics. There were six of us, a Chinese student, an Albanian, two other foreigners, another Russian student, and myself. So this agitator came to our room, to talk to us two Russians and began to give us the propaganda. I began to ask him what they call "provocateur's questions." Discussion ensued and the foreign students had a lot of laughs. So he went directly to the Party bureau of the faculty and made a report. I was called in and threatened with expulsion from the University. I said that I was ashamed of the man's ignorance before the foreign students. They called in witnesses, the foreign students, who because of their ignorance, also said something not in my favor. So I quickly asked to be transferred to the status of "correspondence student" and they preferred that to a scandal of expulsion.

Q. But then you lost students' privileges?

Yes. I had no right to propiska, no right to work. I had nothing to eat, so I got on a train and went to a forest, about 900 kilometers away, in the Vologda Region. Then I took a ride on a track. In short, I arrived at a place where I could work in a forest. There were two kinds of workers there: either people who were in prisons before, and thus had no right to live in the cities, or people who were recruited to work there because there weren't enough workers. I was the only one without a prison past and not recruited. This was 1958. I came without the "workers' book," but they were provincial there and they believed that I had lost it and gave me another one.

Q. What did you do there?

I was cutting down the trees and then had to cut off all the branches. I was penniless, but my roommates gave me some food.

Q. How long were you there?

About two months. Spring came and it smelled so good that I decided to move south. I wanted to see the Black Sea. I felt myself rich because I'd made 150 rubles there and went to the Crimea. I met another wanderer and together we went around the Crimea.

Q. Isn't there a Soviet law against wanderers?

Yes, but that was issued only six years ago. I wanted to see my father who was in the Ukraine, so I sold my coat for 30 rubles and went. My father was rather shocked by my appearance. Then I decided to return to Leningrad. I didn't really care to get the diploma, but my mother very much wanted me to have it and my mother's wish was rather like a heavy stone around my neck. So I went back, and in 20 days passed 16 exams. It was just a circus. The next year I passed the others and got a degree in philology and journalism.

Q. Did you use it?

Well, at first I worked as a floor-layer. Then I met my wife, who was living in Pushkin (22 kilometers from Leningrad). So I moved there and worked as an insurance agent—life insurance and property insurance. It was very easy and very exciting; I met some very interesting people this way.

Q. How long did it last?

Two, three weeks. Soon I was bored with the money business and the talk. But since I turned out to be very successful in that field and brought them a lot of money every day, they didn't want to let me go.

Q. Did they have the right?

They have no right not to let me go, but they had the right to demand that I remain on the job two weeks after my resignation. They tried to reason with me. They said, "Look, you are a 'flier'; you won't get another job; look at your worker's book, it's full of different places of employment." But I sat down and wrote, "I am asking you to fire me for a *progul*." And this son of a bitch, though I never actually missed a day, wrote down in my worker's book: "Fired for progul," which made it almost impossible to get work anywhere for a long time. My wife was a student; it was a terrible situation. I became a specialist in looking for work. I took jobs that no one else wanted to take. Worked as a carpenter, at the factories. . . . Once I worked in an ironworks where most of the people were drug addicts. In between working they ran to the bathroom and injected themselves.

Q. With heroin?

They don't have heroin there. Morphine mostly; sometimes cocaine. They wouldn't even wait to clean the black oil off their arms, just pushed in the needle, through the oil and the steel dust. Then the needle and the syringe goes back to their locker.

Q. How did the administrators take it?

They ignored it, because they knew that no one else would work there. The work was maddening.

Q. What did you do there?

I made steel vessels. It was hard, and from 8 to 11 I worked very diligently. Then I would go to my boss and say, "I ran out of iron; I need to go to the warehouse for more." And he gave me a note so that I could leave the premises of the factory since the warehouse was outside. But I didn't go to any warehouse—I used to go home to read. I worked out this scheme so I could do that. When they asked me a few times why I didn't come back, I replied that I was certainly there, any worker here can testify to that. And they were good fellows and wouldn't rat. At times the boss had to attend political meetings, or else he was drunk and didn't show up. And then the permission to leave had only to be shown, not given, so if it was dated the fourth, I would redate it 14 on the fourteenth, and so on. This way I managed to work only half-time for six months. It was like a physical exercise, and then from noon I could go to the library and read. But these aren't the important facts of my biography. These were just daily details, at times indifferent, at times unpleasant, at times more than unpleasant. In 1958 I made another important discovery, Hindu philosophy.

Q. Vedanta?

Yes, Vedanta. But the interesting thing was that when I read this philosophy, I recognized my childhood states of ecstasy in it, so it wasn't something new in terms of knowledge, but a return to childhood.

Q. But how did you come upon the Hindu philosophers?

Russian interest in Hindu philosophy began at the end of 1957. At that time I was about to be thrown out of the University. One night I met a young man, about 17, who said he had nowhere to sleep; he was a student, but didn't have his dorm assignment yet. I talked our janitress into letting him sleep in my room. But in my room there were many people; we couldn't talk, so we went to the ironing room. We sat down on the table in that tiny room and began to talk about philosophy, as it always happens in Russia and in one's youth. And when he told me about Hindu philosophy, I felt as though I was hit by an electric current. I felt something familiar in all that. But strangely enough, I didn't right away run to seek those books; it took some months till it reached my consciousness. Once I went to the library and asked for Vivakananda. It made one of the strongest impressions on my life. And later, when I had to prepare a lot of nonsense for graduation, I kept, instead, reading those books. I found books; I found others who were interested in that subject, and for months I didn't even feel the world I was living in. So to this day I have these two sources: the general cultural one and the Hindu and Buddhist philosophies. It's not only my road; this is the road that thousands took.

Q. How many converts, so called, did you make?

About a hundred.

Q. Were these books available?

In 1958 when I asked for Vivakananda there wasn't yet this mass interest in Hindu philosophy. At that time in the city of Leningrad perhaps 40 people asked for such books, so it wasn't dangerous for them. When, about 1960–1961, there developed a mass interest in the idealistic, Oriental, and mystical philosophies, then they quickly hid all this literature.

Q. How did you manage then to read those books?

There were ways. A friend who worked in a library would give a book to me for a day and I'd go to another friend who had a camera so we could film it. Then there are museums of religion and atheism; one can get a note from one's work and get to read a book that way, as if for research. In this way there developed a Samizdat of those kinds of books. If someone is interested, I could provide a bibliography. In my estimation there are about 1000 titles. Perhaps you heard of the Buddhist Affair? They've placed some of my friends in insane asylums for that. There was even one among my friends who wanted to organize his own religion. He is now in the psychiatric ward, too, and I was questioned by the KGB for his case.

Q. What about the present—is the interest in Buddhism still alive?

Yes, very much so and it is much more qualified now because people have educated themselves. They became erudite and even certain personalities have appeared.

Q. Gurus?

Not exactly gurus, but people with a certain spiritual development. And, yes, others do come to them to study, and for them it is a new stage in their rebellion. Among the people who are interested in the Oriental philosophy there are many who, as they immerse themselves more and more in those interests, become more and more indifferent to Russian social problems. There is a percentage of them who have the Intelligentsia as their base, despite their preoccupation with Oriental studies, and they continue to concern themselves with Russian culture, with philosophy of history, with the destiny of Russia. With all the so-called "damned questions of the Russian Intelligentsia." So that from the wisdom of the Oriental philosophies they partake knowledge for the clarification of the "damned questions."

Q. Can you say then that you are no longer interested in the Russian problems?

I don't renounce my Russianness, I am 50 percent Russian and I grew up there. I still need to learn a lot about Russia in order to learn about myself. But there is another matter. You see, every nation has its own national idea. Berdyaev formulated the "Russian idea" and so there is a German idea, the English idea, and so on. If we look at it on the mystical-visual plane, we can say that the natural idea is a guardian angel of a nation, or it is its demon; in any case it's a spirit which is the essence of a given nation. Among these spirits there exists a hierarchy. So for a person to be born in a certain nation is to go through a particular education. On the level of morality or ethics, there is no such thing as the worst or the best nation. But on the level of spiritual essence, there are nations that are worse or better. In the history of mankind there were times when over one or another nation a higher spirit was present. In the best time of the Egyptian civilization it was Egypt. If we look at the monuments of the blossoming Egypt, we can see that the very spirit is in it. To my mind, the most spiritual monuments in all of Leningrad are the Sphinxes on the shores of the Neva. One must know how to see them. During the time of the prophets, Jerusalem was such a place. China, India, Italy all had their periods. For example, one didn't have to be super-talented in Italy in the fourteenth and fifteenth centuries in order to partake from this power; one had to make contact with it; all the seeds of one's talents would flourish. Between 1906 and 1916 such a spirit was over Russia, when the very atmosphere was such that even small talents were nourished by it and grew into big talents. In the same way there are times when certain nations are the vessels of Satanism. At the present time Russia, by its karma, deserved to be the carrier of Satanism. It deserved it because of psychological reasons. I think that one system or another does not depend on concrete leaders or revolutions, nor on concrete historical events, but is based on the national psychology. I don't want to paraphrase the French saying that every nation deserves its leaders, but the national psychology reflects its socio-political system. Using mythological expressions I want to explain to you why I wanted to leave that kingdom of Satan. If I were writing, perhaps I would use a more philosophical terminology, but in an interview I have to use the first images that come to mind.

Q. When did you make the decision to leave?

On New Year's Eve, on the eve of 1971. I was always ready to leave. From the time that I became a self-conscious person. Before I got married I was seriously considering an escape. I had fantasies of leaving by boat via the Gulf of Finland. After I got married these risky dreams became secondary. But the moment the wave of Jewish emigration started I began to plan to leave.

Q. Did you have Israel in mind, or any other country?

I had in mind to leave. I didn't have in mind where to but only where from.

Q. Did you have difficulties?

Yes, it took me a year and a half to get the visa. Usually it takes three months. They didn't accept my application 11 times.

Q. Did they tell you why?

They said, "According to your passport you are Russian, so you have no business in Israel. I said, "All right, I'll change my nationality. I have the right to." They told me that in the case of a mixed marriage the nationality is chosen only once. I asked them to show me the article of the law so I could fight it legally—to which they replied that this article is classified and cannot be shown. Then I asked my son to spill black ink on my passport so that the nationality would be wiped out. But they gave me a new passport in which they underlined Russian. So the battle continued. But they let us go when the October war began in Israel. As though to send us to the scaffold. Actually, I went to see the director of OVIR, the Soviet bureau that gives exit visas. His name's Suvorov, a kind of energetic alcoholic. I said to him, "Look, drop the comedy. You'll have to let me go anyway. And you will let me go not because I want to go to Israel or some other place, but because I do not want to live in the Soviet Union. You don't need people who don't want to live here. And I felt that something snapped; he told me to come back and soon afterward they telephoned to come and get the documents.

Q. You arrived in Austria?

Yes, there we told them that we did not want to go to Israel, and SOHNUT transferred us to the International Rescue Committee.

Q. Do you remember your first impression of the West?

Oh yes, very well. Since they gave us the visa sooner than we expected after not accepting our documents for a year and a half, and we had to produce 3000 rubles—a sum we had never seen in our lives—it was an absolutely maddening departure. So we arrived totally exhausted in Budapest, where we had to wait for an Austrian plane, and there the Hungarian customs man who was standing by the Austrian plane smiled at us so happily, so compassionately, with such human understanding that we are going somewhere where we want to go that it remains the first impression. Then when we sat down in the Austrian plane everything was different. Not that I was bought by what must be just a cheap charm (if one looks at it soberly) but the very interior, the slow music that was playing, the way they served us orange juice, the very manner of the stewardess, the de-serfed manner, the very spirit of the difference from everything Soviet. At that very moment I felt this new spirit, my physical fatigue disappeared, I sensed that some mountain fell off my shoulders. This was my first and most important impression of the West. When we came to Schönau I was already very tired. In Vienna there began a kaleidoscope of new impressions, but I didn't experience anything as strongly as I did in the plane. I walked around town, looked at the architecture, was impressed by the difference in expressions of people's faces, was enchanted by the Saint Stephan's Cathedral. I went to a bookstore and with great joy saw the books of Sakharov and Solzhenitsyn and Nabokov, my favorite writer. Once someone asked me about my impressions of the West and I replied—something I can repeat now—that I'm not at all surprised, that is I felt that I was encountering something very familiar and very close to me.

Q. How do you picture your future?

I don't picture it at all. Not at all. I'm not afraid of it because my position is that of an open person. I'm open to everything. I'm immune to nostalgia. Absolutely. My wife and I still have nightmares that we are still there. As for America, I have only one dream: to meet people who are interested in the same things.

Q. As to your son? Have you an regrets that he will not grow up Russian?

The idea of nationality is our burden, a forced one. Unfortunately, the forms of human relationships are still nationalistic. I've talked to you about the hierarchy of national ideas, not people. You may encounter 15 million disgusting Englishmen, but they still wouldn't tarnish the English Idea. You may meet as many—but it is doubtful—wonderful Russians—probably a million and a half—and they still wouldn't be able to elevate the Russian Idea. I'm not talking about political ideas now, but metaphysical ones. So whether my son will grow up to be of one nationality or another it is his affair. Ours is to make him an ethical man.

Q. Were there any negative impressions of the West?

Nothing that really touches one's soul, just small details, small unpleasantness. Someone cheats you out of something—things like that. Irritating things. . . . But there was one separate event. After I was here a few days I saw a demonstration. There must have been 10,000 students or whoever they were. . . . They were marching down the street here, waving red flags and Communist slogans and singing "Katyusha," a Russian World War II song. I stood there . . . then I turned to someone next to me and tried to tell him that I was from there, that I knew. I wanted to explain to him . . . but he was a sympathizer and he turned away from me.

GLOSSARY

agitka	propaganda on a mass low level
Chekists	name of secret-police men in the first years after the Revolution from the time when the KGB was called Cheka
dokhodyagi	prisoners who are on their last legs; goners
etappes	transport stage, from prison to camp or from camp to camp; moving in stages under police escort
glasnost'	to make public; to bring into the open
kartser	dungeon, punishment cell
KGB	Committee of State Security; the secret police
Obkom	a provincial Party committee
OBKhSS	a police division for Struggle against the Theft of Socialist Property
OVIR	Department of Visas and Registration
parasha	a prison bucket that serves as a toilet
podpisanty	the signers of protest letters
povestka	summons
progul	walk; missing a day's work
propiska	permission to live in a certain location
Raikom	a county Party committee
raspredeleniye	"distribution"; a system of assigning jobs to students immediately upon their graduation for a certain period of time